MW00618345

RUDOLPH VALENTINO:
A WIFE'S MEMORIES OF AN ICON

BY NATACHA RAMBOVA

1921 PVG Publishing
(in conjunction with **The Rudolph Valentino Society**)
Hollywood

Proudly Reprinted by

THE
RUDOLPH VALENTINO
SOCIETY

(RUDOLPHVALENTINO.ORG)

70% of the profits from this book go directly to the Society. With these funds we are able to promote and enhance the legacy of Rudolph Valentino through such projects as preservation, restoration, releasing of rare works, and The Rudolph Valentino Film Festival. We thank you for your support.

RUDOLPH VALENTINO
RECOLLECTIONS

By
Natacha Rambova
(*His Wife*)

ABOUT THIS BOOK

After the death of her ex-husband, Rudolph Valentino, Natacha Rambova found herself on the receiving end of much negative speculation and publicity. It had been going on for years, ever since Rudy's "One Man Strike" in 1923. After their separation in 1925 it intensified, yet Natacha did not say much. Natacha ran away to Paris, seeking a quickie divorce. That's where she still was when Rudy took ill in New York, the divorce now official. According to both George Ullman and Natacha, a reconciliation of sorts had taken place via telegram during Rudy's final hours. Believing Rudy would be well, Natacha was certain they would reunite in no time.

George Ullman had been Rudy's manager since the Minervala Dance Tour in 1923. Ullman and Rambova did not get along, battling for control of Rudy's career and loyalty. Ullman was the only person with Rudy when he died, and as Rudy's next of kin rushed to the States, Ullman was put in charge of his estate.

To help cover costs, dispel rumors, tell his own tale, and keep Rudy's name in the spotlight (to keep generating money for his deeply indebted estate) Ullman wrote a book titled, **"Valentino as I Knew Him"** in 1926. Though the book isn't too harsh in its assessment of Natacha (in fact Ullman defends her in parts), Natacha felt something was amiss and decided to release her own book. According to her writings, it was because the spirit of Rudy 'asked her to'.

Her writings were first released as a hardcover in the UK in 1926 through Hutchinson & Co. Ltd. (London) under the title, **"Rudy: An Intimate Portrait of Rudolph Valentino"** (also referred to as **"RUDY: An Intimate Portrait by his Wife"**). A slightly abridged paperback version, **"Rudolph Valentino Recollections"** was released in the US in 1927 via the Jacobson Hodgkinson Company. Both books only received one pressing, and subsequently, have become very hard to find in the past 80 some years. The US version is almost impossible to find, and the UK version brings upwards of $3,000 on the resale market.

"Rudolph Valentino: A Wife's Memories of an Icon" presents the UK text and pictures in full. In addition we have added some new photos, footnotes, new forwards, biographies, and bibliographies.

1921 PVG Publishing
Hollywood, CA

Library of Congress Cataloging-in-Publication Data
Rambova, Natacha
Rudolph Valentino: A Wife's Memories of an Icon/by Natacha Rambova
    p. cm.
ISBN: 0-9816440-4-X
        978-0-9816440-4-2
    1. Valentino, Rudolph   1895-1926
    2. Rambova, Natacha
    3. Naldi, Nita
    4. Mathis, June
    5. Motion picture actors and actresses – United States – Biography

rudolphvalentino.org
1921PVG.com
Colorized Photos by Kevin Scrantz

THANKS

A major thanks to the anonymous donor of this text; as well as the anonymous donor of the photos. Without your help it would have been impossible to make this project. Thank you to Kevin Scrantz for so kindly donating his wonderful colorized photos.

Also a thank you is due to Natacha Rambova herself for not only recording her thoughts, but also for the faun, Young Rajah, and Blackfeather photos. For this alone Valentino fans should adore her! I'd also like to thank JJO...I miss you. For some reason this project reminds me of you. I think I know why.

TABLE OF CONTENTS

(*continued on the next page*)

Natacha and Rudy on their wedding day 1922

NATACHA RAMBOVA: THE FAIR SHAKE
BY HALA PICKFORD

Silent film fans are a passionate bunch. Each star has a story and fans take it to heart, they know who to cheer for, who to boo. In the case of silent film icon Rudolph Valentino one might cheer on June Mathis, Norman Kerry, or Joseph Schenck. The one to boo, the villain, usually falls to either Famous Players-Lasky…or more often than not, his second wife Natacha Rambova.

Every time I speak to some sort of Valentino fan, from those who know his story by heart to those who don't, they all tell me one thing: they don't really like that Natacha chick very much.

When I first heard Rudy's story via "Dark Lover" by Emily Leider, I can't say I was wild about her myself. Mrs. Leider paints a mostly balanced picture; compared to other biographies, she doesn't paint Natacha one way or another. But even Mrs. Leider makes a few leaps and conclusions, which other Valentino authorities have made. Combined with the general narrative, Natacha does indeed come off as some sort of villain.

The common story goes something like this: she took control of Rudy's career, denied him children, humiliated him, cheated on him, and got him into Spiritualism which led to the kookiness that we now have with the antique and self promoting Memorial Service every year.

In reality the picture is more complicated than that, more complicated than any biography or book has yet to explore. While there are at least two good books out there on Rudy (and a slew of not so good ones), and one solid biography for Natacha; other characters and events in their story are overlooked. In my opinion a biography is sorely needed on June Mathis, Rudy's mentor and as the story goes, a key Natacha casualty. Without knowing June's story you can't even begin to fit the pieces together.

Had I ever had the chance to know Natacha, I don't think we would have gotten along. Some of her decisions are still quite baffling to me and some of her beliefs or actions aren't things I agree with. As a new fan, as said above, I did not care for her (she vaguely reminded me of the Wicked Queen in Disney's Snow White). But the more I learned about her the more I kinda liked her. She kind of reminds me of myself in some ways, which is why we would never get along (consider us the Louise Brooks type: stubborn, dominant, talented in our own ways, and sometimes self destructive without realizing it). She was a rebel, she loved mythology, she was quite girl power-esque, and she was extremely talented. Also she posed Rudy in the Faun photos. For that alone I think female fans owe her one.

In all my research and writings about silent film and Valentino in particular the least I can say of Natacha Rambova is this: despite the small attempts already made, she does not get the fair shake. She's still blamed for things she didn't do, and credited with things she didn't do.

Many accuse her of wanting fame, power, and control. Many say she used Valentino for just that. While indeed his string of flops, his only flops during his stardom, literally started with their marriage (The Young Rajah was filmed right after the bigamy scandal began, and Cobra was filmed slightly before their marriage began to crumble), I don't think its fair to blame her alone. We only have two full films out of those five to judge, yet the ones that remain aren't anything too terrible.

In fact I was pleasantly surprised by Monsieur Beaucaire, it's by far one of my most favorite Valentino movies (and if copyrights could ever be sorted out, I'd love to see an official DVD release). A terrible move for his career at the time, but not as misguided as one would think (he-man action hero Douglas Fairbanks had almost filmed that very movie a few years before).

Rudy, by all accounts, was a very sweet man. He bristled when it came to power struggles with men, yet he loved to let women run his creative life. June Mathis, Nita Naldi, Alla Nazimova, and yes Natacha. Rudy loved art and fashion long before Natacha came into the picture (he was said to have spent $3,000 on costumes for Four Horsemen, while only making $350 a week). By no means could she 'make' him do anything. The string of flops follows his usual pattern: arty films (Camille vs. Monsieur Beaucaire, Hooded Falcon), Latin Lover films (Blood and Sand vs. A Sainted Devil), Spiritualist films (The Four Horsemen of the Apocalypse vs. Young Rajah), and of course a crappy film he was forced into by the moguls (Uncharted Seas vs. Cobra).

On the flipside Natacha had been in film before she met Rudy. As Alla Nazimova's 'art director' she made a handful of films before their meeting, some of which were Nazimova's most successful. Nazimova strove for artistic films herself, and had made a name doing just that. Natacha didn't need Rudy for a platform, she already had one. Interestingly people also forget she and Rudy were together during some of his most successful films including "The Sheik" and "Blood and Sand". Their relationship had no negative impact on those productions.

I think one of the great mysteries will always be what transpired between the two, just what set them off, in 1925. In this book Natacha describes it as the evil public turning against her, which was indeed true. It is my personal belief those seeds had been sown the moment after they married, as Rudy went on his 'one man strike' and his popularity began to go downward. True, he had legitimate complaints (he was making peanuts, and he wanted better control of his films so he could make quality pictures), but the public didn't see it that way. They jumped to the conclusion it must be Natacha's fault, and Rudy's return in a powdered wig comedy did not help matters.

One thing I would like to see is the story of June Mathis and Natacha Rambova sorted out. Each woman is credited with, or blamed for various things, the other one did. June gave Rudy artistic parts before he had met Natacha. Natacha may have driven away some of his closest friends and co-workers, June being one of them. However that story is still yet to be told, and sadly Natacha doesn't give many details here. The rift between the two women must have been quite great as she always mentions June by her full name, and leaves her out of all of Rudy's 'spirit' messages (despite his naming of 'psychic' friends and a whole spiel on writers.) The more I research June, the more ridiculous it is, as the things Natacha mentions over and over again match with things June said years before this book came into being. For her part, Mathis claimed to see Rudy's apparition the moment he died. She was also the one to 'loan' him the crypt he is still in to this day. Sadly June would die a year after this book was first published.

One thing in particular that startled me most about reading this book for the first time was Natacha's explanation of their entry into Spiritualism. June Mathis was a heavy spiritualist (for more on this topic please see page 275) before she met Rudy. Every film of hers seems to contain some sort of Spiritualist message, even when it was a comedy (Turn to the Right is a good example). Every biographer cites Natacha as Rudy's entry into Spiritualism, something that would affect his career, his life, and the insanity that followed his death. In this book Natacha cites the death of June's mother Virginia ('Jenny') as the moment they became convinced and began learning various Occult activities. I find this particularly interesting, as first off it makes sense, and secondly Natacha is usually 'blamed' for his Spiritualism…something that I'm not sure she (or June or Rudy) meant to be negative.

17

When I first began learning about Rudy, all signs and resources seemed to cite Natacha's book as the start of cult that has sprung up around Valentino since his death. Ever since 1927, a tacky Memorial Service has been held, becoming more outlandish as the years passed. Along the way many people, self proclaimed psychics, and some mentally ill types, have claimed to speak to Rudy, see his ghost, or communicate with him via séances. While spiritual beliefs should be to each their own (I personally find the topic fascinating, but that doesn't mean every person who claims something should be believed,) this community has come to overshadow anything else associated with Valentino, usually writing books to sell on the matter (or recordings).

Even worse, self proclaimed authors like Kenneth Anger have taken such 'telepathy' and turned it into things like "Hollywood Babylon", turning their sick delusions into 'fact'…or legend. Either way it's malicious, hurtful, and damaging to the man and his legacy. If Rudy had somehow lived long enough to hear such things, he'd surely be livid (case in point: look how he felt about the pink powder puff article). And if indeed these types could receive spiritual communications, I'm sure they would get an earful from the proud Italian-French man.

I was particularly surprised to find in this book that Natacha was against such things. Yes she was a Spiritualist (well maybe more a Kemetic type, again see page 147), who believed in the Occult and everything that went with it, including séances to speak with the dead. But beyond some blatant promotion of Madame Blavatsky, most of her psychic beliefs seem quite sincere and in step with more traditional new age beliefs.

True, she 'spoke' to the deceased Rudy and wrote half of this book about it. But she was against celebrating death, and in 'speaking' with Rudy she wanted to show there was something more once we are gone. She goes out of her way several times to say the death circus that followed his departure 'held him back' and 'upset him' as he could not move on. Indeed, she never attended the Memorial or really spoke about Rudy after the 20s. I think with this book she wanted to show the type of person he was in real life, and the type of soul she thought he was in death. In fact through her so-called 'spiritual communications' she goes on to show that many of the things these kooky types are claiming (such as constant hauntings, messages about nothing, and a focus on death) , are in her belief system, inaccurate.

In her later years Natacha became an Egyptologist of some renowned. In addition she taught many Occult and spiritual classes well into the 1950s, never using Rudy's name to promote her work.

On several occasions she turned the press away, threatening to sue if they said anything bad about her or Rudy. I think it is interesting to note most of the more salacious stuff ('books' and films) came out once she passed in 1966.

I am very proud to release this book through The Rudolph Valentino Society. Not only does it give Natacha a voice she has long been denied (with many misinterpreting her own words), but it tells about the life and work of Rudolph Valentino as well. The very thing I wish to see more of.

I am very, VERY against the Memorial Service and those who wish to erase Rudy the man with Rudy the dead Sheik ghost. If indeed Natacha's beliefs were true than something like the Memorial Service has been 'holding his spirit' back for 80 some years. While you don't necessarily have to prescribe to such a theory, it is quite startling to see Rudy and Natacha's spiritual beliefs put back in a more proper context. The goal of the Society is to restore the legacy, life, and work of Rudolph Valentino. I could think of no better book to do just that.

-Hala Pickford
Founding Sheba of
The Rudolph Valentino Society

Rudy during the filming of Blood and Sand, 1922.

HOW TO USE THIS BOOK

"**Rudolph Valentino: A Wife's Memories of an Icon**" is divided in sections, just as the original book was.

In **Recollections,** Natacha recounts her time and life with Rudy. This section is very similar to a memoir or biography. In certain sections her mother, Winifred Kimball Hudnut (also known as 'Muzzie') takes over, giving her own recollections about her 'children'. This section should be considered factual as far as memoirs go. Notes have been added where we can provide more information, proving or disproving something mentioned.

Revelations is a bit different. In this section Rudy's spirit is supposedly speaking in a first person narrative, via séances with Natacha and an American psychic, George Benjamin Wehner. Wehner was said to go into 'nap' like trances, receiving his messages from his deceased mentor, Madame Blavatsky, Founder of the Theosophical Society. Natacha and Rudy were both Spiritualists who dabbled in the Occult. For more information on this please see that sections foreword, "Rudy, Natacha, and the Occult" on page 147. This section should not be considered a factual biographical text, but a spiritual one. Whether it is to be believed or not is up to the reader's own personal beliefs. However it is an interesting read.

Rediscovering is completely new text, not found in the original book. This section is written by Hala Pickford. Here you will find further information and resources on Natacha and Rudy, as well as some other important people mentioned in this book. For the first time in print are biographies on Nita Naldi and June Mathis. This section has been added as a sort of reference, with the hope that it will encourage fans to learn the real story of both great artists.

PART I

REVELATIONS

Natacha Rambova, 1920s

ORIGINAL FOREWORD

NOW that Rudy's earthly presence has left us, I want to give to the world my recollections of him. In writing these pages I have shared with you, his public, my most treasured possession – the memory of my happiest days, days never to be forgotten and beyond recall.

This memory of Rudy, the real Rudy as I knew and loved him, is being shared by me because I do not feel I have the right to keep it to myself. After all, he belongs to you, who also loved him, is being shared by me because I do not feel I have the right to keep it to myself. After all, he belongs to you, who also loved him, as much or even more than he belongs to me or to any other one person.

So when you read this story, just understand that I am only trying to take you with me through a few years of the past, that you also may know him as I did – Rudy the man, the boy at heart that would never grow up, the companion, the friend, the sweetheart, in other words just Rudy as he was.

Many stories have been written of his life – some true, some not – but at least enough to acquaint you with his early history; his childhood in Italy and his first struggles in America. The period of his life that I shall tell you about begins the year before "The Four Horsemen" was released – the beginning of his fame – and ends a few months before his death.

In letting you read these pages of his private life and mine, I shall undoubtedly be severely criticized by many. But criticism is a petty thing and soon dies out, while I hope this memory will live to record for the future the character of the true man.

You knew him as the dashing lover; the Sheik, Gallardo the bullfight, the swordsman Beaucaire, as he was upon the silver screen – the artist. If you wish to know the man beneath the grease paint, you will find him in these pages.

You will see him at play, at work, at rest, and you will love the man as you did the artist.

Of one side of his life you have heard but little – the side which had to do with the psychic things.

Few people knew that Rudy was himself a medium and clairvoyant and had many wonderful experiences on the "borderland".

In these pages I have told you of some of these experiences personally recounted by him to others beside myself, but never before published.

At the time of Rudy's passing, my family and I were fortunately blessed by having with us, as a guest at my father's château, or friend Mr. George Wehner, a most remarkable psychic.

It was Mr. Wehner's clear instrumentality as a deep trance subject which made it possible for us to communicate with Rudy almost immediately after his passing. Rudy's unusually rapid return for communication is due partly to his own psychic development and knowledge of the Hereafter before his death, and partly to the help and guidance given him by that Great Soul, H. P. Blavastky, founder of the Theosophical Society.

The messages, which comprise the second part of the book, were dictated by Rudy directly through the deep entranced instrument. They are reproduced here as they were taken down by me, many in the presence of my mother and father, Mr. and Mrs. Richard A. Hudnut, and a few intimate friends.

In these messages, Rudy has given to the world the benefit of his own personal experiences while passing through the Great Gateway to the Beyond, and also much knowledge that he has gained in the after-life.

It is his hope that by giving forth this knowledge he may still serve and help to repay in a measure that love which was so generously shown him while here.

I am indebted to my mother for some of the incidents written by her in the Recollections, and to Mr. Wehner, who psychic faculties made possible the Revelations of Rudy.

NATACHA RAMBOVA.
New York,
December, 1926.

CHAPTER 1

IT was a hot winter's day in Hollywood. One of the few places where on can say such things. The old Metro lot was still pretty busy, but now that the strain and excitement of turning out "The Four Horsemen" was over, a certain calm and relief had settled down upon it.

At this time I was working as art director for Nazimova's Unit.* We were just about ready to start the filming of Camille, but there was one small detail which held us up. We had no leading man. We had looked at Armands tall and short, fat and thing, dark and light, but as yet none pleased Camille.

There was a knock at my office door.

"Come in." I was more or less annoyed as I was sure I was going to have to look at some other poor miserable Armand. Then there would be the usual questions. If the unfortunate creature happened to be blond he would be asked if he would mind dyeing his hair black, as Frenchmen were never blond. If he were short inner lifts were suggested.

What was his last picture? A comedy! Then of course he would not be sympathetic enough to play Armand. So sorry. Maybe some other time. One more passed out.

The door opened. Nazimova entered followed by a bulky figure dressed from head to foot in long fur "artics." What I could see of the face was not exactly prepossessing. Two dark slanting eyes with eyelashes and eyebrows white with mica – the artificial snow of the picture realm. This, I thought to myself, was the worst yet.

"Natacha, I want you to meet Rudolph Valentino. Rudolph, this is Miss Rambova, my art director."

---

*Natacha became Metro Star Alla Nazimova's art director in 1920. Under this title she was in charge of set and costume design, both of which she excelled at. Natacha was making $5,000 a week at the time. Despite Nazimova's notorious bisexuality, she never had a relationship with Rambova, though she did have one with Valentino's first wife Jean Acker. Rambova would claim well into her later years she 'despised lesbians' despite having many gay and bisexual friends and co-workers.

The figure in fur advanced and shook hands. At least his handshake was firm. I might add, a little too firm for comfort. I looked at his face. There were little streams of perspiration running down and mingling with the now spoilt make-up and mica.

It was a very hot winter's day! This melting vision in fur was hardly one's dream of a romantic Armand. Then he smiled. That flash of even white teeth had certainly something very winning about it.

"Natacha, this is the young man who played the lead for Rex Ingram in the 'Four Horsemen'*. What do you think of him? June Mathis says he can act."

The figure in fur laughed and then spoke, a little nervously and with a slight foreign accent.** "I do hope you will pardon the way I look. You know I am working with Alice (Lake) in 'Uncharted Seas' and I have just been standing before the sun taking close-ups with her for about two hours. I cannot stay now; they will miss me on the set. Please say for me a good word with Madame." Another smile, a click of the heels, a bow, and he was gone.

So this was the patent-leather-haired leading man I had heard so much about on the lot. The new discovery of June Mathis. Well – he didn't look it. But then sometimes our outer garments are deceiving, especially under such conditions.

Nazimova explained that she had seen some of his "rushes." They were really very good. She was convinced he was the one person to play Armand, but – of course there would have to be some buts, there always were. And this time they were bad ones, only for once, not the fault of Armand or his parents.

What were we to do? He wouldn't be through with Alice for at least three weeks by schedule, which would probably mean four or five. He was leaving in a few days for Arizona on location, so it was out of the question to work him in two pictures at once, which was sometimes done. Then besides what would Charles think? Here Madame confided that Mr. Bryant – her husband and manager*** who was at present in New York – did not like him because he was supposed to be a rather wild young Lothario, and he couldn't bear his patent-leather hair.

---

*Rudolph Valentino had been in b pictures for a few years, usually playing a heavy. Metro Film Executive June Mathis 'discovered' him in the 1919 film "Eyes of Youth", though it is possible she might have seen him in a shelved Julian Eltinge picture beforehand.

June picked Rudy to play 'Julio' in her epic production 'The Four Horsemen of the Apocalypse'. Though not exactly a lead it was a major role, and launched Valentino into stardom, though Metro didn't feel that way. They quickly threw him into a string of b pictures including this one, the now lost, 'Uncharted Seas'. For more on June Mathis see page 275

**To hear Valentino speak please see http://rudolphvalentino.org/speak.html

However, Madame generally got her way, and after many conferences with Alice's director, June Mathis, and the head office, it was finally agreed. We were to wait for him for three weeks and they were to rush their shooting.

As this day in my office was the first time I had ever seen Rudy, I personally found it very difficult to understand why so much fuss was being made to get him for Armand. But then, Madame at times had strange ideas.

The weeks passed, and finally our leading man returned from location. One problem was solved and put aside, but there still remained the patent-leather hair. How was this to be dealt with? We all met in my office to deal with this weighty question.

The Armand of Madame's script, being an unsophisticated young man of the French provinces, would certainly not have used hair pomade. Besides, Mr. Bryant had to be considered.

After much discussion we decided to see how Rudy would look with the naturally wavy hair that all good country boys are supposed to have.

Rudy was sent to his dressing room to remove the patent-leather glaze by a good shampoo; while I collected curling irons and alcohol lamps from the hairdressing department. Why this operation was not detailed to a real hairdresser I cannot now remember, although I think it was to appease Rudy's avowal never to appear with curly hair. I assured him that with the irons I would merely fluff it slightly.

At last the transformation was accomplished. Madame was delighted. I reserved judgment. Rudy was horribly upset and very doubtful.

After a test was taken, however, and he saw for himself the good effect on the screen, his love for characterization, combined with Madame's arguments, finally won him over.

As I look back on the Rudy of those days, I remember him as a strange child, for child he was always, and always so remained. In his work he was so intensely absorbed in trying to please by telling jokes and playing pranks. This was the side of Rudy that used to annoy me frightfully, for so often his American jokes told in his funny Italian way were perfectly pointless. This continued and forced joviality upset me, as in those days I took life, work, and myself terribly seriously.

***Despite usually being titled a 'lesbian' Alla Nazimova was indeed married to Charles Bryant and had on and off again relationships with various men, including Paul Ivano. A more accurate term for her would probably be bi-sexual.

Later we often joked about this, after Rudy had confided the reasons for this strange behavior. His best friend at this time was Norman Kerry*, who had been the means of his coming to Los Angeles and entering pictures.

Norman was always very popular with everyone and very successful, so Rudy, hoping to arrive at the same results, tried to pattern his ways after Norman's as much as possible. Anyone who knows Norman knows his wonderful sense of humor, his spontaneous gaiety and his love of jokes. Hence Rudy's anxious attempts to do likewise.

When I learned to know Rudy better I began to see, underneath all his forced happiness, the lonely and often sad young man he really was. Being a foreigner and unknown, his way was not the easiest. The same people who then considered him beneath their notice, later, after his success, were the first with their attentions and flattery. Long after, this was a source of great amusement to us both.

A kindness done at this time was, however never forgotten by Rudy. To Pauline Frederick and her mother, Rudy always carried a debt of gratitude and love – I know to the end – and for their great kindness and understanding when he most needed it. He often spoke to me about them, and always with a catch in his voice; how they had championed him on many an occasion.

There were also some who traded on this quality of his, as a future means of support. A twenty-five dollar loan of those days – meant the return of many a thousand.

Having both been brought up in Europe, and speaking French and Italian, we soon found a common ground for mutual friendship and understanding. Many were the memories exchanged of our experiences in France and Italy, which always ended in happy plans for our return, although at the time we did not dream of every revisiting these scenes together.

I was living in a little bungalow on Sunset Blvd of which I was very proud. It boasted a bedroom, bathroom, living-room and kitchenette. I had decorated it in bright colors. The furniture, consisting mostly of second hand kitchen tables and chairs,

---

*Norman Kerry was a man of some wealth who wished to enter pictures. He met Valentino in San Francisco around 1916 or 1917, convincing him to go to Los Angeles and give film a try. Kerry paid for Valentino's stay at The Alexandria Hotel. Kerry would eventually become a star in his own right during the mid 20s, notably playing in some of Lon Chaney's best films. Not much research has been done on Kerry, though he is occasionally lobbed in as a supposed lover of Valentino. This seems quite preposterous and no such proof has ever been found. Those who knew Kerry said he was a hard drinking womanizer who was part of the Marshall Neilan and Jack Pickford playboy crowd. If a woman rejected him he'd pretend to not know her.

was painted in black and red; as near as possible to Chinese lacquer, of which I have always been fond. This lacquering was usually done on Sundays in the backyard with Rudy as an able helper.

After work was over at the studio, Rudy often returned with me to the bungalow to cook spaghetti and to prepare, as he explained to me, a real Italian dinner. Before these mighty preparations were completed, however, it was often near midnight than dinner-hour. But what we lost in time, we made up in enjoyment with well-sharpened appetites. June Mathis and her beloved mother, Mrs. Virginia Mathis, would sometimes honor us as guests at these feasts.

One particular scene in "Camille" I shall always remember, as it gave me my first insight into the extraordinary sensitiveness and sincerity of Rudy's character, which was always to me the true secret of his great success.

The scene* I speak of was the auction scene taken from the book version. After the death of Camille, Armand, overcome with grief, returns to Camille's apartment where an auction of her things is being held. He bids for a book which he had given her in the early part of the story and which she had kept with her even to the last.

Before playing any scene of pathos I noticed that Rudy invariably went away by himself, to be alone, where it seemed he could absorb every feeling and emotion of the character he was portraying. Each character to him was always a living, vibrant entity.

Even during the long-shots of the scene I could see that Rudy was struggling with his emotions – to keep back the tears. By the time the close-up was taken we were all crying. From the director to the extras. Even Birkie our camera-man, whose one acknowledged interest in life was his home-made still, was mopping at his eyes.

Sincere grief, like spontaneous laughter, is inevitably catching.

After the last shot was over I found Rudy in his chair behind the set, his head buried in his arms crying like a child, as later I used to find him in some despondent mood, weeping about his mother** of whom he had been passionately fond. This was surely no make-believe, this was real grief, for temporarily he was indeed that character.

---

*Reportedly Alla Nazimova had the scene cut as it upstaged her. This particular ending appears to have never been screened.
**Valentino's father had died when he was 11. He was extremely close to his French mother Gabriella. She passed in 1918, something Valentino would never quite overcome.

It will always be my regret that the picture was not shown with this ending. It would have added greatly to the sincerity of it. Instead, it ended with many feet of the dying Camille. Originally the story was to have been of a modern Camille, to show that the history of such characters is of no period, but of all times. The picture released under the title "Camille" disappointed many who expected to see the charming atmosphere of the original "Dame aux Camelias," and consequently caused much undue criticism.

It was just after the filming of this picture that the Los Angeles opening of "The Four Horsemen" was announced. We were so excited we could hardly wait for the eventful evening to arrive. Rudy, of course, secured tickets the first moment they were available.

"The Four Horsemen" had already been released in New York and had been accorded a tremendous ovation, but even then we could not realize its future success. June Mathis had telegraphed Rudy from the East congratulating him on the reception his performance had been given, but even this seemed too far away to be true. After so many years of hardships and struggles it did not seem possible to Rudy that the day of that long-dreamed-of success had actually arrived.

At last the momentous evening came! The expectant audience was an impressive one. The entire film colony was represented, although many, I fear, had come to scoff and say "I told you so"; as this film was supposed to be the ruination of the Metro Company. Everyone had foreseen and foretold it. Such expense and such extravagance had never been heard of. But what could one expect with a woman at the head of it; a practically unknown director and an unknown actor in a leading role!

During the running of the film not a sound could be heard in the theatre except here and there an occasional stifled sob as the story unfolded. About the middle of the picture Rudy reached out and took hold of my hand, which he held tightly in his own until the end. I knew he wanted to feel that there was just someone who cared and understood. We were both weeping from mixed emotions – joy at the success which could even now be felt on all sides, and sorrow for the tragedy of the story.

When it was over, there was a moment of hushed silence, and then tremendous applause. Sincere and spontaneous appreciation of a thing well done. Rudy was surrounded and congratulated by many of his fellow workers and by many whom he did not know; but his aim seemed to be to reach the door. He wanted to be alone. I understood. During the ride home to my bungalow I do not think a word was spoken. Just a "Good night" when he left me to return alone to his little apartment on upper Hollywood Boulevard.

Another evening comes back to me – equally characteristic of Rudy, but with what a different ending!

Charles Bryant was returning from New York and Madame was most anxious that Rudy should meet him and make a good impression to wipe out his former prejudice against the sophisticated Latin lover with the patent-leather hair.

All was beautifully arranged. Just a small friendly party. We were to dine and spend the evening at Sunset Inn, Santa Monica, in those days the delight of the picture colony, where all the brightest stars of the firmament could be seen enjoying unguarded moments of pleasure and relaxation with their chosen friends. These were happy pre-Vigilance Committee days.* Viola Daniels and Alice Lake, in life, the inseparable star comediennes of the Metro lot, were soon located by the laughter arising from their slangy and ridiculous chatter. Over there, Priscilla Dean was amusing her friend with her sparkling vivacity. Little Buster Keaton with his big pal Fatty Arbuckle were as usual convulsing the entire room with their antics on the dancing floor. If only a camera could have caught them then! Little Bebe Daniels, the new De Mille find from the comedy ranks, was there, surrounded by her ever faithful band of admirers. Gloria Swanson, already the exotic De Mille star, but not yet the clever artist of her future work, could be seen the focus point of my many an envious glance; and others, many others, stars now gone and stars then in the making. Poor Old Sunset Inn, scene of many a happy episode, whose doors, alas, have long since been closed by Prohibition's stern defenders. Enough of reminiscing.

Rudy had been warned beforehand that Mr. Bryant was an Englishman, and therefore not inclined to facile friendships. But all undaunted, he assured us that he already liked Mr. Bryant and saw no reason for their not being friends. We, however, were more doubtful.

The evening started off. Charles was somewhat wary. Rudy cheerful, but somewhat anxious. To break the ice, Prohibition's favorite brand was somewhat freely passed. All looked well! All were happy!

---

*This was shortly before the Fatty Arbuckle scandal erupted, causing massive overreacting and censorship in the film community. Roscoe "Fatty" Arbuckle was falsely accused of raping and murdering b star actress Virginia Rappe. The media sensation that followed would be comparable to the O.J. Simpson trial in the 1990s (however, unlike O.J., Roscoe was acquitted on all charges three times). Valentino had known both Arbuckle and Rappe, and remained friends with Arbuckle until his death.

Then – I began to notice that Rudy had had enough. I kicked him under the table. No avail. Every time Charles filled his glass, Rudy filled his. Determination was in his eye. He was going to show Charles that he was a hell of a good fellow. No one could get ahead of him! They became chummy.

Madame and I were horrified, foreseeing disastrous results. Charles, being an Englishman, was used to the harder variety of refreshments, while Rudy, being Latin and brought up on wine, was most evidently unable to keep up the pace. More kicks under the table. Still no results. I was furious and glared whenever Rudy deigned to glance in my direction, which was not often, as he and Charles seemed to be entirely engrossed in each other.

Madame gave them up and ignored both. As far as we were concerned the whole affair was ruined. Rudy was making a spectacle of himself, and after all our warnings too! It was insufferable! Tail ends of Rudy's countless stories wafted across the table to us, drowned not infrequently by deep English guffaws.

Madame decided she could stand no more; it was time to leave. Ignoring them completely we rose and marched to the door, leaving as we thought, the ruination of our hopes behind us. I was so furious and disappointed by Rudy's actions I could hardly keep back the tears. I had never seen him drink before, or at least, to excess.

As we were stepping majestically into the new Rolls-Royce, in hurt and dignified silence, whom did we see coming towards us down the steps, swaying slightly, but Charles and Rudy arm in arm! Rudy, delighted with his conquest and new-found friend. Charles in evident amusement, supporting him like one.

Once inside the car I burst into tears. I had never thought to see Rudy drunk. It was more than I could bear. I stormed. Rudy fell asleep. Madame retained her aloof and dignified silence while Charles roared with laughter at us all and begged me to forgive Rudy. Being a man and a very real person, Mr. Bryant of course, saw through Rudy's boyish attempts at mannish sophistication. They delighted him and entirely wiped out his former prejudices and opinions. Few indeed there were who could withstand Rudy when he wanted to be liked.

Rudy had succeeded – but how differently from what we had planned and imagined!

Rudy, at last awake, was determined to drive me home. I, still furious, was equally determined he should not. I insisted he was in no condition to drive anything or anyone. He furiously declared that there was nothing the matter with him; he had never been more sober in life.

This was too much for Madame and Charles. They burst into peals of laughter at us both. The more they laughed, the more indignant we became. Both always stubborn – neither of us would give in. In this instance I happened to have advantage. The car was mine. So in I climbed, and off I started, leaving Rudy to run beside the car declaring with every breath that he was sober and perfectly competent to drive me home. I stepped on the gas, the car sprang ahead and Rudy was left behind in the night.

So ended our party, our first quarrel, and the first and only time I ever saw Rudy – shall I say – "under the weather"?

CHAPTER 2

SHORTLY after "Camille" was finished, Rex Ingram started preparations for a new picture – "The Conquering Power," adapted by June Mathis from Balzac's *Eugenie Grandet*. Rudy was asked to play the lead opposite Alice Terry. He was delighted; but thought after his success in "Horsemen" that he was entitled to a raise. He asked for fifty dollars more*. This was flatly refused him. After much unsuccessful argument and no other propositions in sight, he finally agreed to play the part under the conditions of the old agreement.

As usual, he became greatly interested and absorbed in the preparations for his new characterization. He re-read the book and then studied his script. Every detail of costume must be correct, even to the monocle worn in one of the episodes, which gave him untold delight. Hours and days were spent practicing with it to attain just the correct amount of ease and nonchalance.

From the time Rudy finished studying a script until the actual shooting of a film was completed, he had an uncanny peculiarity of never being able to quite throw off the character he was playing. It seemed somehow to dominate him. At times this used to bother me. I would feel uncomfortable, as if in the presence of a stranger. It was due, I think, to his sensitiveness to thought and surroundings. I do not think he quite realized or understood it himself. Even his ideas and opinions of different subjects used to change with his mannerisms. He seemed unnaturally affected by new conditions and atmosphere. This was the cause for his facility in characterizing. It was not acting. It was living.

Many amusing incidents happened during the filming of this picture. I was not on the lot myself at the time, but I would hear all about the day's work during the lunch or dinner hour – as he still continued to take most of his meals with me at the bungalow, which was near the studio.

---

*Valentino was notoriously bad with money and contracts. He had only been making $350 a week during this time, though someone of his stature should have been worth thousands a week..

One evening he stamped in in a fury. His eyes were flashing and he was shaking with excitement.

Rex had insulted him!*

What was he to do?

At such moments his Italian ancestry cropped out with all the force of a dozen Borgias. His thoughts always flew to a duel. This was one of his secret and most cherished ambitions. At last the story came out.

He had been all dressed for the midnight entertainment scene – a gala event both on and off the screen, as he loved to wear his full-dress clothes, of which he was very proud – when just as they were about to start shooting Rex suddenly stopped and bawled him out before all the extras. It was something about a vest, a black one or a white one. Whichever it was, Rex said it should be the other one. Words flew. Rex said Rudy should know better. Rudy told Rex he knew nothing about clothes, a trench coat being the only thing he ever wore. More words.

The question was finally decided by calling in Frank Elliot, an English actor, who was considered the last word on gentleman's fashions.

Mr. Elliot, to Rudy's glee, pronounced him correctly and perfectly turned out.

But this was not all! Oh no! Rex had from that moment on ignored Rudy completely. He had even cleaned his finger-nails with his penknife all during Rudy's most serious and important close-up! How could he act under such conditions!

There were many such squabbles. As I look back now, I realize that they were both little more than children; each with a great deal of talent – and a great deal of but recently acquired success.

---

*Ingram and Valentino had almost never gotten along. June Mathis had 'discovered' them both, giving them important parts in "Four Horsemen" which launched both men to fame. But Ingram felt it should have been his picture, and was quite miffed that Valentino was the one who got all the attention. In addition it seems very likely Ingram and Mathis were in a romantic relationship, causing him to become even more jealous at her attention to Valentino (whether she and Rudy ever had a romantic affair is not as clear). Valentino and Ingram would work on two films together, before Rudy left Metro. Ingram would spend the rest of his career trying to upstage Valentino, showing indeed it was he who had made Valentino a success (even going as far as discovering, with some help from Mathis, Ramon Novarro. Novarro only met Valentino once.) In later years the only people to have anything bad to say about Rudy would be Ingram and the woman he left Mathis for, Alice Terry.

Rudy the snazzy dresser

A few weeks later, an official dinner was to be given by the Metro Company. Rudy was not invited, being on an actor, but Rex was; and he had no evening clothes. Where was he to get them? Rudy? Of course, as they were both about the same size. He immediately sent his assistant director for the desired outfit, so recently scorned. Rudy without hesitation complied. This to me was screamingly funny, but neither of them saw anything funny about it. Rudy, in fact, was totally at a loss at my laughter, and not a little bit piqued. After all it was but a most natural procedure.

Automobiles from the first were Rudy's downfall. At this particular time he was without one, and this is how it came about.

With his first picture contract in his pocket and the hopes of money to come, Rudy's thoughts immediately flew to an automobile. How he had longed for one of his very own, and now that wish could be gratified! No time was wasted in uncertainty. His mind was already fully made up. He would have a racing Mercer. (Rudy always had expensive tastes and would have what he considered the best or at least as near it as possible.)

The arrangements were at last completed. He bought it on the installment plan of so much a week.

In the joy and excitement of this first real possession, he dashed about from work to play and from play to work. But the weeks also dashed by. His contract finally came to an end, as all good things seem to do, and then there were no more weekly checks. He went from studio to studio looking for work, but work was scarce.

After some time of dodging the dealer who had sold him the car, he was at last forced to acknowledge his inability to continue payments.

His car was taken from him and he lost all that he had already paid on it, which was at least half of its value.

When he told me about this, I remember exclaiming, "But, Rudy, surely you could have done something so as not to lose all the money you had paid out!"

He looked at me in surprise and answered "Well, I did the best I could, didn't I?"

Rudy had a philosophical turn of mind. He refused absolutely to worry or to be unhappy about anything already in the past, and this same answer was always to him the satisfactory conclusion to any such affair.

This experience cured him momentarily of buying automobiles.

Being then, at this period, without a car, he, of course, used mine, which was a little Buick runabout. This car I had bought when

I first went to work at the Metro Studios. In my opinion, it was a little beauty, and since it was also my first car, I had fitted it out with all kinds of extras – mirrors, spotlights, canteens, etc.

But Rudy thought otherwise. You see, it just would not speed. As Rudy, in disgust, expressed it, it had no "pick-up". He immediately started out to remedy this error by looking for another car which had the desired speed and for which he could exchange the Buick. He knew I must want a car with a "pick-up".

He haunted all the second-hand car shops, read all the advertisements of "Sale or Exchange" and had all the "props" at the studio on the lookout. Rudy was nothing if not thorough in all that he did.

One day, shortly after this first commotion, while I was calmly eating my lunch at the bungalow, I received a telephone call from Rudy. He was downtown now, but was coming right out! I was to be sure and remain at home as he had a big surprise for me! No, he would not tell me what it was; I must wait!

About half an hour later, my attention was attracted by many loud "honks" coming from the front yard. I ran to the window in great expectation, certain that this must be the surprise Rudy had spoken of, - my imagination quickly picturing a beautifully smart little "sport" car as he had so often described.

A surprise, yes! There was Rudy, wreathed in smiles, waving excitedly for me to come out and view his "find".

The "find" turned out to be a 1914 Cadillac roadster with faint traces still left of having once been painted a dingy blue.

My expression must have betrayed me, for Rudy speedily informed that the proof of a good car was all in the motor and this motor was quite beyond comparison. (I later found to my sorrow that this was indeed correct.)

The "pick-up," he continued, was marvelous. He had tried it on all the hills. The speed was better than anyone could want from a car that was not a real racer. It did not even "cough" at seventy, and the cut-out – well, I must hear it for myself. There was no other like it! As for the outside, that was a mere detail; it could be made like new in a week.

Nothing would do but I must come at once to try it with him. Then I would realize myself what a jewel the motor was.

This all ended, of course, with Rudy exchanging the Buick for the old Cadillac and receiving four hundred dollars to the good, for which amount, he assured me, we could make the Cadillac look like a "real" car.

Rudy was a wonderful salesman, as with his childish enthusiasm and sincerity he could make you see wonders in anything in which he was interested at the moment – wonders which really never existed, except in his own fertile imagination.

By this time "The Conquering Power" was finished and he was now able to devote himself entirely to his new toy. He worked untiringly on the transformation of this ugly duckling, fitting it out with two strong "spots" on either side of the wind-shields, a cigarette lighter on the driving board, and many other improvements, all installed by himself.

After a good coat of black paint – egg-shell finish – and much polishing of the nickel trimmings, it really did not look so bad. But then our trouble started. It would suddenly stop at the most inopportune moments – all of which incidents Rudy declared were liable to happen to any powerful motor. Its capacity for oil and gas was truly remarkable. However, we both agreed that we at last owned a real car, which was a great improvement on the old Buick, and left it at that.

Then once again the hunt for work began.

Although the "Horsemen" had now been released for many months, the producers even yet did not seem to realize Rudy's value. There were several "possible" offers, which for one reason or another all fell through. Rudy, who did not know the meaning of saving, was consequently always hard up between pictures.

I, myself, was working on the designs of the sets and costumes of Nazimova's next film "Salome," for which I had received an advance. Then Madame suddenly decided to postpone the actual filming of this picture in favor of "The Doll's House," which was made first.

We were both in a bad way.

Rudy daily made the rounds of the studios – apparently to say a few "hellos" to friends, but in reality to recall himself to the mind of any directors or producers who might be about. When our expense account allowed, we lunched at one of the favorite haunts of the directors on the boulevard.

In the meantime I took a few private pupils for instruction in the art of designing. This, with the occasional sacrifice of a few of the "family jewels," kept us going.*

---

*Natacha's mother Winifred 'Muzzie' Kimball had married her way into high society when Natacha was a young girl. Her current stepfather at this time was Richard Hudnut, the perfume magnate on par with companies like Chanel or Max Factor (the company still exists today, mainly in France). Though Natacha could have easily asked for some money to help get by, she always refused. In fact Valentino did not learn of her parent's wealth tell after this episode of poverty.

When our appetites grew a little too healthy for the meager ice-box supply, we would resort to an early morning hunt on the old Robertson Cole ranch.

These rides through the dawn fog were always a delight, as well as a necessity. The thrill of "poaching" was exhilarating, as there was always the chance of a possible arrest, which lent an added charm.

Once past Santa Monica, the houses grew scarcer and then we turned in to the quiet of the country roads. Here we stopped and prepared for action. The gun was brought out of hiding, the cartridge belt strapped on, and the hood of the car let down.

For these "hunts" Rudy would sit on top of the let-down hood at the back of the car, with his legs dangling over the side, while I drove. As soon as I saw a quail or a dove out for their morning meal, I would slow down the car until it barely crawled along, and then Rudy would take a "pop" at them. We discovered that if we stopped the car altogether they always flew away, while as long as we kept moving they paid no attention to us.

As Rudy was a pretty good shot and the game plentiful (we were shooting out of season), it was not long before we had eight birds, which was the limit of our "kill". Then we would change tactics and start after rabbits.

This necessitated entirely different maneuvers.

We would drive up any small path and leave the car hidden in the bushes. The birds were concealed somewhere in the grass, in case any too zealous game-warden might be prowling about. Then, with our guns under our arms, we would set off across fields and down ravines. Rabbits were also in abundance here, as few people ever came this way. The ranch itself was now seldom used, even for "locations".

Our limit for rabbits was four. As soon as these were had we would stop and return. Sometimes, however, we would have to leave before our limit was complete, as it would get too light for comfort and we were afraid of being caught.

Several times we had quite narrow escapes. One morning I remember in particular. We had just hidden the car and were about to start on our rabbit hunt when we saw a man emerge from the trees across a nearby field and walk rapidly toward the road. We rushed madly for the car and, throwing all our guns, birds, and cartridges into the rear baggage compartment, drove out and down the road as fast as our car would take us.

When well out of sight we stopped for breath. To avoid meeting the man we had to drive in the opposite direction from Hollywood, and now to return home it was necessary to turn about and drive back over the same road. We waited until we thought it safe and then set out.

As we approached the danger zone, we saw that the man was still there. It was too late now to stop or turn around without arousing suspicion. All we could do was to go on, right for him. Would he stop us? He did, of course. We slowed down, with out hearts in our mouths, wondering frantically who would bail us out. He asked if we had passed anyone on the road with a gun. He had heard some shots. Rudy found his voice first. Yes, we had passed a man – quite a way down the road – but he had not noticed if he had a gun – on second thought, maybe he had. He turned to me. Maybe I had noticed. Being afraid to trust my voice, I tried an unconcerned shrug and a shake of the head.

The man muttered a "Thanks," and moved on. Needless to say, we did too.

For some time after this we decided that we were rather tired of game, so temporarily our hunts were abandoned for another favorite "sport," known to us as "muttiola-ing".

By way of explanation, muttiolas were mussels, of which we were both very fond, especially when boiled with garlic and olive oil. "Muttiola-ing" then meant an expedition to the beach when it was low tide at early dawn, where we would collect pails of mussels off the rocks. These mussels would compromise our chief diet for the next few days to come and, being taken to a house of true Italian taste, they would sooner or later be sure to find themselves in a stew of a tomato sauce.

In this way our love of "outings" was gratified and the larder kept filled.

How often, in later years, we looked back with regret on those happy times. We were both poor, still unknown to the world in general, and glorifying in our freedom. They were days of laughter, days of dreams, and of ambitious planning for the future.

For myself, I know they were the happiest days I shall ever experience in this life.

Chapter 3

RUDY and I were both great lovers of animals. Whenever we could, we would spend the day at one of the many zoos in or around Los Angeles – one of our cherished ambitions being to one day have a small zoo of our own. The old Selig Zoo was a favorite, but most of all we enjoyed paying a visit to "Curley" Stecker, the head trainer of the animals on the Universal lot.

Here we would spend hours listening to Curley's yarns and experiences. After a generous allowance of these tales of hairbreadth escapes, he would take us to pay a visit to our more particular animal friends – Joe Martin, the famous old chimpanzee of countless Universal comedies, and Ethel, the tame lioness. Ethel was often encouraged to perform some of her many tricks, and then, as the main feature of the day's program, we would see Tom, Dick, and Harry, the three big lions, fed.

Knowing my weakness for all young animals, Curley informed us on one of our visits that he had something he knew I would like to see. He led us across the lot to the leopard cages. There, in the end case, were four adorable lion cubs. Just six weeks old!

Of course, Rudy and I shrieked for joy and insisted that we be allowed to buy one. Curley at first refused, saying that they were not playthings and had already a decided will of their own, which was not very friendly. We, however, declined to take "no" for an answer, so at last Curley went in search of a box and we selected our cub. After much clawing, spitting and yowling she was safely boarded in her cage and deposited in the automobile. We left Curley shaking his head and declaring that we would bring it back again before the week was out.

We could hardly wait to arrive at the bungalow to turn our little spitfire loose.

The first thing that faced us was to somehow clip her nails. This was managed by means of a gag. After this was accomplished, Rudy insisted on christening her with a good scrub of soapsuds in the bath tub – and then we set her free.

I have never in my life seen such indignant rage in anything so young. She strutted all about the house, giving vent to yowls of resentment.

Many were the amusing experiences we had with "Zela," as she was afterwards named. Temperament or temper was her strong point, as Curley indeed had warned us. Her greatest characteristic seemed to be an indomitable pride. She would not tolerate any patronizing on our part, but often, when Rudy was sitting quietly on the couch reading, I have seen her crawl up on his lap to be petted and caressed.

She became a great pet and was devoted to us both, but particularly to Rudy, whom she followed around like an adoring puppy.

Curley never recovered from his amazement at not receiving the cub back into the fold. Poor Curley himself has since passed on, eventually a victim of one of his own lions.

Animals always seemed unable to resist Rudy's sympathy and understanding. He loved them and consequently they loved him. They spoke the same language.

I remember an instance of this mutual and instant friendship. It happened in San Francisco, some time later than the period of which I have been speaking. He was there on "location" for some scenes of "Moran of Lady Letty," in which he supported Dorothy Dalton.

While there he became acquainted with a gentleman and his wife, who were also great lovers of animals. They told him of their police dogs, of which they were very proud, having raised many of them themselves. Rudy was immediately interested to see them. This culminated in an invitation to their home for an inspection of the pets.

One beautiful male dog, shut off by himself, particularly attracted Rudy's attention. He was told that he was too ferocious to be invited to meet strangers. This, of course, only made Rudy the more insistent to be presented. With the hair standing up on his back and with many ominous growls, the dog was last led forth.

Rudy started to talk to him, absorbed in overcoming his apparent animosity. After a while the dog quieted down and stopped his growling to sniff inquiringly at this curiosity, whom he had been unable to daunt by his ferocity. To the astonishment of his own owner, he made friends with Rudy.

After this there were many such visits – Rudy and the dog "Marquis" becoming fast friends. When the time finally arrived for Rudy to leave San Francisco, he was presented with the dog – the owners, declaring that this attachment on the part of their pet, who had been up to now unapproachable, was so extraordinary that they felt he really belong to Rudy more than to themselves.

Another time, while he was taking a short vacation at Palm Springs on the Mohave Desert, he heard from one of his cowboy friends of a horse which was to be shot. According to "Pete" it was just a "bad hoss." It wouldn't be harnessed and it wouldn't be saddled, and as feed was high, it was going to be shot.

Rudy asked to see the horse.

It was a dappled grey desert pony with obviously no family tree to brag of, and with mean eyes, but still Rudy could not bear the idea of leaving it to its fate. He bought it for twenty-five dollars.

With animals Rudy always had infinite patience. With this patience and understanding he finally won the confidence of this same "bad hoss," who became a saddle companion for many future desert expeditions.

When our finances were at the lowest ebb and most of the family jewels were paying for a prolonged visit to "Uncle," Rudy was suddenly engaged to play the "Sheik".

Little did anyone realize what a godsend this was to us.

Loving riding and all outdoor life as he did, Rudy was in his element while making this picture, especially on locations in Oxnard, where here he could be in the midst of cowboys, camels and horses, as all the company camped out in tents.

When he returned from Oxnard he brought, to add to our collection of pets, a beautiful and huge gopher snake. We were both fascinated by snakes.

Our family now consisted of "Sheik," a police dog puppy which had been given to Rudy during the filming of this picture, two Great Dane pups, Zela the cub, a little green moss monkey and the snake.

My unfortunate neighbors, at last refused absolutely to have Zela in their midst any longer. Being now over four months old, she had grown very large. Besides, she had a most annoying habit of disappearing to take a walk by herself down the street.

You can imagine the fright and indignation these prowls caused. Finally I was sweetly but firmly requested to remove myself or my cub from the vicinity.

Rudy and I were both heartbroken, as it was impossible for him to keep Zela in his small apartment. We decided to board her out with Nell Shipman's trainer, who kept her animals on a ranch about thirty miles from Los Angeles.

Many tears were shed at this parting, but nothing else could have done.

The last time we saw Zela was about four months later, when we drove out to pay a farewell visit. The trainer was taking all the animals up to Oregon where Miss Shipman was, I believe, to make some films. Zela was going with them.

The trainer warned us not to go too near her cage as she would not remember us. She had, it seemed, become very treacherous. As he saw we were unhappy at this change in our pet, to distract us he led us off to view some new arrivals which had just been shipped there for training. These turned out to be some lovely baby bears. While I was busy playing with them, I suddenly noticed that Rudy had disappeared. I called him, but he did not answer. Wondering what was keeping him so engrossed, I went in search of him.

I found him, inside, sitting on the floor of Zela's case. He was talking to her and calling her by her old baby names. She was crouched on the other side of the cage, looking at him doubtfully. Then quite slowly I saw her crawl towards him on her tummy, as I had seen her do a hundred times before when wanting to be caressed. She came to Rudy and put her head on his knee, letting out little yowls of pleasure.

Rudy sat this way with her for some time, caressing and talking to her, while the tears streamed down his cheeks.

This was the last time we saw her.

After the "Sheik" was completed, Rudy was engaged by Famous Players for "Moran of the Lady Letty," while I again resumed my work with Nazimova. It was about this time that my mother and father returned from Europe. Their first meeting with Rudy and their impressions, I will let mother tell in her own words.

"In the year of 1921, early in May, we had left San Francisco for Europe. When we reached New York, we received a telegram from Natacha, asking us to be sure and see 'The Four Horsemen' and to let her know what we thought of it. After we saw the picture we replied that we thought it an unusually good film and we were quite enthusiastic over the acting of the new star, Rudolph Valentino.

A few weeks after we reached Paris, we received a cable from Natacha announcing her engagement to Rudolph Valentino and demanding our congratulations. Most modern children have so well trained their parents that they are supposed to sanction every action without question. So we did the expected thing, and forwarded our congratulations at once.

In October we returned to America, and from New York went direct to Hollywood to meet our proposed son-in-law.

Natacha had written glowingly about her first little home, which she had furnished entirely from her own earnings. At this time she was working with Madame Nazimova as art director at a very good salary. From the description of this cinema mansion I expected it to compare favorably with the John Jacob Astor Fifth Avenue brownstone palace.

Natacha met us at the station at about seven o'clock in the evening. She said that Rudy was on location but would be able to dine with us at eight.

We drove up Sunset Boulevard and stopped, as I supposed, at an empty lot. 'Come along,' said Natacha cheerily, 'this is home!'* Being quite dark, it was a little difficult for us to find our way. From the sidewalk we went down several steps and along a narrow path which led to the mansion.

This turned out to be so much in miniature that I mistook it for the garage. Natacha rang the bell and the door was opened by a neat little maid**. We now entered a two-by-four, which appeared to be divided by four closets. The front room was quite large enough for four people if you happened to edge in right. The rug, a creation of the most brilliant modern colors and design, was painted on the floor. Four kitchen chairs, lacquered in red, a small comfortable sofa tables which held lamps with cheery paper shades, bookcases which had been originally packing-boxes but now transformed by red paint into things of beauty, comprised the unique furnishings of this room.

I now entered a room at my right. The windows were small and curtained to the sills in mauve taffeta. The floor was covered with a black carpet. A kitchen table painted black, with a mirror top, stood to one side of the room. On it reposed two glass-beaded baskets filled with glass-beaded flowers, such as one sees by thousands in cemeteries in Italy. On the opposite side stood an oblong black casket affair; having neither foot nor head, it took a good guesser to ascertain its real identity. Two small taffeta chairs stood on either side of the casket.

This room reminded me much of a chapel in a morgue, but I decided it must be Natacha's bedroom.

Entering her white porcelain bathroom, I ran unexpectedly into a snarling cub lion! This was the constant companion of Natacha, but it was necessary to lock him up when she had guests.

*This house still stands at the corner of Sunset and Seward in Hollywood, CA. As of this writing it has been repainted and remodeled into a wine bar.
**Hoping to impress her very wealthy parents, Natacha and Rudy hired the maid for one night. Despite his new found success with Famous Players, Rudy still wasn't making very good money.

I was taken through the tiny kitchen into the garage to be introduced to her two Great Dane pups, an engagement gift from Rudy. They were at present suffering somewhat from rickets as their mistress had stubbornly made up her mind that her dogs should be vegetable fed.

We entered the house just as Rudy arrived for dinner. I saw a slender, boyish, athletic-looking Adonis, with the dark, fervent eyes of romance and a frank, honest smile that completely won my heart. As he had come right from location, he apologized for not being dressed for dinner.

Rudy, in accordance with Italian custom, embraced both Mr. Hudnut and me, kissing us affectionately on both cheeks. It was impossible not to love this impulsive, naïve child.

The kitchen table was now brought in and we all sat down to a delicious little dinner.

Mr. Hudnut and I left our hard-working children with a promise that Rudy would visit us in San Francisco as soon as his picture was finished.

A few weeks later he came for a visit of two weeks. During this visit we learned to truly love him and accept him as one of our very own. While with us he related the fascinating story of his childhood days in Italy and of his subsequent struggles to achieve his ambitions, all of which the public has been acquainted with through his own telling of it in one of the photoplay magazines."

The Whitley Heights Home

CHAPTER 4

AFTER the completion of "Moran of the Lady Letty," Rudy began work almost immediately with Gloria Swanson in "Beyond the Rocks."

It was at this time that we decided to buy the little house on Wedgewood Drive, Whitley Heights*.

As the cash amount to be paid down on the contract was about all we could both manage to scrape together, there was not much money left for furniture. But this did not bother us; we would do it gradually as we could.

A friend of Rudy's with whom he had shared an apartment before, was also living now on Whitley Heights, a few doors down the hill. They arranged it between them to share apartments again so that we could be near each other and Rudy could continue having most of his meals with me**.

These were temporary plans, as we hoped to be able to marry in the Spring.

Of one thing we were determined, and that was that we should have our first Christmas dinner and celebration together in the new house.

The little furniture I had at the bungalow was carted up the hill and I finally moved into the new abode two days before Christmas. It was dreadful – no hot water and no gas, but we were so excited to be in our own real home that nothing else mattered.

The only furniture in the living room was a good Christmas tree and one chair. But what a good time we had decorating that tree. It was the first either of us had had for quite a few years. There was also a bulgy stocking for each of us tacked on the mantle. Wreaths were hung in all the windows and red bells and Santa Clauses made up for the lack of other furnishings.

The Christmas dinner was cooked entirely on a little electric stove, but at that we thought it was the best we had ever eaten.

---

*This house was torn down in the 1950s. The foundation can still be seen from the 101 Freeway by the Vine and Cahuenga Exit sign.
**This was a press lie to keep the morality police at bay. Both Natacha and Rudy moved into this house, sharing it with Paul Ivano. They would only separate once the bigamy scandal had occurred and they had no choice in the matter.

Natacha and Rudy at Christmastime

At midnight we were to open our presents.

We lit the candles on the tree and were just about to begin untying the packages when Rudy suddenly grabbed me by the arm and dragged me upstairs. I was then pushed into my bedroom and told not to dare to move until he called me down.

Next I heard him racing out of the house and down the hill. I couldn't imagine what had happened.

After about ten long minutes, he returned. The outside door banged and I heard him rush downstairs. This was more than my curiosity could stand. I opened the door and called down, asking if I might now descend.

No answer. Silence.

Then a tiny muffled bark – and I too ran downstairs.

The head of a Pekinese puppy with two little paws were just visible, peeping out over the top of my stocking hanging in front of the fireplace. Rudy stood beside it, waiting in childish expectation to see my surprise.

I screamed with delight. I had been longing for another Peke, having lost my last one nearly a year before.

This is how little Chuckie became a member of the family.

We opened out packages, laughed, cried and played with the puppy until the candles on the tree burnt out. Then, tired out from all the excitement, Rudy left and went to this apartment down the hill.

Such was our first happiest Christmas together in our first little home.

After the holidays, preparations were begun for "Blood and Sand," which was to be Rudy's first starring picture under his new contract with Famous Players.

June Mathis adapted the story for the screen and made it from a truly wonderful script. No one ever understood or wrote for Rudy as she did. She gave him his first chance in her version of the "Horsemen," and now again she wrote for him the role which was, in my mind, to be his greatest characterization, and in which he gave his best work.

Real torero costumes and complete outfits were sent from Spain.

Motion pictures of the big Corridas both in Madrid, Seville, and Mexico City were sent to the studio to study from.

During these days Rudy lived and moved in a world of his own creation.

Jean Acker

He took lessons in bullfighting from a retired matador, who later became his dresser. With him he talked Spanish* and discussed many events and incidents of the old bull fighter's past.

He grew his sideburns, learned to walk like a torero and even to eat like one. If ever a character had come to life, it was Gallarado as he was lived by Rudy.

Of all the characters Rudy ever interpreted, I know that of Juan Gallarado appealed of him the most.

He and Gallardo had much in common, as his own life has proved. Maybe, even then, subconsciously he knew he was but interpreting himself. His own childhood and career were but placed in another setting.

This living of the character in which he was absorbed was not only noticed by but by many others.

To quote from Mr. Ullman's book about Rudy:

"As I have said before, when Valentino was filming a picture he enacted his brief role at all times. Once, when we were on the train going to New York, he read 'The Sea Hawk,' which afterwards Frank Lloyd produced with Milton Sills in the leading role. Rudy went wild about this part and declared it was made for him. Under its spell he was indeed The Sea Hawk. His manners were rough. When he wanted me to move aside, he shoved me out of his way with his elbow. He ate like a pig. Considering Valentino's fastidious table manners this ability to get inside the skin of a character greatly interested me.

Again, when he was filming 'The Sainted Devil' his habitual courtesy left him entirely and he was rough and swaggering. I shudder to think what would have happened if he had ever been called upon to play a cut-throat Apache. His friends would have had to run for their lives!"

---

*Valentino spoke at least 4 languages fluently: Italian, French, Spanish, and English. He may have spoken more.

The wedding party: Douglas Gerrard, Natacha, Rudy

During the filming of this picture Rudy was granted his interlocutory decree of divorce from Jean Acker*. It was handed down on March 4th, 1922, but the decree would not become final until March 4th, 1923.

We wanted to marry as soon as possible, so we asked Mr. Gilbert, Rudy's attorney, his advice on the matter. He explained to us the law and told us that we would have to have patience and wait one more year.

This, of course, was not to our liking. The more we thought about it, the more foolish it seemed. There were so many people we knew who had married out of state, long before the year was up, and no one had apparently considered it worth bothering about*. Then there were Dagmar Godowsky and Frank Mayo who had been married, right after Mr. Mayo's first decree at Tijuana, Mexico.

Everyone seemed to have done the same thing, so why on earth should we wait?

We decided not to. As soon as "Blood and Sand" was finished we also would go to Mexico. In the meantime I finished my work on "Salome" with Nazimova. A few days after the last scenes of Rudy's picture were filmed we left with a friend, Douglas Gerrard for a vacation at Palm Springs.

From here we motored south to Mexicali, accompanied by Doctor White and "Gerry".

Our marriage, which took place on May 13, was a wonderful one even thought it did cause many heartaches and worries later.

The ceremony was performed at the Mayor's house, with a stringed orchestra on the porch and the Civil Band in the yard to lend a musical background. The whole town turned out for the festival.

I shall always love the Mexican people for the happiness they gave us that day. There was nothing that was too much for them to do.

---

*Valentino had impulsively married b actress Jean Acker at a house party in 1919. Acker was a lesbian, caught in a love triangle with Nazimova and Grace Darmond. Both women threatened to destroy her career. So she agreed to marry Valentino, who was unaware of her orientation. After dancing all night at the Hollywood Hotel she locked him out of their bridal suite and refused to see him. Valentino wrote her love letters for months pleading with her to 'forgive him' for whatever it was he must have done. Eventually it must have been explained to him as he quit trying and Jean moved on as well...until she seen how famous he had become. After the divorce she toured the country as "Mrs. Rudolph Valentino" a name he had not been using when he married her. They would reconcile before his death, with Jean being one of the last people to see him alive. After his death she immediately released her own song and once again began capitalizing on the Valentino name.

The wedding "breakfast," composed entirely of real Mexican dishes and refreshments, was also held at the Mayor's house. This lasted until seven in the evening, when we finally took our leave amidst much shouting and the band playing, the Mayor and the Chief of Police accompanying us to the border in their car.

The tragic and immediate ending to all our dreams came the next day. From the studio, by long-distance telephone, we were frantically summoned back to Los Angeles. We left without even a coat or suitcase, motoring continuously until we arrived that evening at nine o'clock.

The trumped-up charge of bigamy, Rudy's arrest, and my hurried departure for New York*** on the advice of Mr. Gilbert, are too well known to be gone over again.

The agony of mind which we both went through at this sudden and heartrending parting can easily be imagined

The "test" case, which was nothing but a contemptible "publicity stunt" on the part of the District Attorney's Office, was dismissed after a police court hearing, dear Mr. Gilbert again defending us with his usual, but otherwise unusual, ability and wit.

As soon as the Lasky people were assured that Rudy's pictures would not be barred, he started work on "The Young Rajah".

"After Rudy's and Natacha's marriage in Mexico, Natacha immediately came to us at the Biltmore Hotel in New York. We were here for a few days, intending to sail for Europe.

When we saw how wretchedly unhappy Natacha was we cancelled our passage and decided to open Foxlair, our country home in the Adirondacks.

**The law of the time in most states was one must wait 1 year between divorce and remarriage, or they could be arrested as a bigamist. Indeed many stars had skirted this with no repercussions. Most famously America's Sweetheart Mary Pickford divorced her first husband Owen Moore March 2nd, 1920; and married Douglas Fairbanks 26 days later. Though segments of the public were in an uproar most embraced the couple, making them the most famous celebrities of all time in a way that is hard to compare in the modern era.

***Valentino was imprisoned on a Friday, so he could not be bailed out until Monday as the banks were closed. Natacha learned of this at a stop in Chicago and was said to be devastated. Famous Players-Lasky refused to help him at all, with June Mathis, George Melford, and Thomas Meighan raising his bail funds. This episode would eventually lead to his 'one man strike', causing the public to look at Natacha unfavorably.

Thomas Meighan, Valentino, and June Mathis on the day he was
bailed out of jail.

After being settled in the quiet of all that mountain loveliness, we found Natacha's grief inconsolable. She worried constantly for fear that the newspaper notoriety might ruin Rudy's career. The children wrote and telegraphed back and forth daily, and Natacha rode for miles two or three times a week to put in long-distance calls to Hollywood. Rudy was at this time doing 'The Young Rajah' which was expected to be finished in a few weeks."

I am giving here one of Rudy's letters written at the time, as it will do more to let you know Rudy as he was than anything I might say.

Tuesday, 5:30 p.m.

MY VERY OWN AND ONLY BABYKINS,

As I came home I found your two letters instead of telegrams I still expect, and it did my heart good to receive that long one of Wednesday night. If you only knew how I devour them and desire to read some more, you would stop apologizing for the length and make them a little longer. Though no matter how long they were they would seem all to short, as the real happy moment is when I read your letters. I feel you are just talking to me, and I assure you, babykins, you have not spoiled anything at all, but I am happy and also proud in a way for being the cause of bringing out the adorable femininity which I knew you possessed. But false pride and a wrong idea of reserve kept you from giving it free vent. Only through the suffering of separation it came forth, soaring through the skies, from which now you can see how people seem foolish when they try to stifle the genuine sentiments and tendency which are a legacy of our race, simply to adopt a ridiculous modern theory of independence which implies the scorning of any romantic impulses and feminine charm, defining them as weakness.

The more I read you letters the more I admire in you those lovely qualities of femininity I admired in my poor dear mother. Some people might call me old-fashioned, but really I am not. I am very human and proud to possess that traditional feeling of admiration and respect for a womanly woman, a thing which nowadays seems to be a thing of the past upon which the cynics of our generation cast their blasé glances with a faint smile of superiority.

Do not be afraid of my misjudging your sweet spontaneity for a second childhood, for I simply adore it, as I know that in moments of seriousness there is a very strong womanly character in you, which renders you to me doubly beloved.

You embody for me all that there is of lovely and ideal and sacred. You are to me the most precious jewel God ever gifted me with, and any suffering, privations, and hardships for your sake and our happiness I shall gladly bear with a smile, for it is through suffering that the best of our nature comes forth or is molded.

Do not think, darling, that I want to receive only the happy letters from you and keep the tears to yourself. If you did that I should feel that you had stopped loving me. I want to share your tears as well as your joy.

You know, darling, the night we came back from Palm Springs and you cried in my arms at the thought of having to go to New York. I loved you and I will love you as I never did before, while I used to get furious when before you would send me away and cry all by yourself, because I felt I was only welcome when happiness reigned, but when sorrow came you estranged yourself from me as if I were not worthy of sharing your tears. I felt cheated and was mad because I felt you were not mine while you were suffering, as if you had retaken yourself from me.

I am sure my poor darling Mamma loves you from the other world as much as if you were her own child, and she will protect us and guard us from harm and help us to be together for ever and ever. I must leave you now for a moment to take my fencing lesson and will resume this night after dinner.

I drank the coffee so quickly to be back here talking to you that I burned my mouth, but I am happy talking to you, so nothing else matters.

I can't tell you much about the picture except that the photography is good, as we have not got into the drama as yet, but I believe it is going to be very good.

Tomorrow or the next day I will receive a set of the publicity stills taken last Sunday and will send them to you. The fan mail has doubled and is still growing very strong, so much so that Margaret mails now 1,500 pictures a week and is way behind, having a sack full of mail waiting for her. If it keeps up I believe I shall ask Lasky to come in on it fifty-fifty or raise my salary, as it is getting to be tremendous.

I cannot understand why you have remained without news of me a stretch, as I have written you most every day, but I suppose it is delay of mail.

Please, darling, tell Muzzie and Uncle Dick how much I love them and how grateful I am to them for all they have done and intend to do for us both. Their affection and loyalty is a very rare treasure, and I know you will, as I will, guard it very jealously and carefully.

Oh! Darling, what a bliss to go to Nice. Well, if we cannot do it now we shall in a few years, but anyway I am counting if we do not go abroad for Don Caesar*, to go for our honeymoon next Spring. Anyway I shall be in your arms, darling, inside of six weeks. Ti strongo al cuoro forte forte.

Sempre, sempre, sempre il tuo Bambino che ti adora e vive per te sola.

Rudy

---

*Don Caesar was supposed to be a follow up to The Young Rajah, eventually becoming "The Spanish Cavalier". Famous Players promised to let the couple shoot on location in Spain, since they had reneged on that same promise for "Blood and Sand". June Mathis wrote the script, but after the one man strike, the film was given to Pola Negri and became "The Spanish Dancer".

CHAPTER 5

I WILL now let mother go on with her story:

"In order to avoid further newspaper notoriety Rudy tried to arrive incognito. But it had been telegraphed from Hollywood that he was en route for New York, so at every station he had been met by newspaper people.

It was the first good laugh Natacha had had for weeks when Rudy arrived at Foxlair. His own mother would hardly have recognized him. His face was covered with a dark heavy beard and his eyes hidden by big dark goggles. He wore a tweed golf suit, with a golf bag slung over his shoulders, and a soft grey cap pulled well over his face. He also wore a smile that reached from ear to ear.

Douglas Gerrard, an English actor, came with him. Our small party was now complete. Foxlair was an ideal place for a happy vacation. Its twelve hundred acres of mountain land, with its large lake, fishing pond, private golf links and deer hunting, gave the children plenty of opportunity for good sport.

They practically lived in their bathing suits, swimming, boating, and golfing the whole day long, never thinking of dressing until it was time for dinner. I used to sit up in my boudoir and hear those three screaming and laughing as if no cloud had ever come to shadow their happiness. This exhilarating country life, with good food, alternative exercise and rest, soon brought the ruddy glow of health to their cheeks. They were no longer the fretful, anxious children of a few weeks before.

At Foxlair we never troubled to close or lock the doors and windows at night. But at about six o' clock one evening, one of the maids saw a man drive up in a Ford car, which he parked in the heavy shrubbery below the kitchen. This appeared rather suspicious to her but, as Mr. Hudnut had gone to New York that morning on business, and I was in bed with a sick headache, not wishing to worry me, she did not mention the incident but locked up the entire back of the house.

After dinner, the night grew intensely dark and heavy showers came on. It was the blackest night we had had.

Natacha, Rudy, and Gerry were playing poker in the big front living room, which had a screen door leading on to the verandah. This verandah stood twelve feet from the ground and surrounded the house. From where Natacha was sitting she could look on to the verandah but, because of the darkness, could but dimly see through the screen door.

Suddenly this door began to slightly and cautiously open. This started Natacha, and she said in a low voice, 'Don't appear to notice but I think someone is on the verandah – I saw the screen door open a little.'

'Nonsense,' said Rudy, 'it's only the wind.'

'There's no wind blowing,' answered Natacha, 'the night is too sultry.'

Just then she saw the door again carefully opened and back of it the slight outline of a man.

In a still lower voice she said, 'I see a man looking in – Uncle Dickie's revolver is upstairs in his top bureau drawer. You go up and get it, Gerry, and Rudy and I will keep playing as if we had noticed nothing.'

Saying in quite a natural voice, 'It's my turn to get the drinks tonight,' Gerry arose and left the room.

There sat Natacha and Rudy, waiting for Gerry, never dreaming that he had taken the revolver and gone down the back stairs, out of the kitchen door, and tiptoed stealthily along the verandah to the front of the house.

Suddenly they heard Gerry's voice ring out, 'Damn you, hold up your hands or I'll shoot!' Gerry had taken the eavesdropper by surprise. The man now rushed to the edge of the verandah and as Gerry thought he was about to jump over, he clutched him by the coat.

Catlike the man turned on him and, seizing him with both hands by the back of the neck, pitched Gerry over the porch railing to the ground, twelve feet below. Gerry fell flat on his back, but as the rain luckily had softened the earth, no damage was done. Strangely enough, in all this scuffling the revolver was not discharged. The fall quite knocked the wind out of Gerry and it took a few seconds for him to collect himself. Springing to his feet and turning toward the sound of the man's departing footsteps, he fired in rapid succession three shots.

Out of the darkness, there sounded an agonizing scream. Then dead silence.

The children, who had been standing spellbound listening to this, rushed to the window and loudly called for Gerry. No answer.

Then Rudy, knowing there was a shotgun upstairs in my room, rushed up to get it, Natacha at his heels.

At Foxlair we had no electric lights, depending upon oil lamps and candles. As I had had one of my bad headaches I was lying in the dark, terrified at all this excitement.

Rudy rushed in saying, 'The shotgun, the shotgun – Gerry's been killed!'

'The gun's in the bay window,' I answered.

In a second Rudy had it in his hands. 'Don't you do it,' screamed Natacha, 'you may be killed or disfigured for life! Remember you belong to the screen – the public!'

Then another tussle began in the dark. Natacha was trying to get the gun away from Rudy. Chairs and tables crashed to the floor. I could hear my photograph frames and bowls of flowers smashing. I jumped from the bed and tried to find the matches to light a candle, but trembled so from intense fright that it was a minute or two before I succeeded.

By this time the children, like magic, had rushed down the stairs, Natacha hanging on to Rudy's coat tails. I followed, holding the candle, only to see them madly dashing out the front door and down the side path. As I entered the living room there stood Gerry. And this was my greatest fright of all. I mistook him for the burglar – the murderer – the spy – or whatever he might have been.

It was impossible to recognize Gerry, as he was soaked to the skin and so covered with mud that only the whites of his eyes and his white teeth shone through. At the sight of him I threw up both arms and let out a shriek for help.

In a mud-muffled voice he piped up, 'It's Gerry. Don't you know me? I hit him all right, but I can't find him!'

Then we both called from the verandah for Natacha and Rudy to come back. But there was no answer.

In a short time the rain-bedraggled children returned. They had found nothing. Gerry was still convinced he had killed or seriously wounded the man. So, taking lanterns, the three of them went out again in search of the victim.

I remained, huddled in my dressing-gown, and in my bare feet, chilled through and through, but too frightened to return to my room. After a vain search they all returned. The man had evidently escaped. It was useless in the pitch darkness to search further.

After all had quieted down and the children were fast asleep, I heard in the early dawn the chug-chug of a motor. Stepping out on the upper verandah leading from my bedroom, I saw a little Ford disappearing rapidly down the drive and out the big front gates.

That morning we found the man's footprints and the imprint of his body where he had fallen over a low wall. Several broken cigars had tumbled from his pockets and lay in the mud.

After breakfast the three young people motored to North Creek Station and inquired of the stationmaster if anyone had left by the early train. There were so few homes around North Creek that this man knew everybody. He told them that a stranger had driven up in a Ford with another man. The man, he said, was well dressed, tall, slender, and good-looking. He seemed to be in pain, as he walked with two canes, holding one foot front the ground. This man, having bought a ticket for New York, boarded the train, while the other drove quickly away.

Who and what this man's mission was – whether a burglar or a detective – I am sure he hopes never again to meet Gerry!"

CHAPTER 6

SOON after this we left Foxlair for New York. My aunt, Mrs. Werner, came from the coast to join us here while my mother and father at last, after many postponements, sailed for Europe.

I have not mentioned the trouble which had been brewing since "Blood and Sand" between Rudy and Famous Players Company. Their treatment of Rudy and the litigation that followed are too well known to go into detail*. I shall only refer to this case briefly, when necessary, to show its direct bearing on our personal lives.

Our marriage in Mexico having been declared illegal, it was necessary for us to have separate residences.

Auntie and I took an apartment together on Sixty-Seventh Street, to be near Rudy, who was now living with an old friend of his Frank Menillo. Their apartment was the Hotel des Artistes on the same street.

Here we lived during all of our first months of the fight with Famous. Rudy was under strict injunction which prevented him in any way from earning a living, so our finances were again in a precarious position.

A friend in need, in the form of Joe Godsol, came to our rescue. We shall both be eternally grateful to him for his kindness and generosity, which was given entirely free from any security on Rudy's part.

---

*After the bigamy scandal, Valentino was livid with Famous Players for refusing to help him out (he also perceived it as an insult to his new wife). The Young Rajah did not do well, being his first flop since superstardom. When Famous Players reneged on their promise to shoot "The Spanish Cavalier" on location in Spain, Rudy considered it the final straw. He began a 'one man strike' against Famous Players-Lasky, demanding more money (he was still severely underpaid) and control over his films so he would not be forced into b rate films as he had been at Metro. Famous Players refused and sued him, barring him from any employment at all until the matter was legally settled. This was eventually lessened to just work in film, keeping Valentino off the screen for almost two years. Public favor was not won, as the press assumed he was being a whiny diva when in reality his demands were just. Many blamed Natacha, though she had very little to do with the matter.

As indeed we had none. This unselfish proof of friendship will never be forgotten. His help was not given, as is usually the case, in return for some mercenary agreement, but without even interest being asked or accepted when offered. Although this debt was paid immediately the injunction was modified to permit Rudy working, we will always be indebted in a way that money cannot repay.

It was during the first few months of our stay in New York that we became interested in psychic things. It came about in this manner.

After a very severe illness, a dear and beloved friend of ours*, who was staying with her daughter and mother at Astor Hotel, passed away. We were all, naturally, heartbroken. During her illness, her daughter, and a devoted friend who was staying with them told us of many peculiar and unaccountable rappings they heard – particularly just before her mother's death.

This was the first time that either Rudy or I had come into personal contact with anything of this kind, and we were both inclined to believe that these happenings could easily be explained in some ordinary way. We had many talks about phenomena and psychic experiences, as it appeared that both "Jenny"** (as I shall call our friend) and her daughter had been interested in this study for a number of years. We were still far from being convinced.

Suddenly one morning a few weeks later, we heard from the daughter that she was sending Rudy a message. The message had come through the automatic writing of the friend who had been staying with her at the time of the mother's death. She said she did not know whether Rudy would believe it or not, but she had been instructed from the other side to send it to him and she was doing so. The message proved to be for Rudy from his mother who had passed away in Italy a few years before.

We were frankly puzzled. The purported communication referred to several familiar incidents of Rudy's youth which no one in this country could have known of.

We had the opportunity of again meeting "the lady of the automatic writings" (C.M.G.)*** shortly after this. We told her that we had been very interested in the message and would be grateful if she would have dinner with us one evening so that we could talk it over.

---

*The woman was Virginia Mathis, who passed away in 1922. She was the mother of June Mathis, Valentino's mentor. June was a firm believer in Spiritualism and the Occult. When Valentino passed away she claimed to see his apparition in her living room.

**The spirit 'Jenny' referred to numerous times in this book is Virginia Mathis.

***Cora McGeachy (sometimes credited as Cora MacCreachy) was a costume and daughter of actress Cora Macey (sometimes credited as Cora Macy). She and June had been friends since at least 1919.

I have not given the names of these friends, who were the means of interesting us in this study, as they are all professional people in the public eye and may feel reticent about being openly connected with this work.

Some, however, may recognize them. We will hope that at a not too far distant date, they will acknowledge publicly the belief to which we all owe so much*.

The more we investigated this remarkable gift of automatic writing, the more convinced we became of the great truth which lay behind it. The truth of life-ever-continuing on its path to progress and evolution and the truth of communication with the so-called death.

As we became more interested, we formed the habit of meeting at my apartment one or two evenings a week to obtain messages and discuss this subject.

C.M.G. although possessed of a truly rare gift of mediumship, made no use of it except to entertain or help some personal friends. She was herself a well-known artist and never in any way used this faculty professionally.

I must describe something of this particular phase of automatic writing, as an itself it was so convincing.

After a little music had been played, C.M.G. would hold the pencil in her hand on the pad of paper. Usually the writing would begin almost immediately. Once it started, her hand literally flew across the pages. As the writing came backwards (from right to left on the sheets of paper) and she knew nothing what was being written, she would often keep right on with us in any conversation we might be having. To be read, the messages had to be held before a mirror.

Long forgotten incidents of Rudy's childhood were told be an old Italian woman who had looked after Rudy in his early youth.

All of these incidents were verified by Rudy, as also was her name, which she gave at the time but which I have since forgotten. Messages were received from Rudy's mother, Gabriella Guglielmi, over which he often shed many tears of joy, and from countless others. Much wonderful and helpful advice given to us by "Jenny" in her same loving and familiar manner.

---

*It's odd Natacha would feel the need to hide names. June's films were full of Spiritualism and Occult from the moment she met Valentino. "The Four Horsemen", "Blood and Sand", "The Young Rajah", and even non Valentino films such as "Turn to the Right" all blatantly showcased these themes. In addition June spoke openly of her beliefs in interviews. This book was originally published in 1926 and 1927, June died in late 1927 making the call all the odder. As for Cora McGeachy and Cora Macey neither went on to do much of importance other than work on a handful of June's films including Colleen Moore's "Irene".

It was through these same writings that we first consciously contacted Meselope, an Old Egyptian, and member of the Hermetic Brotherhood. He, like all the higher Teachers, never gave advice on material things, but confined his communication to spiritual guidance and prayers.

Black Feather, an Indian "guide", of Rudy's, whom he was later to see many times, also became a dearly loved member of these "pow-wows" as he described them.

It was through these writings that we were told, weeks before it happened, of the modification of the injunction against Rudy, and also of a long and extended trip which we would make to many cities. In fact, most future events of importance were prophesied to us in this way.

These prophecies were the facts which did the most to convince us of this truth, as no prophecy of future events can be explained by the usual theory of mind reading – conscious or subconscious.

After several months of these wonderful communications I remember one night as C.M.G. was writing, she suddenly stopped and explained, "Oh look, they are not writing backwards any more!" Then the writing continued, telling us that "they" would no longer write backwards as it was now unnecessary for proof; besides, this way it would be much less trouble for us to read. From that day on the writings came in the usual way.

Rudy soon made the discovery that he also was mediumistic and could receive automatic writings.

This, however, at first he did not like to do, feeling that C.M.G. was so much more developed an instrument.

The long journey to many cities, which had been prophesied to us long before, turned out to be the dancing tour on which we embarked with Minervala*.

It was on this tour, that we became acquainted with George Ullman, who we soon discovered to be the man, described to us psychically, that would eventually be led to take charge of Rudy's business affairs**.

---

*The Minervala Dance Tour was one way around the injunction as both Valentino and Natacha had been professional dancers at some point in their lives. They made $7,000 each per week. The tour traveled across the US and Canada. The program consisted of the couple dancing, a beauty contest, and a tirade against the Motion Picture industry by Valentino. Footage of the final beauty contest at Madison Square Gardens still exists under the newsreel title "Rudolph Valentino and his 88 American Beauties"

**George Ullman had worked at Minervala and came up the idea of a dance tour to promote his company. Valentino and Natacha asked him to take over Rudy's business affairs, to which Ullman declined. Eventually he changed his mind and would be with Rudy until the end.

Valentino posing as Black Feather

I will quote his own version of this phenomena, written by himself on page 69 of his book Valentino As I Knew Him.

"I had observed that both Rudy and Natacha were interested in something supernatural. Just what it was I did not know. Afterwards it turned out to be automatic writing and a form of the psychic. Before making any move they consulted this power. Not knowing this, I was at first surprised by the quietude with which they received what appeared to me to be startling developments. When surprising things occurred, I naturally expected them to share my own amazement. But this they seldom did. Instead, I would be very likely to hear something to the effect that they had expected it and knew it would come. For example, they had known that they were to go on a long trip, that they were to take a new business manager, and that Valentino would change his attorney. It turned out that these things had come to them through automatic writing.

When Valentino became sufficiently acquainted with me to explain things, he naturally wished me to share his interest in them. Being open to conviction, I very willingly listened, and to my surprise I found that a number of things predicted by this psychic force actually came to pass.

It was in San Antonio, Texas, that Valentino, after many false starts and some show of nervousness, first broached the subject to me of taking over his affairs and becoming his business manager. I refused. I had a family, whereas Valentino was $50,000 in debt and had an injunction again him which prevented him from appearing on stage or screen; his salary of $7,000 per week he owed many times over. Where, then, would my salary come from? He waved this aside and with a sublime confidence in his guiding star he told me that he would pull out of this, that he would make plenty of money, and that he wanted me to manage his affairs. But I could not see it that way. I needed to know where my income was coming from. Yet when, ten weeks later, I suddenly and without any further assurance decided to become Valentino's business manager, I looked for some expression of surprise at my 'volte face.' Both Rambova and Valentino smiled inscrutably, and said it had been predicted before they embarked on the tour that they would change business managers and that I would be the man! These things at first rather gave me the creeps, but later, because of the sublime confidence of the Valentinos and their psychic control, I became less skeptical and more confident."

CHAPTER 7

MARCH 1923, found us dancing in Chicago. We were in constant touch with Mr. Gilbert on the coast, anxiously awaiting his telegram announcing the signing of the final decree of divorce. This at last arrived, but our troubles, it seemed, were not yet over.

We now discovered that we could not be remarried in Chicago, or at least not for another year. Illinois had some sort of law to the effect that marriage was illegal if performed before one year after the final decree. This was too much!

Mr. Michael Romano, assistant district attorney, and a close friend of ours, helped us to solve this problem.

The solution resulted in a night trip to Crowns Point, Indiana, where the ceremony was finally and legally performed* on March 14th, my aunt, Mrs. Werner, and Mr. Romano acting as our witnesses.

It was also during this dancing tour that the poem book *Day Dreams* was completed.

When this book was published in May, many of the newspaper articles and criticisms caused us much amusement. Some of these poems were dedicated to various initials, which seemed to greatly intrigue reporters. I remember one instance in particular about the poem called *Cremation* and dedicated

(To G.S.)

I

Just a packet of letters tied with a bit of blue,
Just a packet of letters that once were sent by you
To one who proved unworthy
Of the love inscribed within.
The tiny packet of letters, a witness of my sin.

II

Just a packet of letters, but they are not mine own.
I dare not claim one thought in them

---

*This courthouse still stands. In addition they have a 'Valentino's Café and Ice Cream Parlor' which proudly displays Valentino memorabilia and the original marriage certificate.

Natacha in costume for the dance tour, 1923

Not even as a loan,
For to the one you thought I was
In all sincerity
You bared the secrets of your soul
Now I send them back to thee.

III
Just a packet of letters,
A monument of love.
You lie within the fireplace,
In smoke you'll rise above
The sordidness of all deceit,
The grime of earthly thought,
Yet, in this flash of living fire,
The flame of love is caught.

IV
Just a packet of letters a while ago you were,
Now in vaprous symphony of grey
I send you back to her,
For the spirit of true love that's penned
Must rise to meet her soul
In pearly glory 'round her head.
Love's halo – is its goal.

To rake over the dead ashes of a burnt out love one must use the pen point of poetry.

The poem the reporters were sure was addressed to Gloria Swanson – as a "memorial" to some of episode of the past.

The reason some of these poems were dedicated to initials, I will explain. All of these writings were psychically received (as indeed are all poems, only some writers are unconscious of the fact) and the initials stood for the name of the soul who had inspired them. G.S. was George Sand.

On the title page you will see drawn a black feather. This was in memory of Rudy's guide, Black Feather. The little poem underneath, addressed

(To M.)
The serenade of a thousand years ago,
The song of a hushed lip,
Lives for ever in the glass of to-day,
Wherein we see the reflection of it
If we but brush away
The cobwebs of doubting faith.

Was given by Meselope.

You will also notice that neither on the cover nor the title page will you find the word "by" – just

DAY DREAMS
RUDOLPH VALENTINO

"The Gift Book" (To J.R.) was inspired by James Whitcomb riley

"The Love Child" (To B.) – Byron
"Gypsies" (To R.B.) – Robert Browning
"At Sunrise To-morrow" (To E.B.) – Elizabeth Barrett
"Sympathy" (To. J.) – "Jennie"

The following poem was, I believe, Rudy's favorite:

GLORIFICATION
(To W. W.) – WALT WHITMAN
The arms of the earth broke through the sod
And clenched his fist in derision,
For clay knows not the might of God,
It has been but an earthy vision.

The finger of God wrote in the sky
A sign of mighty fire:
"Reach up to me for I am Life,"
But earth could reach no higher.

With strength to muscle, with might and main,
Earth struggled and then defied,
But God stretched forth His hand of Love
And Earth was glorified.

CHAPTER 8

IN August, after the dancing tour was over, we sailed for Europe.

No one will ever know the wonders and happiness of this, our first trip to Europe together. It was the culmination in reality of all our dreams and plannings. Auntie, who had been with us through so much trouble and anxiety, and to whom Rudy was so loyally devoted, accompanied us.

We sailed on the *Aquitania*. It was a wonderful crossing. George Arliss and his wife were also on board, and many delightful hours were passed in their charming company.

Auntie left us at Cherbourg, journeying to Paris and then on to the château, where we were to join her in a few weeks.

I shall pass over our arrival in London, the crowds which met us at the station, although it was pouring rain, and the other incidents already told by Rudy in the articles of *My First Trip Abroad*.

For the first three days of our stay in London, Rudy was held prisoner in our suite at the Carlton Hotel by the endless stream of interviewers and photographers. Then at last we were free to revel in all the old historic spots we had so often roamed through in our imaginative wanderings – The Tower of London, Westminster Abbey, Windsor Castle and many others. Rudy and I were both very fond of history, especially the period from the Crusader - King Richard to the Virgin-Queen Bess.

Of all the places of historic interest, I think we enjoyed most the haunting beauties of Hampton Court. The Cardinal Wolsey apartments had just been opened to the public. I myself had been here many times before, but seeing it all again with Rudy's fresh enthusiasm, it seemed even more inspiring than ever.

There was also much rushing to tailors, boot-makers, hatters, shirt makers, etc, as London is to men what Paris is to women – the paradise of fashion shops.

We had a letter of introduction to Mr. and Mrs. Richard Guiness, friends of my mother and father, who did all in their power to make our short stay in London a pleasant one.

Mrs. Guiness has one of the most interesting "salons" in London. Here, in this home of exquisite taste, you are apt to meet anyone from Michael Arlen and Edmond Dulac to Lady Diana Manners or Morris Gest. Mrs. Guiness herself is a woman of great brilliance, refreshing and fearless frankness – one of the few women I have met of the social world "big" enough to disregard the usual hypocritical and snobbish standards of conventional etiquette. At this house on Great Cumberland Place you will meet genius from every walk of life, the hostess requiring only that you be interesting.

I remember one luncheon at which we were present and at which Rudy was guilty of an amusing *faux pas*. Among the guests were Lord and Lady Birkenhead and Arthur Rubenstein, the pianist.

During a moment of silence Lord Birkenhead inquired of Rudy if this was his first trip to London. Considering that the papers had been full of this eventful first visit for the last two weeks, we considered this a rather stupid question.

Rudy, however, explained that it was. To continue the conversation, Rudy politely asked Lord Birkenhead if he had ever been to America.

The naïve question greatly delighted our hostess (who considered it a rather good comeback, however unintentional) as Lord Birkenhead had but recently returned from one of his many trips to America, where his speeches had caused, in diplomatic circles, little less than a sensation. But what was Lord Birkenhead, famous as he might be, to Rudolph Valentino or Rudolph Valentino to Lord Birkenhead? They both lived and moved in different worlds. Neither had probably ever heard of the other until this meeting, or at least, I am certain on our side that we never had – although I supposed I shouldn't admit it.

We were also invited to the beautiful country estate of Mr. and Mrs. Benjamin Guiness – where Rudy had his first glimpse of English country life – this branch of the Guiness family proving equally charming to us.

Mrs. Bridget Guiness is an artist of great talent and here we had the opportunity of seeing some of her beautiful work. In particular the dining-room, the walls of which were entirely decorated by her own hand.

Before leaving England we drove down to Bletchingly, Surrey, to see the world-famous Pekinese kennels of Mrs. Ashton Cross.

On our way there we passed by my old school, Leatherhead Court, near Epsom, where I had spent so many years of my childhood. We stopped here long enough to wander through the old gardens, which now look deserted as it was still the period of the summer holidays.

From here we drove through the hedge-lined country roads of Surrey to Merstham. In front of the old Inn we found two of the Misses Cross awaiting us to act as our guides through the many winding lanes which lead to the house and kennels.

I shall never forget the sight which met our eyes as we drove through the old gates of Whitehill Roughets. The beautiful lawns around this country house were literally bouncing with Pekes. We were certainly in Pekinese heaven. There were Pekes just about to toddle, to the old and disdainfully feathered champions of many a famous show. Pekes of every size and color.

We spent a delightful afternoon. When later we motored back to London, we left Mrs. Ashton Cross and her daughters with a family now diminished by the loss of two woolly six-week-old infants.

After three wonderful weeks in London, one grey morning found us on our way to Croydon. From here we took the plane to Paris.

Paris was again another fast round of interviewing, entertainments, sight-seeing, and shopping. Here Rudy ordered his specially built Voisin racing car. Much of his time was spent in selecting the right shade of grey for the paint and the vermilion morocco for the upholstering. As it could naturally not be ready for several months, the Voisin people loaned us another sport car to use in the meantime.

In this car, about two weeks later, we left for the château. This was the first time either of us had motored from Paris to the Riviera. For myself, I later hoped it would be the last. Unfortunately, this year the roads were in splendid condition, I say "unfortunately" as it gave Rudy the marvelous opportunity of testing the speed of the racer. I shall never forget that trip! Rudy was happily a clever drive, but, oh, what a reckless one!

Every car that Rudy saw ahead of him on the road was to him a special invitation to prove our superiority in *vitesse*. And we did. Our trip was one mad dash through suffocating dust. The climax was reached as we rushed around twisting and twining the roadway of the Alps, nearing our destination.

By this time I was so weak I couldn't scream any more protests, which were only drowned out by the thunder of the open "cut-out."

We rounded one curve at breakneck speed – only to find apparent nothingness before us. It was a double curve! Rudy wrenched at the wheel and stood up on the brakes. The car bumped to a standstill with one back wheel over the edge of a yawning precipice.

I looked at Rudy. He was trembling and deathly white. The first thing he said was, "Did you see Black Feather?" I shook my head, being beyond speech. Then Rudy told me that he had seen him lean over him and help him give the wheel the wrench that had saved us. We certainly must have had guardian angels to have saved us from his dare-devil driving.

For the first time in my life I felt like having hysterics. Indeed, I would have liked to, to teach Rudy a lesson, but he was so shaken himself by our narrow, miraculous escape, that I merely wilted into silence.

The rest of our trip was slow and uneventful. We reached the château at about ten o'clock that night, worn-out, hungry and beyond recognition. Home and family were never so appreciated. Filthy as we were, we literally fell into the waiting arms of dear Uncle Dickie, Mother, and Auntie.

As we had never before seen the château, we soon quite forgot how tired we were in our excitement of exploring. Inside the house was decorated almost entirely in the eighteenth-century period, as both my mother and father love the old atmosphere of the Louis'. But mother, knowing our love of bright colors, had furnished our apartments in gay modern things. She was very nervous that we would not like it, being her first attempt along these lines. She later confided that her friends had thought it dreadful, but we, however, were delighted with it.

Rudy was indefatigable. Bright and early the next morning he was out investigating the garden, the guest house, the greenhouse, the small wharf at the foot of the gardens, and planning all kind of improvements. By the time I had dressed and set out to look for him, he had already discovered just the spot for a small zoo, a kennel for his large dogs (that he had not yet bought), a boat-house, an outdoor picture theatre, and goodness knows what else.

We were here only about ten days when he decided that it was time to leave for our motor trip to Italy. His first trip home in ten years! So one bright sunny morning a few days later, Auntie, Rudy and I waved a farewell to "those being left behind" and started on our way.

At Ventimille, the frontier, we had to stop to pass the Italian customs and show our passports. We inquired of one of the guards where we were to go and what there was to do. He informed us that the customs was now closed as it was lunch "hour" and we would have to wait until two o'clock. Rudy look at his watch – it was five to twelve!

We fumed and argued but to no avail – nothing was allowed that might interfere with the digestion and siesta slumbers of the officials. All we could do was to wait.

About two-fifteen the customs were finally opened. Rudy's ardour and excitement at the idea of returning to his native land were by now a bit cooled. We were asked if we had anything to declare. Rudy explained that we were just motoring through Italy for a few weeks and had nothing dutiable but a dozen boxes of cigarettes. These he was asked to produce.

Much chatter followed amongst the officials, who at last demanded a certain sum as duty on his cigarettes. This made Rudy (whom the long wait in the grilling heat had made somewhat short tempered) furious. He declared he was an Italian returning to his own country and should pay no duty. Besides, the sum was ridiculous! Enough, in fact, to buy all the cigarettes in Italy!

One of the officials then jokingly nudged Rudy in the ribs, winked at him and pointed with his thumb at Auntie and me. We were too far off to hear what he said, but for answer we heard Rudy yelling at the man indignantly in Italian.

A few minutes later he stumped up to the car, jumped in and slammed on the gears. We shot ahead.

Had he paid? Was everything all right? Yes, he had!

Then we heard what the trouble was. The officials had dared to insinuate that after going to America and marrying an American heiress, he could well afford to give a few of his American dollars to his country. This struck Auntie and me as being terribly funny, but Rudy with his pride refused absolutely to see anything humorous in it. He had been grossly insulted and by his own country-men! And on his first visit home in ten years! The idea of anyone accusing him of marrying for money! Our evident amusement only made him recede into an indignant and hurt silence. We succeeded in muffling our laughter and peace was once more restored.

The route along the Italian Riviera is very beautiful. The road winds in and out and around the base of the mountains, with the deep blue of the Mediterranean nearly always in view. We enjoyed every mile of it, regardless of the dust.

For an early dinner, we drew up to a little wayside inn, where tables were laid on a terrace overlooking the water. The terrace itself was covered over by an arbor of grape-vines through which the rays of the lowering sun cast a reddish glow. Big bunches of purple and yellow grapes hung heavily down over our heads. The inevitable drone of flies! Only now in this quiet and sleepy setting did we realize that we were once more back in Italy.

Rudy was very silent. Both Auntie and I could see that many episodes of the past were picturing themselves before his eyes. Once in a while he would have to furtively brush away an unwelcome tear.

That evening late, tired out from our long drive, we arrived at Genoa, where we were to pass the night.

Tired as he was, Rudy took out his pencil and paper to talk to his mother, whose welcoming presence he had felt strongly for some time. Many were the messages of love and comfort that flew across those pages between this mother and son. Such true adoration the veil does not lesson or divide. Yet there are some who deny this communication of love. Rudy fortunately knew better and was comforted.

CHAPTER 9

THE next morning early we motored out to Rudy's old school, the Dante Alighieri College in the hills on the outskirts of Genoa.

It was still vacation time so we were able to wander through the school at our leisure. Rudy showed us the schoolroom, his desk and the corner in which he stood most of his time in punishment. The dining-room, with its long wooden tables and benches, and the dormitory recalled to Rudy's mind many childhood pranks. He had been the despair of his teachers and his mother.

The schoolhouse itself is built on the top of a hill surrounded by terraced gardens, laid out in rows of fruit trees and vegetables. The children help to keep up these gardens as one of their outdoor studies. What they do not gain in knowledge, they at least gain in health.

We spent an interesting and amusing two hours in this old spot. On our return drive down the steep hill of the school we passed by a little lace shop. Filling the doorway was a black-haired Italian woman of very generous proportions. Hanging on to her skirts were the usual six or eight children with as little difference in their ages as kind Mother Nature would allow.

The instant Rudy saw this model of motherhood, he slammed on the brakes, jumped from the car and made straight for the shop. It was all done so quickly Auntie or I could hardly realize what had happened.

We saw him address the woman inquiringly, which resulted in exclamations of astonishment, chatter, laughter and an inspection of the children. Then they all disappeared into the shop.

A little later he reappeared with many bundles and was sped on his way with more laughter and the waving of many hands, large and small.

Could we believe it? It was Maria! (I am not sure of the name, but this one is always safe to use.) Shades of his first romance with the gardener's daughter. Of course she had remembered him. She had been such a pretty little thing. To think, if he had remained in Italy he might now be the owner of the lace shop and the generously proportioned Maria; not forgetting the fathership of the eight children! Such is destiny!

Rudy had practically bought out the shop in this rush of sentiment, so that the whole family enjoyed lacy mementos of this early romance for some time to come.

From Genoa, we motored on our way the following morning. We paused at Bologna long enough to have lunch and visit the famous Piazza with the sculpted monument of Neptune by Giovanni de Bologna.

Rudy was most anxious to get to Milan, as here we were to meet his sister Maria, who was to accompany us on the rest of our trip.

When we at last arrived at our destination, we found at the hotel a telegram waiting for us from Maria. She had, it appeared, gone to Genoa to surprise us, had missed us and was now on her way back.

She arrived the next morning while we were having breakfast. There was a touching meeting between these two who had been separated now for more than eleven years. What changes time can bring!

Maria was instantly overwhelmed with pride in her handsome and successful brother. Rudy, on the other hand, after the first tenderness of their meeting, was rather appalled by his sister's old-fashioned ways and ideas[*]. These he immediately set out to remedy. Our first task was to buy her clothes and, above all, a box of face powder – hitherto unknown.

I am afraid I was a terrible shock to her properties. Not only did I use powder, but lip rouge and kohl as well! Not to speak of the brilliant coloring of my clothes and an extensive use of perfume. All of which, according to Maria, was simply not done except by an unmentionable class of persons. She was frightfully concerned over her brother's reputation, and could not refrain from the suggestion that I at least should not wear a glove over my wedding ring.

Nothing could have been funnier than the endless arguments of these two, totally opposite in viewpoint, yet so much alike in character. They were both very stubborn, but also very quick to change and learn, once they were convinced they were in the wrong.

---

[*]In fairness one must wonder if it was Rudy or Natacha who was appalled by her old fashioned ways. Maria and Natacha didn't seem to get along, as each represented a world the other was not familiar with.

It was no time with the help of a smart new wardrobe and a little face powder, before Maria blossomed forth into a very attractive young woman. She had beautiful large eyes and Rudy's same perfect white teeth and charming smile.

All of the time not spent in shopping for Maria we spent in visiting churches. Maria was of a religious turn of mind and insisted on showing us the beauties of Milan Cathedral which we had all seen before, but which were, nevertheless, well worth seeing again. Apart from the triumph of its architecture and its stained-glass windows, the truly amazing collection of jewels in the treasury alone merited the visit. These fascinated Rudy, who always had an Oriental's love of beautiful jewelry.

We also visited the crypt (for this privilege you again pay extra) to see the famous solid silver casket of some pope or cardinal, which is a masterpiece of the silversmith's art.

On certain festival days, we were told by the old priest who acts as guide to this region, the top of the silver casket is raised on chains and the skeleton remains may be viewed. These remains, decked in more jewels and regal robes, are in an inner glass casket.

This glowing description made Rudy eager and insistent to see the inside of the silver casket. After much cajoling and the exchange of a few crisp bills, the doors of this sanctuary were closed and barred and we became privileged spectators. There was also, of course, some miraculous story attached to it, all of which I have since forgotten.

After five days spent in Milan we left for Rome.

On our way we passed through the old town of Sienna, where, we are told, the purest Italian in Italy is spoken. Here we found an antique shop with many interesting things and one small painting in particular of Anne of Cleves, signed by Holbein. This attracted our attention. We bought it for a small sum and continued on our way.

We were tremendously excited. Had we accidentally run across an original Holbein? It certainly looked like it. What can equal the thrill of the collector who thinks he has found an undiscovered work of art!

That night we stopped at a little farmhouse inn on a country road somewhere between Sienna and Florence. It was an attractive place and fortunately clean. Our room had an old red-tile floor at least a foot higher in some places than others.

We were very anxious to do some automatic writing to see if we could possibly find out whether or not our picture was an original. As there were no chairs in the room, nothing but one wobbly little stool, we resorted to the bed as the only sitting place available. And this was only just available, being one of those old-fashioned affairs with a step-ladder as its only means of ascent. Here on the heights with our legs crossed under us and by the light of one candle, Rudy wrote.

Before writing we minutely examined our treasure. The wood it was painted on was unquestionably old. A hairpin soon proved the genuineness of the worm holes. We were just about that we were the proud possessors of an original Holbein.

After waiting for awhile the writing at last began. We spoke that night (by means of the pencil) with Rudy's mother, Jenny, and with many other of our friends and relations. We inquired if they could tell us anything about the picture and were told that a little later a friend, who made study of such things, would speak to us about it.

To our disappointment we finally learned that the picture was not an original, as we had thought, but an old copy. At least it was old; that was something. On our return to Nice this was confirmed by an expert.

As our time was limited we only stopped in Florence for a day or so, but long enough to pay a visit to Pitti Gallery for a glimpse of the favorite Botticelli.

The leaning tower of Pisa was, of course, also inspected on our way to Rome.

I for one greeted Rome with a sigh of relief, the thought of a bath to come and a rest from dust and Rudy's driving having kept me alive for the few days past. The roads in Italy at this time of the year were always bad and dust in an open car unbearable. Those who are addicted to hay-fever may understand my feelings.

We spent a delightful ten days in Rome, which more than made up for the trip in the automobile. Our pleasures and entertainments while here were mostly arranged by Baron Fassini, who had also been kind enough to put at our disposal his beautiful palace in the hills near Florence during our stay there. This opportunity of living in an historical setting we had declined as our visit to this city was so short.

One amusing day in Rome I shall never forget. A day spent watching the filming of "Quo Vadis" with Emil Jannings as Nero. We arrived on the outdoor set just in time to see the meticulous Petronius being carried in his litter to the entrance of his palace. This might appear to be a simple thing, but it was not. Far from it.

Four huge black slaves bore the reclining Petronius. Every time the rehearsal started, a pandemonium broke loose.

Having just arrived we were all completely at a loss to explain this apparent uproar. We were not at all sure but what we were witnessing a fascisti uprising, until we noticed the calm and boredom with which those on the outer circle watched this excitement.

Our minds were finally relieved by Baron Fassini, who disclosed the identity of the main participants in this noisy drama. We were in the midst of a veritable Tower of Babel.

This picture boasted two directors. A German director and an Italian director, each possessing many various German and Italian assistants and interpreters. Neither director spoke the language of the other.

Jannings, the star of the production, although an American by citizenship and birth, spoke no other language but German.*

Nero's favorite, Petronius, was a Frenchman who, as fortune would have it, spoke no other language but French.

The leading lady was an English girl who spoke nothing but English and a little weak French, and who was consequently unable to understand anything going on.

The Negro slaves, of which there seemed to be an amazing number, had been especially brought from Arabia or Egypt and spoke nothing but their native tongue.

Hence the apparent confusion.

One director shouted through a megaphone in German, while the other did likewise in Italian. The interpreters did their best to outshout them both, and the poor actors and extras, making nothing of the hubbub, ran in all directions. Then both directors would throw down their megaphones, tear their hair, look to heaven for help and shortly become sufficiently pacified by the sympathies of their respective assistants to enable them to begin all over again.

To us it looked as if war would be declared any moment between Italy and Germany. But such was not the case.

We lunched that day with Mr. and Mrs. Jannings and all the principals in the drama at the restaurant Borghese Gardens. What was our surprise to find all in a jovial, happy frame of mind. All on the best of terms. Food was at least one language they could all understand.

---

*Emil Jannings was born in Switzerland to a German Father and an American mother. He grew up in Germany, though he had some command of English as he later made a few English talkies.

94

Mrs. Jannings, who has an amazing gift for languages, was the interpreter de luxe for the table. Rudy and Jannings, who sat side by side, seemed to get along famously without any help by speaking in their language of pantomime.

We were also invited by Baron Fassini to visit the ancient palace of Nettuno, which is at present in his possession. This palace, about an hour's ride from Rome, is one of the historical monuments of Italy and belonged at one time to Caesar Borgia.

All restorations have been made according to historical documents and under the supervision of the government. The Baron, who is a man of excellent taste, has furnished the entire castle in period, and with the exception of a few bathrooms hollowed out of the thickness of the walls, it stands to-day practically as it was during the occupancy of the famous Borgia family.

This castle was particularly interesting to Rudy as Caesar Borgia had always been one of his favorite characters in history. In fact, it had been his ambition for some time to portray the character of this Borgia on the screen, the story to be written around some of the incidents recorded by Sabatini in *The Banner of the Bull.*

Before dinner our host took us all over the castle. We visited the dungeons and the torture chambers at the bottom of the round towers; we passed through the dark, narrow, damp passageway in the thickness of the walls where, in the obscure centre, there is a trap door down which undesirables fell on to spikes below and thus conveniently ended their interference in Borgia plans. As the castle itself is built on rocks out over the sea, it was not difficult here to be rid of one's enemies. What tales those waters could tell if we but understood the language.

We passed along corridors and through chambers with old red velvet walls, uneven tile floors and furnished heavy but beautifully old carved old Renaissance furniture. In one wing, up a small and at one time secret staircase, we entered the private apartments reserved for Mussolini. Here, in the home of his friend, the Duce spends what hours of rest he may snatch from hectic state affairs.

Although the castle is undoubtedly unique in beauty and historical interest, it is not a place where I should care to live. Its atmosphere is too impregnated with sombre, sinister vibrations of past deeds to give much happiness in repose. As Rudy expressed it afterwards, it was fortunate for the Baron that his psychic facilities were undeveloped or he would not have spent many nights in this residence. Rudy himself had seen many shadowy forms and had felt the presence of many conflicting forces.

Later that evening after dinner our host invited us to remain the night. Rudy, however, declined, preferring to return to our hotel in Rome, where he felt more certain to rest undisturbed by visitors from other periods.

Another fascinating place is the old Castle San Angelo. This monument stands supreme as a document of super-hypocrisy. One example in where, in particular is the bedroom of Pope Clement VII, where, while kneeling "in prayer" before the picture of the Holy Family which hangs on the wall above his prie-dieu, he might raise his eyes to the ceiling and there enjoy the painted scenes of some of the most degraded of Pompeian festivities. On the ceilings in the dining-room of this "Holy Father" may also be seen amongst satyrs and nymphs the famous or infamous Julia Farnese at some of her playful pastimes.

While here we were also shown the tiny chamber where the great Cagliostro was imprisoned and tortured and the cell of the traffic Beatrice Cenci.

We saw the Vatican and wandered through the Coliseum in moonlight and, of course, visited the ruins of ancient Rome.

It was Rudy's intention to motor south as far as Castellaneta and Taranto and to stop on his way for a short visit with his brother Alberto. As the roads were in terrible condition and the dust worse even than what we had already come through, Rudy thought it better for me to return to the château and wait for him there. This suggestion I accepted with enthusiasm, having not yet fully recovered from the dust fever of the first part of our tour.

A little over two weeks later Rudy and Auntie returned, bringing Maria with them to meet my father and mother. They were all worn out and delighted to be home again after a trip which I gathered was more dust and bumps than pleasure.

It was not until one of our future stays at the château that I met Alberto, who came then from Italy to spend a few days with us.

Early in November Maria returned to Milan, and Rudy and I sailed for America, which brought this glorious visit to an end.

Shortly after our arrival in New York our troubles with Famous Players were amicably settled by our lawyer, Max D. Steuer. Rudy once more started preparations for a new film after a compulsory vacation of nearly a year and a half.

CHAPTER 10

Muzzie again tells her story, "I RECEIVED a telegram from the children saying they would spend Christmas and New Year with us and to meet them in Paris. Accordingly I arrived in Paris the morning the boat was due. I met the boat-train, but no children were on it. Mother-like I was terribly worried and returned to the hotel to await developments.

At four o'clock in the morning Rudy rushed in the room, saying that he had come from the boat by motor and Natacha had to remain in America. When he saw my disappointment, he put his arms around me and told me it had been necessary for Natacha to stay in New York ten days longer on business*, so he had come on alone to be with me.

When Natacha finally joined us, the time was so short before Christmas that we had to motor day and night to reach home, at Juan les Pins, the morning of the 24th.

We had made up our minds to have a real American celebration, but such a thing as a Christmas tree on the Riviera had evidently never been heard of. We tried everywhere to buy a tree, Mr. De Langly, a friend of ours, at last took pity on us and had the gardener cut down one of the most beautiful pine trees from his estate. When this was sent over, it took all of us, including the servants and the gardeners, to drag it into the hall. With the assistance of several carpenters, we finally got it placed ready for trimming.

Then a great trouble arose as to how we were to find trimmings sufficient to decorate a tree of this size. But much to our surprise and delight, the children had brought over with them two enormous trunks, filled to overflowing with every conceivable kind of decoration. There must have been very little left at Woolworth's Fifth Avenue Store after Natacha had combed it.

*George Ullman had mostly helped settle the matter with Famous Players-Lasky, which would have Valentino owing two pictures to the company before they would release him from his contract. Natacha negotiated the deal with Ritz Carlton Pictures which would be settled soon after this trip. The deal would be a disaster as Ritz Carlton failed to mention their tiny budget and would not let the duo film on location. The deal was cut short after 'two' pictures: the never made Hooded Falcon, and Cobra.

The Santa Claus which was put on the top of the tree was enormous, and from his arms hung hundreds of yards of glittering gold and silver tinsel. Then there were silver stars, cornucopias filled with delicious chocolates, candy canes, balls of vivid color, and enough other trinkets to rival the wonders of the Arabian Nights. Rudy, Natacha and I worked nearly all night to get this in readiness. Mr. Hudnut insisted on having the tree well lighted with tiny electric globes in red, white and blue, the American colors. The children made no objection to the globes as a decoration, but they were quite determined it should also be lighted with little old-fashioned candles. These candles were placed upon every tip of every branch. The small parcels were tied on the tree; the larger boxes and gifts of importance were arranged around the base of the tree. The finishing touch was fine cotton pulled to a fluff to represent snowflakes, which we sprinkled with gleaming diamond dust. When finished, it was the most gorgeous thing you ever saw.

It was distinctly understood in the house that no one was to see the tree until it was lighted, so the family were made to go to dinner through the back stairs and hallway.

After dinner the family became quite rebellious and insisted upon watching Rudy and Natacha light the candles. Not having the long-handled tapers, they each took a cane and tied a candle to the end of it, so that with the kind assistance of chairs and step-ladders they were able to reach the highest candle branches.

At last the tree was practically illuminated, when Rudy discovered a small unlighted candle quite far back in the branches. In lighting this, a cotton snowflake caught fire. In a flash the entire tree was ablaze!

We lost our heads, with the exception of my sister Teresa, who is always the essence of calmness. Her one thought was to rescue the gifts. While we stood around screaming, she saved nearly all of our treasures.

Mr. Hudnut shouted to Rudy to bring in the fire hose and for Natacha to turn on the water full force. This brought me to my senses.

In a flash I realized this would be the finish of my lovely Gobelin tapestry and my wonderful Saint Cire needlepoint chairs, my most precious possessions. As I saw Rudy coming through the door, it occurred to me that it would be impossible for the hall to burn as it was built of stone.

In my excitement I knocked the hose out of Rudy's hands and shouted for all to get buckets of water to throw on the tree from the upper balcony.

Valentino, ready to kill a bull

Everybody rushed for water – some with buckets, some with pans and some with teacups and glasses. In this way the fire was quickly extinguished, but not the black smoke which filled the hall. The tree was a sorry sight!

Choking and gasping for breath, we began to lament the loss of our gifts. But practical Teresa calmly led us into the salon and there on the table they lay. She had saved everything, with the exception of a few of the small toys which had been tied to the branches for the gardener's children.

Grimy with smoke we sat on the floor and untied our parcels, screaming and laughing with joy, as if we had gone back to our first childhood. Champagne was brought in to restore our spirits and the merrymaking lasted until broad daylight.

New Years, Mr. and Mrs. John Wheaton gave a party for the children at the Negresco Hotel in Nice. Between the dances it was the custom of the Americans to dodge into the bar for an extra cocktail.

Happening to pass by with Mr. Wheaton, we saw that there was an unusual excitement going on. We elbowed our way through the crowd and saw Rudy giving an exhibition of 'Blood and Sand.' He was on his knees stabbing at an imaginary bull with his cane. Looking up with that bewitching smile of his, he saw me and exclaimed, 'My God, I've killed the bull!'

I rushed back to our table and told Natacha that Rudy had already killed one bull in the bar and I thought before he killed any more she had better go and rescue him. 'What!' gasped Natacha, and without even excusing herself rushed from the table and into the bar after him.

I waited fully fifteen minutes, but neither of them returned. Anxious to see what was going on I went back.

On a high stool before the bar sat Jane Day, the dancer, while Rudy stood with his arms around her telling her was a wonderful movie actress she would make. But Jane was so near asleep that Rudy's pleadings were wasted.

Looking around for Natacha, I saw her being embraced by at least eight young men. She was giving them a long talk on the picture business, but none of them were listening.

I now thought it was wise to insist on their return to the table, as the Wheatons would probably forget they had invited them. A trifle unsteadily they followed me.

Natacha, being in one of her benevolent moods, kept leaving the table and bringing back different pretty girls for Rudy to dance with, and through this, of course, made herself very popular.

The band was playing 'Home Sweet Home,' but the children were far from ready to leave. So our agreeable host and hostess suggested we go to the Perroquet and finish up the morning. Eight of us got inside the big Renault, while Rudy and a friend of his climbed up on to the top and dangled their legs in the chauffeur's face.

After one or two dances at the merry Perroquet, we wound up with egg and ham sandwiches and hot coffee. Dead tired, we slept most of the way home, arriving not long before luncheon.

This New Year's Day ended with the children's happy but rapid holiday, for the next day they departed for America. They hurried back to commence 'Beaucaire,' as there had been an amicable settlement between Rudy and Famous Players Company after a fight over one year. Their one thought was to finish 'Beaucaire' and to return as soon as possible to the château where they had made so many plans for their future happiness.

Rudy decided while in New York to buy and send over a projection machine, so that we could have the pleasure of seeing his pictures as soon as they were finished. In this way he was also able to keep a record of all his work.

Rudy was always very generous and wanted the best of everything, so in selecting the projection machine he chose a duplicate of the one used in the Capitol Theatre, New York. They told Rudy that the machine was far too large and could never be used in a private house, but he insisted the hall of the château was large enough for anything. Nothing but the largest would do for him.

The thing arrived in great boxes that looked like caskets. It came down with three men in a van and took ten men in all to get it into the house.

Rudy had written us that the machine was on the way and also a print of 'Blood and Sand.' They arrived at the same time. Of course, we were terribly anxious to put on a real performance. But how to get the thing put together? Every electrician we ever heard of we sent for, but they had never seen a projection machine before and refused to tackle it. We were in despair. Oscar Colcaire, one of Jean de Rezscki's pupils, had the brilliant idea of digging up a young man who had at one time run a machine at the Ideal Theatre in Nice.

The young man worked daily at this task for weeks. Each time that he thought he had it perfected we sat breathlessly in comfortable chairs waiting for the treat. But the performances were either given upside down, or the figures were so large they could not possibly get on the screen, or when they did they were headless. He did the funniest things.

Valentino in Monsieur Beaucaire

In despair we sent to Marseilles, asking as a great favor if the Lasky people would send us a special to put this damn machine in running order. They ignored our pleadings entirely!

Regretfully, we were forced to let the whole matter drop until Rudy's return in the summer.

Early in August 1924, the children arrived from Paris in Rudy's new Voisin sport car, which he had ordered the year before. It was magnificent affair. The exterior steel grey, the interior a brilliant red morocco leather of the finest quality. On the back seat sat Natacha in a new fur coat with five highly pedigreed Pekinese.

At the wheel sat Rudy in a high fur-collared leather coat and his life-size goggles, traveling incognito to escape his admirers. At his side sat famous Kabar, the huge Doberman given him by MM. Herbertot, director of the Champs Elysees Theatre.

Descending from the car they entered the château with the menagerie. It was almost impossible to walk without stepping on dogs. Natacha evidently thought it necessary to apologize for bringing us the kennel. The little white one, she said, was bought because it looked so sad; Utie, the sleeve champion, was taken because they had wanted three thousand dollars for him, and finally let them have him for fifteen hundred. The three little baby Pekes were so cunning they could not decide which to choose, so they bought them all.

Everything was 'Beaucaire, Beaucaire, Beaucaire!"

The children had brought the film over with them. Because of the glorious settings and the marvelous costumes they were impatient for us to see it.

Immediately after luncheon Rudy started work on the now famous projection machine. He damned all the foreign electricians and called them stupid idiots, as in America this machine would have been put in running order in less than a day. 'I know nothing about it, but I'll them a thing or two,' he shouted. 'Look here, Uncle Dick, they didn't know enough to put the parts together with the corresponding numbers.'

Then he tore the entire machine apart and before dinner had it reconstructed and almost in working order. He promised that after dinner he would show us the exquisite 'Beaucaire'.

But Rudy, being so excited, couldn't wait for dinner. He called us into the hall to witness the showing of the first reel. It ran along beautifully for about ten minutes, and just as Rudy was to make his entrance on the screen, there was a flash – and the whole château was left in total darkness! Every fuse in the house had blown out.

Not being prepared for this blow-out there were only about six candles in the house, and our grouchy old chef insisted on having them all, declaring that otherwise his kitchen would be too dark to prepare dinner. We compromised by giving him four, the other two being divided equally amongst the family.

The next day the fuses were replaced, while Rudy and Natacha spent most of their time at Nice searching for old ivories and armor in the antique shops. These were their two extravagant hobbies.

In the evening, as we were all waiting for dinner to be announced, Rudy decided to give another trial on 'Beaucaire.' Rushing into the library which had been turned into a projection room, he turned on the current. Bing! Again we were submerged in darkness!

At this moment we heard shrieks and screams coming from the kitchen. It was the chef threatening to leave. Fortunately, Mr. Hudnut with uncanny foresight, had purchased several boxes of candles. The soft lights wavering shadows of the eighteenth-century rooms brought back the real atmosphere of that period, making one almost regret the discovery of electricity.

The second blow-out, with the now perfected machine, caused Mr. Hudnut to realize that expert advice was necessary as he was unwilling to live in total darkness any longer. He called in the head electrician of the Antibes office. This man explained that the machine required two extra cables, as there was not sufficient voltage to run both the machine and the house.

A week later this was completed and the machine worked to perfection. At last we saw 'Beaucaire!'

In the evenings Rudy had been giving Tango lessons to his sister Maria and my niece Margaret Dinwoodey, who were both staying with us. He grew impatient because the electric piano would not mark time to suit him. So while the cables were being laid for the projection machine, he busied himself with pulling the piano to pieces.

The hall was strewn with every conceivable part of the mechanism, which he was never able to put together again so that it would work. He had neglected to number the pieces. Refusing to acknowledge that it was too much for him, Rudy kept insisting that he would finish it up when he had time. But that time never came. It was necessary to write to England to have the Duo-Art Company send a man over especially to put the piano in order.

Rudy used to get the wildest ideas. He expected to make millions in order to make his dreams come true.

He was always crazy over motor boats, and it was perfectly remarkable how easily he handled them when he knew practically nothing about them. This seemed to be one of his many gifts. He rented one and took us on many wild cruises all over the Riviera. It was a beautiful sight to see him standing at the wheel, bareheaded, in his black bathing suit, the white spray dashing up in his face.

We often stopped at the beautiful island of St. Lerins and spread our lunch in the deserted medieval castle which juts out into the Mediterranean. One of his extravagant dreams was to buy this castle from the French government and to restore it as a dwelling-place for himself and Natacha, filling it with the wonderful old treasures of that period.

I will never forget the morning when Rudy took me to a corner of the château grounds overlooking the public highroad and the sea. He said, 'Muzzie, this is where I want to build my boat-house.' He then began telling me his plans for it. The boat-house would have to be an enormous affair, large enough to hold a yacht and a couple of motor boats. It would also require a tunnel under the road to the sea so the boats could be hauled up on the tracks into the boat-house for the winter. He took from his pocket a pad and a pencil and gave me the dimensions, which, when the boat-house was finished, would, in comparison, have made the château look like the gate-keeper's lodge.

A short distance back of the château stands the 'dependence' or guest house of thirteen rooms. He turned one of these chambers into an ideal darkroom, said by several well-known photographers to be the best equipped darkroom in France.

Cameras were a mania with Rudy – large, small, and medium-sized of every make. In dead earnest he used to tell us this was his only extravagance. He spent hours a day taking pictures about the château, and we spent hours a day posing for him, only to find after the negatives were developed that there were from two to three pictures on the same plate. Then Rudy declared it all the fault of the camera and rush off to buy a new one."

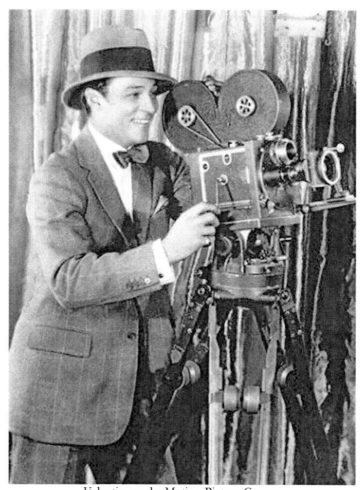

Valentino and a Motion Picture Camera

CHAPTER 11

Muzzie continues, "IN September, with its cooler days and autumn splendor, we decided to journey through Spain. It had been Rudy's intention to make the tour by motor, but on account of bad roads he at last reluctantly gave up the idea and we traveled by train.

Natacha and I had taken this trip before, but we now looked forward to it with new joy in seeing it through Rudy's eyes. His viewpoint was always so new, refreshing and enthusiastic, in its child-like wonder and love of beauty.

On trains, Rudy always insisted upon taking three compartments, a double one for himself and Natacha, one for me, and the third for his numerous cameras and voluminous hand-luggage. We looked for all the world like a troupe of wandering minstrels! Traveling through Spain with a lot of unnecessary baggage is no joke, as we soon found out, for one usually has the pleasure of hauling one's own baggage from train to taxi – porters being scarce.

Rudy's first impression of Spain was Madrid. We arrived on a day that was not too warm and gloriously colorful. It took two taxis to get us to the Hotel Ritz. We rode in one, the hand-baggage in another.

We and the baggage were all dumped in the lobby, and Rudy, refusing to look at rooms or even to register, insisted upon rushing off to see a collection of armor that he had read about in some paper. So letting him go, we selected a bright and cheerful suite overlooking the lovely gardens.

After we had taken our refreshing baths and dressed in cool muslin gowns, having had no breakfast, we came downstairs for an early luncheon. We sat waiting until two o'clock, but no Rudy. Unable to ward off starvation any longer, we ate alone. We were perfectly furious and hardly knew what we had ordered. Having forgotten to take a camera, we knew Rudy would turn up sooner or later. In the midst of rehearsing just what we were going to say to our deserter, in he rushed full of hunger and old armor.

Now that we had finished our luncheon, it was not too difficult to listen to yards and yards of enthusiastic description of something we knew nothing about. To women, all armor looks alike.

Rudy never believed in wasting time. He wished to see everything in a day. So after he had had a few mouthfuls to eat, like excited maniacs we flew off to view the wonders of the Prado. Having decided to have his portrait painted by several of the best modern Spanish artists, his intention in going through those galleries was to choose which school of the ancients he wished the moderns to imitate.

However, his plan was frustrated for the day, as we arrived just in time to have the doors closed in our face.

Rudy was a thorough sightseer, never missing anything of interest. By the time we left Madrid he could have rewritten *Baedeker.*

One full day was given to antique hunting, as Rudy was collecting armor; Natacha, old ivories; and I, jade. We found so many treasures, we thought it unwise to remain too long in Madrid or our money-bags would be too diminished to continue the trip.

From Madrid we went to Seville. This city was found more fascinating because of its old memories and being less frequented by tourists.

Seville thrilled Rudy more than any other city, because of its association with his then enormous success in 'Blood and Sand.' Rudy had actually lived the character of Gallardo in the fictitious action of the scenario, but now he seemed to re-live it in reality. Ibanez had drawn this character from the life-history of a famous bull-fighter who had once lived in the city.

From the concierge of the hotel, Rudy learned the name of the street and the number of the little house where this fascinating character had lived. We obtained permission to go through it. It was a forlorn little dwelling. This is where the bull-fighter had lived and dreamed his dreams of fame in his early days. It was now occupied by very poor and slovenly peasants and an air of neglect was upon it. It was with a strange sadness in our hearts that we left the place. In the same street lived a man who purchased the clothes

Valentino dressed for Blood and Sand, 1922

of the toreadors and matadors after their death. It is a superstition among the families connected with the bullring that the clothes of their dead heroes must be gotten rid of as soon as possible. Otherwise they are believed to bring bad luck.

From this man these gorgeous suits, made of silk velvet, hand embroidered in solid gold thread, can be purchased for a mere song, while to have them made to order costs a small fortune. Rudy bought from this man the most beautiful toreador costume I have ever seen. The bolero was of black velvet, so heavily and closely embroidered in gold one could scarcely see the velvet. The trousers were of plain black velvet with gold stripes down the sides. The stockings were of flesh-colored silk and the cape of royal purple silk-velvet embroidered in gold and lined with a lighter shade of purple satin. The fine muslin hand-made shirt had rows of tiny pleated frills down in the front, and the broad silk sash to be wound around the waist was of purple silk to match the cape.

Whether true or not, the man convinced Rudy this costume had belonged to the most intimate friend of the famous toreador.

The foremost thing now in Rudy's mind was to see a real bull-fight. The next day being Sunday, a gala bull-fight was to be given under the auspices of the royal family for the benefit of the Red Cross. We were fortunate in getting our seats directly under the royal box.

Rudy took with him to the arena a motion picture camera and another for 'stills' slung over his shoulder. Had it not been a gala day and a great deal of excitement going on, I doubt whether he would have been allowed to have enter with this paraphernalia.

On this eventful day all the nobility and the better class of people were seen driving up to the gates in their beautiful carriages with spirited horses, almost a thing of the past in this age, and, of course, thousands of autos. The vivid sunshine falling on the colorful crowds was dazzling. We stood by the gates, jammed by the throng, until the royal family entered.

Our seats gave us a wonderful view of the entire arena. It was a magnificent sight to watch the beautiful women of Seville taking their places in the upper tiers surrounding the royal box. They were dressed in almost the costume of the olden days; black silk dresses made with frills, ankle length, tight bodices and short sleeves. Their high Spanish combs were very beautiful, some solid gold studded with precious jewels, others of tortoise-shell handsomely carved. Over these combs were gracefully draped their wonderful old mantillas of real lace, some black and some creamy white, which had been in their families for generations. Over their arms they carried their magnificent silk shawls, hand-woven in the brightest colors, embroidered in bright birds, flowers, and foliage of every description. Unlike the heavy modern shawls, these older weaves are almost light as gossamer, and it is a saying among the nobility that a shawl is not acceptable unless it can be drawn through a wedding ring. Taking their seats, the ladies threw these gorgeous creations over the balcony rails upon which they rested their elbows.

There was a certain nobleman whose great desire it was to revive the ancient method of bull-fighting. This method was to fight the bull on foot, and thus do away with the terrible cruelty of torturing and slaughtering the pitifully bony worn-out horses which are used for this purpose. These poor dumb creatures haven't a chance for their lives. They are often gored by the bulls till their entrails drag on the ground. After this, if they are still able to stand on their feet, their entrails are shoved back and sewed up, and the tottering animals are once more led into the arena. Times do not seem to have changed so much after all from Nero's day! The terrible part of these bull-fights is that one becomes physically hypnotized by the tremendous thought-force of the crowd until the bloody spectacle is a thing of enjoyment. Then you dangerously excuse yourself, losing sight of the hideous realities, and fall entirely under the spell of the perfected art to which the Spanish have exalted their national sport.

At first, Natacha had refused absolutely to go, declaring her love for animals made it impossible for her to sit by and see them tortured. This so took the joy out of Rudy's day that at last I consented to join him. It was not until we had got in the carriage that Natacha weakened in her resolve, and so under the spell of this hypnotic influence did she fall later, during the course of the bull-fight, that she lost her former sense of horror and became as enthusiastic as any Spanish woman in the crowd. This sport is, indeed, an insidious thing!

This nobleman had obtained permission to give, before the regular bull-fight, an exhibition of this ancient and more humane method – if the word 'humane' can be used in connection with such a brutal sport. It is some consolation to know that by this method the only animal tortured is the bull.

This man was very tall and slender, extremely handsome, and looked every inch an aristocrat. He wore long black trousers which flared at the ankles, a black velvet embroidered bolero, and a broad-brimmed hat of grey felt held on by a black chin-strap. I am not sure, but perhaps this was a costume of the olden day.

We understood this gentleman to be a cavalry officer and an athlete, and his performance was a marvel of grace and accurate precision, ending the animal's life without further suffering.

The uproar from the multitude was deafening. People stood up and screamed, the women throwing their fans and even their jewels into the arena. The men, in a frenzy of excitement, literally showered him with their hats.

The entire royal family arose to their feet and wildly applauded, while the successful hero stood with hat in hand, his fine head bowed gracefully and respectfully before the royal box. His poise, in spite of the flattering applause, was something to wonder at.

In his great excitement, Rudy had entirely forgotten to take his motion pictures, which he had been counting upon doing for days. He stood on the balcony rail, having thrown his hat in the ring, and waved his arms frantically while he screamed himself hoarse. Both Natacha and I had to hold on to him to keep him from jumping into the arena.

Trembling, and with tears in his eyes, he turned to us and said, 'My God, this is the most wonderful thing I have ever seen. From now on I'm through with the movies! Spain for me! I'm going to be a toreador!'

The balance of the performance was much like the usual bull-fight. After one has seen about sixteen bulls killed and more than twenty horses mangled to death, and after the excitement has worn off, a great and wondering sadness fills the heart.

Now that Rudy had emphatically declared his intention of becoming a toreador, many discussions arose between himself and Natacha, which seemed screamingly funny to me. I knew very well this was only a passing fancy, for any character that greatly interested him or won his admiration, either in fiction or in life, caused him to want to become one with it. This ability to throw himself into a character was the reason, I believe, of his great success as an actor.

While Rudy was still under the illusion of wanting to become a bull-fight, he took us one evening in an open carriage miles outside of Seville to the bull-pens. This is a place to which the specially bred bulls are brought from the country the night before the fight.

The evening was very hot and sultry and we were clad in the thinnest of gowns, with no wraps. It took us about three hours to reach the pens. Natacha and I had had a rather strenuous day and consequently we both fell asleep. Upon our arrival, Rudy left us in the carriage undisturbed and finding a most agreeable caretaker spent a glorious hour inspecting the wild bulls to be selected the next day.

It was midnight before we started for home. The night had turned extremely cool, and it was almost morning before we arrived at the hotel. We entered it, sneezing and coughing, and awoke the next morning with very bad colds.

Rudy said this state of affairs would never have happened had we but taken more interest in the bull-pens. He was greatly disgusted that all his glowing descriptions had been wasted, as we had been asleep during the whole trip.

While in Seville, Rudy wished to present us each with a lovely old Spanish shawl. Directly beside the gates leading to the Alcazar was an antique dealer who possessed the most wonderful collection of antique shawls in Spain. It was while looking over these treasures that Natacha was struck by a brilliant idea. Why not buy the most beautiful of this collection and sell them for big profits to the smart Fifth Avenue shops? So glowingly did the children present their wonderful schemes that I, hypnotized by their enthusiasm, always became converted to them.

Rudy, being so well known in the picture world, was never able to hide his identity for long, and the Valentino name, regarded as a dollar sign, often caused extra prices to be added to the purchases. Time after time, when ten per cent had been judiciously tacked on by some shrewd dealer, after long dickerings, this same ten per cent was taken off as though a great favor were being granted the famous screen artist.

Rudy and Natacha selected the most beautiful specimens of the collection and the bill only came to the modest sum of ten thousand dollars! These shawls were shipped to America in bond. Needless to say, none of them were sold, but these generous children gave many away to their friends*. I, myself am the possessor of three of the choicest.

We remained in Seville three extra days to enjoy the beauties of the Alcazar and its wonderful gardens. Rudy took hundreds of photographs. Views were taken in the uncertain light of early dawn, in the bright glare of noon, and at night in all the splendor of the moonlight.

He stood for hours with his pet motion-picture camera, reeling off hundreds and hundreds of feet of film of the Alcazar courtyard, never stopping to realize that as there was not a soul in it at the time there would be no action!

---

*Upon her return to the States, Natacha filed a patent for a 'combined coverlet and doll' which probably utilized these scarves. She was granted patent #1575263 for this invention, which surprisingly has been referenced by several other creators in the last few decades.

While in Paris, Natacha had ordered the costumes, having designed them with great skill and artistry. Nita Naldi had been chosen for her exotic beauty to play the leading feminine role, the part of a Moorish girl. She was now in Paris busily being fitted. The costumes, entirely different from those in 'Beaucaire,' were even more exquisite.

He took everything. Exteriors and interiors. I don't think there was a nook or a corner that he missed in this truly magnificent palace, as this trip had really been planned for a purpose of getting data for his coming film 'The Hooded Falcon'*.

In this film Rudy was to play a role of a Spanish prince of the fourteenth century. We had found in one of the galleries a portrait of this period, which had so impressed Rudy that he immediately adopted it as his model for the make-up of his character and speaking Spanish so perfectly, without the slightest accent, he was continually taken for a real Spaniard. Rudy's former identity had entirely disappeared.

One day, in going to a bank to present his letter of credit in order to replenish his vanishing funds, he was asked his nationality. When he replied 'Italian' the cashier expressed his doubt, saying that his appearance and perfect Spanish was a contradiction. He had to produce his passport to verify his statement.

We were all very much interested in antiques, lovely old furniture, etc. Some of Rudy's handsomest pieces of armor and many of Natacha's most beautiful and valuable old ivories were found here in Seville. They also bought a number of other things, amongst which were a superb pair of Renaissance doors, a Gothic chair, and two very wonderful Gothic chests. If I am not mistaken, all of these objects of art are now in Rudy's Hollywood home.

As Rudy intended to reproduce parts of the Alhambra for scenes in 'The Hooded Falcon' we at last tore ourselves regretfully away from Seville and started on our journey to Granada. This was to be our last stop in Spain."

---

*This film would never be made, and some of the troubles of its production are described in the following chapters. In the meantime the couple had made "A Sainted Devil" which had been another flop for Valentino. He was seriously in need of a hit film for both his future career and finances at this point in time.

Valentino in Costume for The Hooded Falcon

Chapter 12

WHILE in Granada we stayed at the beautiful old
Alhambra Palace Hotel, perched high upon the hills of this last
Moorish stronghold. Far below spread the plains where once had
been encamped the victorious armies of their most Catholic
Majesties, Ferdinand and Isabella.

Many were the stories of romance, splendor and tragedy,
life-dramas enacted long ago, which swept over our consciousness on
our visits to the palace and gardens of Alhambra – that most perfect
pearl of all Muslim art and culture.

In wandering through the shadowy marbled halls, through
arches of fantastical design and delicacy, past fountainhead
courtyards, Rudy seemed above all haunted by the utter sadness of
the place. Was it an impression of some dim memory of the past, or
was it but the force of grief and despair left as an heritage to these
long-deserted walls by the departing Boabdil and his vanquished
court?

Many wonderful days were spent wandering through this
earthly paradise.

Photographs, as usual, were taken galore of every possible
detail which could later be of use to us. In the thickness of the walls
of the arches, leading from one room or court to another, we found
there were always small arched holes about three feet high and two
feet deep. These holes, often covered with tiny beautifully designed
and perforated arches, had been used I believe for bronze lamps and
incense burners. This was but one detail we intended using. It could
have been the means of unusual lighting effects.

In one of the Sultana's rooms of the Generalife, the
summer palace of the Moorish princess, we found the perforated
floor which we had read about in Washington Irving's description of
the Alhambra. It seemed that these perforations were for perfuming
the room, the perfume or incense being burnt and tended by slaves
under the marble flooring of the chamber. This, of course, fascinated
Rudy, who loved all novel devices.

The baths of the Sultana were also a source of delight to us
both. Certainly no modern house of the most up-to-date comforts
can equal the luxuries of this ancient Moorish civilization.

Valentino and Nita Naldi in Cobra, 1925

While visiting these same apartments we were very nearly arrested and thrown out for good, and all on account of the cameras.

The room itself was quite dim, so Rudy decided that it would be necessary to make a flash-light photograph. As this was the first time he had ever used the flash-light gun, he, of course, put in much too much powder. There was an awful bang. In a few seconds we heard running footsteps and much shouting. Fighting their way through the thick smoke, the guards rushed in to find the anarchist who was presumably blowing up the palace. They had never seen or heard of a flash-light gun before, and we passed some anxious moments before Rudy could finally convince them we were not destined for jail.

The Alhambra in the moonlight is one of the most glorious sights I have ever seen, as it seems to cling with whitened fingers to the hills that gave it birth

Rudy's heightened psychic senses made it possible for him to see many shadowy forms and snatches of scenes of long ago, reflected in the Astral Light. But in this realized atmosphere of the Arabian Nights it was not difficult to imagine in these moonlit gardens the faint twang of some lute or the hushed laughter of some Moorish beauty with raven tresses.

It was with sadness and regret that we left this haunted place of dreams, consoling ourselves with the promise of a future visit when we could remain for a longer time.

Muzzie's story continues, "After our return from Spain the children decided to make a tour of the Touraine district, visiting all the famous châteaux of the Loire.

We started off on the glorious but rather cold morning of October 1st in Rudy's sport car. Our party consisted of Nita Naldi*, Margaret Dinwoodey, my niece, Natacha, Rudy and I. The first day was sunshiny and lovely, but from the second day on it rained steadily. When we stopped at Chambord, Rudy courteously rushed us into the palace under an umbrella, and, excusing himself, rushed back to the car. Taking out all the nice warm, dry, rugs, he carefully covered the car with them from stem to stern, the appearance of the motor evidently being of far more importance that the comfort of its occupants.

---

*Nita Naldi was a popular film actress mostly known for her vamping roles (many modern viewers confuse her with the first Vamp Queen, Theda Bara). She was Valentino's most frequent co-star appearing in four of his films. She was also one of the few people around him to befriend Natacha, appearing in Natacha's film "What Price Beauty?" in 1925. For more on Nita see page 257.

Chambord, the largest and most showy of all the châteaux, consisted of over four hundred rooms. Rudy became wildly enthusiastic, and ran us through the long corridors and damp cold rooms until we gasped for breath. But he never tired. At once he pictured himself owning all of this and inviting all of his friends each year for the hunting, and the banquets that he began to give in his imagination would have excelled even those of Frances the First.

Natacha exclaimed, 'That's all very well, Rudy, but as we live in modern times, how on earth would you heat such an enormous place? And how would you ever get servants enough? It would take at least from two to three maids and valets on each floor to direct people to their rooms.'

'Oh that's easy,' said Rudy, 'give each guest a candle, a Cook's guide, a hot-water bag and a bottle of whiskey. What more could they want?'

The thing that most delighted Rudy at Chambord was the mysterious double staircase, which allows one party to ascend and another to descend at the same time without either party seeing the other. Rudy worked out the plan of this most carefully, thinking it a valuable idea to take back to his friends in Hollywood.

It was quite dark when we left the palace and found our way back to the auto. Can you imagine our horror when we found our comfortable rugs drenched through? It was impossible to put them over us. We wrung them out as best we could and tucked them into the bottom of the car and returned to the hotel shivering with the cold.

At Chateaudun, Rudy went into raptures over the Renaissance architecture, which he loved best of all, and spent the entire morning running around to real estate people to ascertain if this almost ruined castle could be bought. When this failed, he tried to impress upon the old caretaker that the property should be sold for very little money of because of its run-down condition.

When we entered this fascinating old place, Rudy was most enthusiastic over the secret passage-ways, secret staircases and dungeons. Rudy, being so psychic in nature, felt the horror, the despair, and the tragic longings for freedom of those who had been confined in these dark prison cells. Who can say that ancient houses do not in some strange way retain the memory of deeds that transpired within their walls?

Because of the dangerous condition of the château, many rooms were shut off. But locked doors only baited Rudy's eager curiosity. There was one old tower with an outside staircase leading to rooms above, shut off by a rickety wooden gate. The caretaker insisted that the staircase was in too rotten a condition to allow of a visitor ascending. But Rudy, whose pockets were always well lined, slipped the old caretaker a generous pourboire and scrambled under the gate, dragging Natacha with him. Nita, Margaret and I stood outside in fear and trembling, listening for the crash that might come at any moment. But the children returned unharmed. They had been thrilled with the old tower rooms who floors had fallen in, and lured on by black passage-ways that seemed to lead to nowhere.

The morning that we visited Chaumont, we arrived just as a party of Cook's tourists was leaving the Château. Nita, with her exotic and striking beauty, attracted their attention at once. While all eyes were devouring her, she suddenly screamed, 'Mimi, Mimi, my darling – my God – we've lost the Chinese princess! The princess with the long nails and the eyes of melting clouds – where is she – where is she?'

People rushed about in every direction in hopes of catching a glimpse of the princess, only to see Nita emerging from a flower bed, holding in her famously beautiful hands a muddy, wet, shivering, snarling little black-and-tan dog!

This little dog caused us many sleepless nights as it was constantly disappearing.

Nita never ceased to be amusing and refreshing. Usually in hotel dining-rooms her shrill voice* could be heard above all others as she recounted her back-stage Winter Garden reminiscences. Her shins must have been raw, as we were continually kicking her under the table, as most of her stories were a bit risqué for the public and too risqué for my young niece.

This castle, with its moat and drawbridge, while not one of the largest, we found to be one of the most interesting, as it is still in its original state. The rooms of Catherine de' Medici and Ruggieri, her astrologer-medium, are furnished and arranged exactly as they were when occupied by them.

These apartments of the Queen Mother especially fascinated Rudy and Natacha because of their interest in psychic matters. We were all thrilled to stand in the bedroom of Ruggieri, the very room in which, one day, as history tells us, he gave a séance to the Queen, during which she saw the departed kings of France.

This bedroom of the astrologer was separated from that of Catherine's only by a small passageway, which caused Nita to exclaim, 'These old guys had nothing on Hollywood morals, only they evidently got away with it!'

---

*Nita was said to have a mouth that would put Olive Thomas to shame. Contrary to popular belief she did not have a Brooklyn accent. To hear her voice see rudolphvalentino.org/nita.html

Very few tourists are allowed to climb the secret stairs leading from Catherine's room to the secret laboratory where Ruggieri made the poisons for his Queen's subtle use. But Rudy always held the Open Sesame which secured admittance to such places.

When the secret wall-cabinets of this mysterious room were opened, Rudy hopefully expected to see some of the old bottles and vials, but nothing remained save the memory of such things which clung to the musty walls. Rudy's sensitiveness to psychic conditions caused him to feel distinctly these impressions of former days.

While at the ancient ruins of Loche, Rudy had a rather startling psychic experience. We found that the old caretaker had recently unearthed some ancient dungeons. In so doing he had brought to light many interesting objects – small iron figures, crosses, and many old coins – upon which he had been complimented by the French government. Rudy immediately insisted upon seeing these dungeons. Because of the quantities of rocks and loose dirt, Margaret, Nita and I thought it too dangerous to descend. But as nothing seemed too dangerous for our two adventurers, we remained in the old courtyard while they disappeared into the subterranean vaults.

It was a dull, cold sort of a day, and it seemed the children had been gone for ages, when Rudy suddenly reappeared, his eyes the size of sauces, his hair seeming to stand on end. In his excitement he had entirely forgotten Natacha, who was left somewhere underground with the guide.

He told us that in going through a narrow passageway leading to the oubliettes, he had heard groans. When he reached the oubliette, a pitch black hole scooped out of the solid rock, and just as he stooped to enter the low door, his blood was frozen by a hideous scream of agony which he swore was far too real for any imagination!

That night in our rooms at the hotel, Rudy told Natacha and me that while wandering alone among the ground-floor rooms he had come upon one which had great rings, hooks and chains hanging from the walls. He had been frightfully startled to see the ghastly white bones of a human skeleton, its neck held by a ring, its arms outstretched, its blanched and bony toes hanging within a few inches of the floor.

Thinking this skeleton to be real when he went closer to ascertain just how it had been fastened to the wall, when the bones vanished before his amazed eyes, leaving only an empty ring and rusty chains! Later, the guide had verified this experience by explaining that this room had been a torture-chamber. The whole place was haunted, he had said, and his wife positively refused to remain there alone, having heard from time to time such horrible noises.

In visiting the remaining châteaux of the Loire, nothing of unusual interest occurred, and it was with real regret that we finished this happy trip and returned to Paris."

CHAPTER 13

AFTER three months of travel in France and Spain, spent mostly in studying and absorbing the atmosphere of past ages, in preparation for "The Hooded Falcon," we sailed for America in early November on board the *Leviathan*. We were accompanied by Miss Nita Naldi.

On our return to New York there were many conferences with J.D. Williams, head of the Ritz Film Company, with whom Rudy at this time was under contract.

It had been the intention of the company to produce the two pictures for which Rudy's services had been obtained, in New York. The studio problem, however, could not be solved; and it was at last decided to return to Hollywood – that fatal capital of Filmdom.*

While in New York Mr. Williams, without our knowledge, bought the film rights to Martin Brown's stage success "Cobra." The first we heard of it was an announcement in the newspapers that "Cobra" had been bought by Williams for Valentino. When we asked Mr. Williams what this meant, he explained to us that he had bought the play on speculation and had used Rudy's name to enhance the value. As this was nothing to us one way or another, we let it pass and paid no further attention to the matter.

"Uncle Joe" Henabery, who had directed Rudy in "The Sainted Devil" and to whose genial personality and careful ability Rudy was very attached, had also been engaged to direct the first Ritz film.

---

*New York and New Jersey had originally been the film capitals of the US. In 1910 D.W. Griffith brought the first legitimate film company (Biograph) to Hollywood. By 1918 almost all production had moved to California. Hollywood was an extremely rural area at that time, causing many stars to lament the loss of 'culture' and 'excitement' they had known in New York City. By the mid 20s more stars tried to bolt back to the East Coast, but found doing so quite difficult and costly (Gloria Swanson was one such star). This indeed had been a stipulation in Valentino's contract with Ritz Carlton, which they would break.

Valentino in costume for The Hooded Falcon

After three weeks in New York we left for the coast. Our party included Nita Naldi, Joe Henabery, J.D. Williams, Joseph Jackson, our publicity head, Adrian the designer*, George Ullman, Rudy and myself.

Before leaving for Europe in August we had seen June Mathis, who had just returned from Ben Hur camp in Italy, and was then in the throes of settling her difficulties with Metro Goldwyn.

We read the story of our next film to June and asked her if she would not try and find time to do the scenario. She said that she liked the story, and would do her best to arrange it.

While we were in Europe Miss Mathis severed her connections with Goldwyn and signed a new contract with Richard Roland of First National. Under this contract she was to write scenarios and supervise feature productions.**

Just before leaving for the coast we received June's script of "The Hooded Falcon." Enclosed was a note – she hoped we would like the script; she had been very rushed with her First National work and had done the best possible with her limited time.***

We read the script on the train going west. Mr. Henabery, Rudy and I, all came to the same conclusion – there was much to be changed. As time was short, it was decided that we would have to work on the scenario ourselves, as we knew June was now far too busy on her own first production to be able to give sufficient time to us. Mr. Henabery suggested that he might be able to obtain assistance of Mr. Anthony Caldewey, who had worked with him before.

The moment that Mr. Williams saw this unsettled state of affairs in regard to the story, he immediately came forward with the idea of producing "Cobra" first.

As both Rudy and I thought "Cobra" in every way unsuitable, we rejected the situation.

---

*Natacha is very rarely credit for this feat: she was the first to hire Adrian Greenberg (better known simply by his first name) to work as a costume designer in film. Adrian designed for both A Sainted Devil and The Hooded Falcon. He would go on to design for Cobra, The Eagle, and What Price Beauty? His career would span the golden age of Hollywood, designing for the likes of Greta Garbo and Mary Pickford. Most famously he designed the red shoes in Wizard of Oz (1939)

**June Mathis had left Famous Players and signed with Goldwyn as an Editorial Director. This stint was disastrous culminating with her attempt at 'Ben-Hur' which was to be under her control similar to 'Four Horsemen'. After trouble with the Director and location shooting in Italy, Mathis resigned from Goldwyn in the summer of 1924 and by August had signed with First National again as an Executive.

***Mathis had just months to get her first project in production, which as described, conflicted with writing for The Hooded Falcon.

After our arrival, Mr. Ullman went to see Miss Mathis to explain to her about the script of the "Falcon." What passed at this interview I do not know, but the results I soon learned.

June refused to have anything further to do with us. As it was the usual procedure to credit all disagreeable things to my account, this instance was not an exception.** Rudy and I, however, were both very distressed at so foolish an ending to such a long and true friendship.

William Cameron Menzies, in my mind the cleverest dramatic architect in the business to-day, had been engaged for the settings of the "Falcon."

If for no other reason than to have given the public a glimpse at the remarkably beautiful creations of "Bill" Menzies, it was a pity that this film was never produced. I must also include in this regret the exquisite costumes designed by Adrian.

When we realized that the preparations for this picture would take at least another two months before actual filming could be started, Mr. Williams again came forward with his suggestion of making a smaller film first.

After much discussion this was finally agreed upon under the condition, however, that this first small story should be held and not released until after the completion of the "Falcon."

"Cobra" was again brought up.

Neither Rudy nor I were in favor of this story, but as Mr. Williams was so insistent we at last gave in against our better judgment.*

Personally I took little interest in this picture (with the possible exception of the sixteenth-century vision) beyond supervising the costumes and settings, as I was far too absorbed in the work on the "Falcon." Besides, it was a modern story and modern stories always bored me to tears – I had neither cared nor understood anything about them, unless by chance they were fantastical or symbolical, which was rarely the case.

---

*Just why Mathis reacted so harshly is unknown, see page 300. This was during the time when Natacha was being blamed for everything wrong with Valentino's career and personal life. With Mathis' departure the criticism intensified. Mathis and Valentino would reconcile months before his death. It is unknown (and probably unlikely) if she ever reconciled with Rambova.

**Indeed Natacha would be given the blame for this film's failure, it would be the last film she and Rudy would ever work on, to whatever degree it may have actually been.

A BREWSTER PUBLICATION

MOTION.PICTVRE.

THE QUALITY MAGAZINE OF THE SCREEN

SEPTEMBER

MAGAZINE
25 CTS

The Valentinos

HUMAN HEARTS

Adele Whitely Fletcher Discloses the Charities of the Stars

129

When "Cobra" was at last completed and we were ready to start work on the medieval Spanish story, we were informed that Ritz was unable to proceed with their financial obligations.*

Joseph Schenck then came to the front as arbiter and settled this complication amicably by signing Rudy to make two productions for him.** These productions were to be released through United Artists.

The "Falcon" was then dropped and work was begun on "The Eagle".

The unhappy misunderstanding between Rudy and myself, which had been hovering over us for the past six or eight months, came to a climax shortly after this.

The beginning of the trouble had been the ridiculous articles and insinuations in newspapers that Rudy was "henpecked," and that I wore "the pants in the family."

This would naturally have had its effect on any man, especially one as proud and sensitive as Rudy. Then it was also continually pointed out that I had ruined his career.

Look at "Beaucaire!" I was to blame for that, and then there were "The Sainted Devil" and "Cobra."

"Beaucaire" was chosen by Famous Players and submitted to us for our approval. We accepted it, yes, but no one ever heard that it had been in the first place their own choice.***

During the filming of "Beaucaire" there was much talk about my "terrible interference," because I had artistic supervision of the film and insisted on the historical data being correct.****

---

*Both Natacha and Rudy had no sense of money when it came to making films. For The Hooded Falcon they had a budget of $500,000. By the time the plug was pulled, and not a bit of film shot, they had already spent half of that. Both claimed to not have been informed of the financial limitations until long after the contract had been signed.

**Natacha leaves out many details here, as this is when their marriage began to crumble. Severely in debt, and his fame in question (his last 4 films had flopped, and another one had been shelved. Movie magazines declared John Gilbert his successor), Rudy was offered the fairest contract he had ever seen: $7,000 a week, a cut of his films profits, and creative control with United Artists. One contractual stipulation, however, was that Natacha could not partake in his films or even be on set. Feeling he had no choice Rudy signed. It strained the marriage irrevocably and as production began on The Eagle, Natacha left for New York announcing their separation.

***In fairness not only might this be true, but other stars had considered filming it as early as 1922. Douglas Fairbanks, the he-man action hero was one such star.

****According to those on set, Natacha came off as icy and asked to be called 'Madam' while Rudy came off warm and asked everyone to call him by that nickname. Indeed Natacha was to be a full partner in Beaucaire, and her insistence on such details were not out of the ordinary. D.W. Griffith had done such a thing for his two most notorious films, "Birth of a Nation" and "Intolerance".

Although by contract I was artistic supervisor, I declined to have my named used on the title cards as I did not wish to obtrude myself on Rudy's public. It had been so often brought to my attention by Mr. Ullman that it was a drawback for a romantic actor to have a wife.*

When the pictured was released, it caused a sensation and was acclaimed by the public and critics an artistic triumph. All those who had been the loudest to complain about my interference now completely forgot that I had ever been at the studio. It was not until about a year later when "the Powers that be" decided that "Beaucaire" had been a mistake (some of the farmers of God's Country had taken unkindly to the white wigs), that my interference was again remembered.**

Rex Beach's story "Rope's End," was submitted to us, amongst others, for Rudy's second picture. The story as Mr. Beach himself read it to us was a story with tremendous possibilities. The plot was motivated by and the result of – War.

When the story had been accepted, bought and paid for, "the Powers that be" decided that for the sake of international policy (or expense) the war must be removed from the plot – in other words, the raison d'etre, the spinal column of the beast, was to be amputated. I objected loudly, but was overruled.***

---

*Whether Ullman said this or not is unknown. However it wasn't necessarily true. In the early days of flickers, Frances X. Bushman suffered as a romantic lead when it was learned he had a wife and children. By the 1920s this would rarely be the case; many romantic stars were in relationships or married without adverse effects. The problem was not so much that Rudy was married but married to Natacha, who the public blamed (sometimes unfairly) for his mistakes.

**This is indeed confirmed by the box office receipts. Beaucaire did very well in the bigger cities, but failed miserably in the smaller markets. Later on many a mogul would pin this picture and its 'failure' on Natacha.

***Possibly true, but also unlikely. War films had been in vogue since Four Horsemen. Only a year after Beaucaire was released, "The Big Parade", an intense war film, would go on to be one of the best selling silents of all time. In 1927 Wings, another war film, would win an Academy Award. Foreign markets occasionally were offended, but that never seemed to stop the moguls.

Douglas Fairbanks, Jackie Coogan, and Valentino

When the spineless excuse for a drama which remained was released, this naturally was also laid to my poor judgment.

Next I was accused of sacrificing Rudy for my own selfish ambitions – I wished "to become a power in the industry!"[*]

Fortunately, my conscience is entirely free from this despicable accusation.

Not that this excuses me from the many mistakes I did make – it does not.

Both Rudy and I were dreamers and too artistically ambitious. He was as great a worshipper at the shrine of beauty as was I. We both took for our model Douglas Fairbanks[**], whose great business ability and commercial fearlessness, forms a combination difficult to equal.

No – my fault was not selfish ambition, but it was conceit. I was conceited enough to imagine that I could force the producers into giving Rudy the kind of production which our artistic ambitions called for – productions such as "Robin Hood," "The Thief of Bagdad," or "The Black Pirate".

I could not understand why, with his ability, romance, magnetism and proved drawing power, Rudy should not have the best – why he should continually be thrust into small, trifling, cheap, commercial pictures, while other artists of much less ability and popularity were given big stories and big productions.

The injustice of it made me furious, and I stubbornly made up my mind that he should not be so used.

Why should Rudy always be a pawn in the hand on the great iron-fisted soulless god of Commercialism? But that same great god only laughed at my puny efforts and clenched his iron fist the tighter.

It was my passionate love of history and beauty which caused all of the trouble, as do all things carried to unreasonable extremes.

---

[*]It is true this claim was lobbed at Natacha, but it was very unfairly so. She had been in film since 1917, long before she had met Rudy, let alone probably heard of him. She also had the vehicle of Alla Nazimova for her artistic ambitions; she didn't need to use Rudy for anything.

[**]Judging by their hard work on Beaucaire, this seems very probable. Douglas Fairbanks was an action hero type who rarely played romantic scenes at all as they made him uncomfortable. Initially he did not like Rudy (throwing him out of he and his wife Mary Pickford's home, Pickfair), but relented and the two men became friends of sorts. Doug tried to be more like Rudy by making films like "The Gaucho" (1927) while Rudy tried to be more like Doug making films like "The Eagle" (1925). Doug however had something Rudy did not, Mary Pickford, the most powerful woman in Hollywood. With the help of Mary, Doug was able to become an astute businessman and together they, alongside Charlie Chaplin and D.W. Griffith formed United Artists in 1919. Doug had the freedom, celebrity, and business knowledge on his side. Rudy did not.

Doris Kenyon and Valentino in Monsieur Beaucaire, 1924

In my intense desire to incorporate beauty into Rudy's productions I lost my perspective. I lost sight of the fact that if beauty is only used as a shallow satisfaction for the eye and not combined with food for the soul as well – then it is but an empty gilded shell.

This I have learned. The public will accept a soul-inspiring or touching story which has no outward beauty, but they will not alone accept beauty which has no soul.

The molehill of petty "henpecking" jibes soon grew to proportions of formidable mountain, helped, you may depend on it, by our many "friends," who lost no opportunity of showing Rudy any articles of the above description. It was also extremely disagreeable for Rudy to be continually pitied for having a wife who would sacrifice his career for her own selfish ambitions.

Another sore point, it seemed, was the fact that we did not often go out in the evenings of attend the usual Hollywood functions.* This was accordingly taken as another proof of my managing; I was jealous, of course, and afraid to allow Rudy to be out with other women!

Rudy's friends insisted that he must reinstate himself in the eyes of Hollywood; I was the cause of his being wrongly labeled "upstage." He must show Hollywood and the world that he was a regular fellow!

Gloria Swanson was no fool when she packed her belongings and moved to New York, establishing her permanent home in the East – the East where there at least plays, operas, concerts and museums as diversions from the continual grind.

We started to go out oftener. We did the expected thing. We joined in the "fun." We danced, we gossiped, we giggled, we flirted, we laughed, we drank, and succeeded in being exceedingly bored.

We even went on "those amusing expeditions" to Venice (the Coney Island of Hollywood), where we ate "hot-dogs," rode on the merry-go-round and pretended we were having a hilarious time.

Hollywood – all the joys of the petty community life of "Main Street" with an additional coating of gold dust thrown in for good measure!

---

*Its obvious Natacha did not think much of Hollywood or its parties; however it is disputable what Rudy thought. He socialized before he met her and he socialized after their divorce. It seems he, to some extent, enjoyed the Hollywood lifestyle.

I am not going to describe any of the widely heralded Hollywood parties with unmentionable details, nor am I insinuating that Hollywood is a "wicked city" – it is not even that – it is merely an imitation gilded hell of a make-believe realm. Nothing but sham – sham – and more sham.

Hollywood (in speaking of Hollywood in this chapter, I am referring only to the picture colony) – one continuous struggle of nobodies to become somebodies, all pretending to be what they are not.

In the technical ranks – jealousy, stealing of ideas, buck-passing, alibis, graft, with here and there a few sparks from the Divine Fire waiting to be fanned in to genius and crushed into oblivion.

Extra girls spending their last dollar on their backs or their hair-cuts to look like some star they are not, but with the ever-burning hope before them of catching the eye of a passing director.

"Bit-players" fighting to become feature players, and feature players fighting to reach the goal of stardom. And when they have reached that goal, what have they gained?

Stars of the past trying to keep up appearances and pretend they are still what they once were.

Stars of the present in public pretending they are what their fans think them to be, in private either empty-headed butterflies blindly jazzing through life or weary, worried, disillusioned fighters frantically clutching their ever-slipping success.

A pathetic race after vanishing illusion.

Work – is the one thing which makes life in Hollywood tolerable.

Wrecked homes, heartaches, frayed nerves, intrigue, bitterness, ill-health, overwork, ruin and tragedy are the heavy tolls paid by hundreds each year to Hollywood.

With companionship and trust gone from the home and only hurt and pride to take its place, Hollywood is not exactly the spot wherein you can fold your hands and continue to dwell in peace and quietude.

When disillusionment opens our eyes to cold hard facts, we generally rush for some anesthetic to deaden our misery – I was no exception to this generality.

It has been said that this earth life is the schoolroom in which we learn our lessons. In Hollywood, like many others, I was given a test to pass and like many others I failed in it. We are also told that we learn our lessons by bitter experience; I think next time I shall pass the test. Rudy is more fortunate; he has already passed into a higher grade.

Muzzie's story continues, "In July 1925, like a thunderbolt out of the clear blue sky, I received a telegram from my sister, Teresa, saying that Rudy and Natacha had separated, and that Natacha was on her way to us in Europe. From their constant letters to me I had received the impression that they were both overworked and getting into a rather nervous condition. But it never dawned upon me that this could lead to so serious trouble. This news was a great sorrow, both to Mr. Hudnut and to me, but we could not help feeling that there would soon be a reconciliation.

We received long and anxious telegrams daily from Rudy, saying it was impossible for him to come over as he was in the midst of his new picture. It seemed rather hopeless for us to smooth over the difficulties between these over-tired and temperamental children. They were both too proud, too hasty, and impetuous, and the unfortunate divorce followed. Immediately after, Natacha returned to America to go on with her work.

Early in December we received a telegram from Rudy saying he was spending a few weeks in London with Maria and Alberto and would come to us later. We answered immediately, inviting them to spend Christmas with us. He replied, 'Dearest Uncle Dick and Muzzie, my heart is too full of sorrow to spend the holidays in the home where the happiest days of my life were spent. I will come to you early in January.'

In January he came back to us, the same sweet, loving boy of old. It was impossible for him to remain many days, as his sadness was too great. He often went to Natacha's room to sit there awhile by himself and when he came out he would kneel beside me and bury his head in my lap and cry like a baby. I was heartbroken. We always hoped there would be a reconciliation, and I am happy to say it came during his last illness, though only a few days before his death.

My many friends have heard me say and I again repeat it, that if I had my choice of all the sons-in-law in the world, I would only choose our dear Rudy. Death has been kind. It took Rudy at the height of his fame, rather than in later days when his exceptional popularity might have waned. Death has been still kinder. It has not separated us. The veil between this world and the next is not too cruelly thick. Its transparency has allowed us to be at one with him.

To prepare us for this great sorrow that was so soon to come, God sent us in May the beloved American psychic, George Benjamin Wehner, who remained a guest in our home for six extraordinary months. 'George' is the most remarkable and unusual psychic I have ever met, and I have investigated many. And why not? For her is the chosen instrument of that most beloved and marvelous soul, Madame Helena Petrovna Blavatsky, who brought during her earth-life the truths of the Wisdom Religion to the West.

At the very time when the doctors thought Rudy to be out of danger, the prophecy came through the instrumentality of 'George' of Rudy's passing out of the mortal body. In a few days this prophecy was fulfilled.

From that time on we have been in constant communication with Rudy. At first he seemed bewildered, and lamented the fact that he had been taken from the work he loved so well. The great tribute paid his memory by the loving public, a tribute no king has ever received, seemed to hold him for a while sorrowfully to the earth

But spiritual light seemed to be given him through the welcome of those who first met him – his mother, his father, and Caruso, his countryman, whom he had always so admired; and those two fellow artists, dear Wally Reid, the favorite of millions, and little Olive Thomas, beloved by all who knew her. These loving friends drew him from his earth-clinging, and led him to the realization of the true life of the spirit.

It was two years before his passing that Rudy himself interested me in the psychic truths that have brought so much happiness into my life. He was extremely mediumistic himself, often astonishing us with the excellent test-messages received him through his automatic writings."

The Last Kiss, 1925

CHAPTER 14

MONDAY morning, August 16th, while at my father's château in Juan les Pins, I received a cable from Mr. Ullman, sent at Rudy's request, telling us of his sudden illness and operation.

This message was a great shock to us all, as we had imagined Rudy to be in the best of health. But knowing his splendid strength we did not for one instant think this illness could prove fatal.

All the proper petty resentments of our misunderstanding seemed to fade from my mind with the anxiety of this new and unexpected sorrow. I cabled immediately. From this time on, until the end, we were in constant communication – Mr. Ullman notifying us of the slightest change in Rudy's condition.

Wednesday evening we had our usual family sitting with Mr. Wehner, the American psychic, who was a guest at the château at this time.

During the sitting, while Mr. Wehner was in the deep trance state, Rudy, using this available instrument, "came through" muttering a few almost incoherent words and calling Auntie's name and mine. For those who have investigated psychic phenomena this will not seem mystifying, as it is not an unusual occurrence for the consciousness of a person still living in the earth-world, to manifest or communicate at a distance while the body itself is sleeping or unconscious. On awakening, the person will often remember these experiences in the form of a dream.

Friday morning my cablegram brought us the cheering news that Rudy had greatly improved and was on the road to recovery.

That evening we were impressed to have a sitting. Almost immediately after Mr. Wehner was in trance, Black Feather, Rudy's Indian guide, "came through" to tell us that he would stay with his "Chief" and would not leave him. Then Jenny spoke and told us that she had been constantly with Rudy since the beginning of his illness. He himself had seen her, she continued, as he was taken in the ambulance.

These communications bothered me. They did not seem happy or hopeful, as I expected they would, after the morning's cheerful cable.

Meselope, the Egyptian brother, from whom Rudy and I together had so often received lessons in the past, now took control. He talked to me for a long while, gently and with such compassion, speaking as I had never heard him speak before, of personal things; of Rudy's life, his character and his career. He made me realize the seriousness and purpose of this earth-life, the schoolroom to which we are sent back again and again, until all lessons necessary for this stage of our development are learned.

If we could only realize this more fully, how differently we would do so many things.

This life is not just a playground to be selfishly enjoyed to its utmost before passing into a convenient oblivion. Meselope explained to us that Rudy's present term in this earth-schoolroom was completed, and that within the next few days he would pass to another plane of consciousness of this ever-continuing Life.

Although we in our Inner Self may realize the great Truth and Reality of Being, it is nevertheless difficult for us, while bound to earth limitations, to use our knowledge when overcome with a sense of loss and separation.

Early the next morning I cabled Mr. Ullman about Rudy's condition.

The cable was not answered. What was there to say?

We had already been told the answer, but what we do not wish to realize we try to stifle in our hearts.

Monday morning I awoke to find the atmosphere of my room heavy with the perfume of tuberoses – and then I knew that Rudy had passed on.

When Tuesday morning the delayed cables arrived announcing Rudy's death, I was grateful for Meselope's kind prophecy, which, with understanding, had softened the seeming cruelty of this news.

Wednesday evening we again had our family sitting, although our sadness and consequent depletion affected slightly the usual strength of the communication.

This third day after Rudy's passing, he came to us for the first time, brought by his mother Gabriella.

His attitude of mind, his resentment at having been taken at the height of his career when he felt his work was not yet completed, made this first and still almost incoherent contact a very unhappy one.

He repeatedly called Auntie's name.

He left suddenly, and his mother then spoke to us. She was almost distracted by his state of mind and said that she regretted the day that she had ever allowed him to leave Italy. She could not see the benefit of a success which only brought him to this bitterness and anguish.

Our beloved H.P.B. then came to comfort us, explaining in her wonderful way that Rudy's present condition was only natural and to be expected with all the force of world thought and grief directed as it was upon him. She told us we must have patience and each try to help in our own way. She would also help him. This darkness would soon pass away.

This same week of Rudy's passing I received a letter from my sister in New York. Among other details of Rudy's illness she wrote that he had seen Jenny, and called out her name just as he was taken in the ambulance from his hotel. She had been told of this by Mr. and Mrs. Ullman who had been with him. I mention this just as one of many tests. This only confirmed what Jenny had herself told us at our Friday evening sitting.

It was not until the last rites had been said in Hollywood that we felt the first great change in Rudy's attitude. He seemed more reconciled to his new surroundings and told us of his meetings with Wallace Reid and little Olive Thomas. He had also seen Jenny again and Black Feather, who he had said was "very good-looking for an Indian."

His mother was also much happier.

From this time on, as he was taken to the "Centres" on the Astral Plane, visited the theatres and Temples, he became not only contented, but thrilled and enthusiastic over the wonders of this new life opening before him.

As his communications grew stronger, he told us that he would like in some way to give to others the benefit of his experiences, to tell them of the marvels of the life to come. If he had during his life here been fortunate enough to bring to some a little joy, a few moments of romance and forgetfulness of sorrow, might he still not be allowed to serve? Could he not try and repay in some measure, with messages of his newer learning, the gratitude he felt to those who had shown him, while on earth, so much love and encouragement?

The following messages, which comprise the second part of this book, were dictated by Rudy himself through the deeply entranced instrument. They are his messages, prepared by him and printed here exactly as they were taken down.

Some I know will find comfort and happiness in their Truth.

From those who are not ready to believe, I ask only that they at least reverence or respect the spirit in which they were given – the spirit of Love and Service.

Rudy, Natacha, and The Occult
By Hala Pickford

It has always been my firm belief that when researching silent film matters one should stick to pure facts. Kenneth Anger infamously declared his research methodology as 'telepathy' (speaking to spirits via the mind) which resulted in such dribble and damage as the art deco dildo rumor (never happened, nor did any relationship with a man on Rudy's behalf).

However Natacha's book puts me in a precarious position. When it was first released there was no split, just the short explanation of why she was relaying Rudy's 'messages' and how wonderful her medium had been in obtaining them. This book is quite literally two different things: the first half a memoir, the second half an odd spiritual text. And when it comes to spiritual texts one must take a different approach. Sure you can give the history of something, the personal beliefs of the participants, and an explanation of the techniques. But just short of doing some hardcore historical and scientific research no one can really declare such things 'factual' or not. Sure we know scientifically Jesus didn't ride dinosaurs, but that won't stop so called 'Intelligent Design' people from embarrassing themselves in US public schools (they even have a theme park!)

Though I have mostly dedicated myself to working on silent film, it is actually an odd coincidence that I have also had a penchant of studying world religions for many years. It's been awhile since I was as immersed as I once was, but it does give me a working knowledge and respect for the topic at hand. Much like Natacha, I am very against people who focus on death, as it offends my own personal beliefs. And much like Natacha, I find mythology and new age-y things interesting. None of these things should ever seep into historical research (a failure many kookies have been guilty of), but when it comes to something like this section, it's quite useful.

First let's start with the strictly verifiable stuff. In this day and age the word 'Occult' usually conjures images of Harry Potter or Goth kids studying a Silver RavenWolf book (I actually had to laugh quite hard when I noticed a Barnes and Noble in Los Angeles…in 2009!...recommending one of her books). Worse yet, it brings to mind all sorts of terrible, weird things to people unfamiliar with just exactly what that word means. Occult does not refer to any religion or religious practice in particular; instead it means a 'knowledge of the hidden arts'. This includes thing such as magic, astrology, divination, numerology, and ESP. Many monotheistic religions (Judaism, Christianity, Islam) look down on such practices while polytheistic or more open religions (Paganism, Hinduism, Shinto, Wicca, New Age faiths, Spiritualists) embrace them. As I am sure there is at least one reader out there asking: No Satanism really doesn't fit any of those categories. Satanism can be divided into two types: the worshipping of oneself, or the more flashy rebellious kid type. Neither has anything to do with anything presented here or involving Rudy or Natacha.

Various forms of Paganism predate all monotheistic religions by thousands of years (Sumerians, Greeks, Babylonians, Egyptians, Celts, so forth). The earliest known culture ever was the Sumerians who likely predate the Jewish faith. These Pagan societies worshipped multiple Gods, practiced what would now be called occult endeavors, and basically ran theocracies (the faith was in every part of life and government). When the monotheistic faiths took over society, these older faiths were banned, and became something quite mythical. While many modern Wiccans (self proclaimed 'witches') like to whine about 'the burning times', such things had little to do with modern variations. However, it does show people of these ancient years weren't exactly open to the idea of 'tolerate all faiths' (of course the Inquisition and the Crusades easily verify that).

In the 1800s archaeologists began to discover artifacts from 'biblical times' including the Sumerian era. This excited them as they were sure they could verify that indeed things in the Bible were scientifically true. However this turned out to not be so (in fact the Bible contains many of Sumer's myths usurped as their own; including the flood story, the story of Adam and Eve, and even the story of the dying and resurrected God).

Sumer had its moment in the Sun, but by the mid to late 1800s other such ancient endeavors captivated society. Many 'new' religions/spiritual associations were created, inspired by the old. These included the Strega, Wiccans, Spiritualists, Golden Dawn, Theosophy, and even Thelema. Some of these faiths claimed ancient roots, though the most accurate way to describe them would be 'inspired by' instead of 'descending from'.

Spiritualism came into vogue in the 1840s. Inspired by the writings of Franz Mesmer and Emanuel Swedenborg, Spiritualists sought a direct understanding of the afterlife. The faith (in fairness it's a very loose faith, but for simplicities sake this is the word we will use) taught that there was no single heaven or hell, but that there were different levels and spirits could communicate with the living.

Spiritualists believe in using various occult methods to speak to the dead. They were and are particularly fond of séances, mediums, clairvoyants, hypnotism, automatic writing (receiving messages from spirits through writing), scrying (divining while gazing into something such as a crystal ball or mirror), spirit guides, telepathy, and faith healing. They don't have a specific deity doctrine, though many drew from Christianity during the early years of the faith. Unlike other New Age types they don't believe in the use of 'magic' or spells, the belief that thoughts can influence an outcome of some kind (no, it doesn't involve killing cats and babies or so my research tells me).

Surprisingly, the official stance is they don't believe in reincarnation (the belief that a soul can continually return to earth to learn lessons), though most Spiritualists then and now (including June Mathis, Natacha, and Rudy) did indeed believe in such a form of reincarnation. For those unfamiliar, reincarnation can mean a variety of things. Depending on who you ask, one might reincarnate only as a human of their particular gender, either gender, or sometimes as animals. From these writings, it appears Natacha and Rudy believed in reincarnation as humans only, with the ability to switch genders (though that might just be a remark from Blavatsky).

Spiritualism peaked in the 1880s, before being revived in the 1910s. It again peaked in the 1920s, this time probably inspired a bit by Egyptomania sweeping the nation (King Tut's tomb had just been found). At its height it was said to have 8 million adherents. Today the faith still lives on.

In the 1920s two particular faiths were extremely popular in Hollywood: Spiritualism and Christian Science. Spiritualism was used in ways comparable to new age faiths now (particularly Kabbalah or Wicca), while Christian Science was similar to Scientology (Christian Science is controversial for their belief in never operating or taking medicine, as illness is 'God's will'.) Mary Pickford, Anna May Wong (who would later become a Daoist), Joan Crawford, and King Vidor were of the Christian Science camp; while June Mathis, Rudy, Natacha, and Sir Arthur Conan Doyle counted themselves as Spiritualists.

One of the most interesting things to come out of this book is Natacha's version of how she and Rudy came into Spiritualism. Natacha is usually cited as the one who drove Rudy to the faith, while in actuality it was June Mathis and the death of her mother, Virginia (Jenny). This is not surprising as June was quite a fervent Spiritualist, inserting her beliefs into most of her films. "The Young Rajah" is probably the most striking example, making it all the more upsetting that it's mostly lost. In the film Amos (Valentino) learns he is an Indian prince who has the gift of psychic vision. He can see the future through his third eye, which sets up the plot.

June believed in reincarnation, telepathy, automatic writing, and divination. I wish more could be found on her thoughts but as it stands her beliefs were probably somewhere between modern Paganism and Spiritualism. Though there is nothing to indicate she was a believer in magic, June was a huge believer in the power of belief to achieve a result. This can be seen over and over again in films such as "Turn to the Right" (1922). June's belief in reincarnation was quite interesting as well.

She believed she had a life in Egypt and that Valentino and Rex Ingram had at some point in her spiritual history, been sons of hers. She believed she had wronged them and in her present life she would fix that. After she had fallen out with both men, (Ingram in 1922 as he romantically left her for Alice Terry, and Valentino in 1924 for reasons still complex. See page 150) she told friends that it didn't bother her, that she had done what she was supposed to do in this life. However she did reconcile with Rudy before his death, so what her further thoughts were on the matter are unknown. June called him her 'Dear boy' and Rudy called her his 'little mother'.

Natacha is much more complex. Though she cited herself as a Spiritualist, via research, I don't feel that term is proper. In this following text it is quite obvious the Theosophical medium influenced his 'readings' and possibly Natacha as well. Madame Helena Petrovna Blavatsky founded Theosophy in 1871. The faith is more a spiritual form of Occult practices rather than an actual religion.

Theosophy is similar to Spiritualism, except for it believes in the use of magic, reincarnation, and a study of the arts. Spiritualists considered Theosophists unscientific, and Theosophists believed Spiritualists 'uncouth'. This would show that Natacha had either changed her mind or had sought something else to suit her beliefs.

However, I believe more than anything she would match the modern description of a Kemite (follower of Kemetism, Egyptian based Paganism). After her second divorce, Natacha returned to the States and decided to study Egyptology. She had been a fan of Egypt since her teenage years, and seemed to believe she had at least one past life in Egypt. She paid for her own travels and research, eventually teaming with the now defunct Bollingen Foundation. Through them she released two academic texts on Egypt, using works she had translated.

She believed in astrology, automatic writing, spirit guides, and séances. In her later life she taught classes on a few of these subjects in her New York apartment. Reportedly she had a belief during the 20s about reincarnation that 'pieces of furniture from a past life must be collected together to find inner peace'. She had wished to write a book on the matter, but thankfully that never came to be.

I think it would be best to say she was a Spiritualist through the 20s, a Theosophists in the late 20s, and an Egyptian Recreationist (Kemite) from the 1940s till the end of her life. For the record she never identified herself as such, but that is what her beliefs appear to match.

As for Rudy, his Spiritual beliefs seemed to have gone somewhere between Natacha and June's. Raised Catholic, he was never wild about the faith, skipping church and only going when his mother asked him to. He was likely introduced to Spiritualism through June in the early 1920s, and did not adapt the faith until 1922 when her mother died. What exactly he thought about God or Gods is unknown. He proclaimed himself a Spiritualist in many interviews.

He believed in Spirit Guides, automatic writing, séances, and ESP. As for reincarnation I have yet to see anything that had him addressing the subject, though judging by his interactions with Natacha and June I think it is safe to declare he believed in it. He adopted June as a sort of mother figure, and was surely aware of her beliefs on their past lives.

According to George Ullman, Rudy didn't speak much of his Spiritualists beliefs once he and Natacha separated. However, as Natacha noted, George and his wife did mention Rudy calling for 'Jenny' when he was taken in the ambulance to the hospital (odd side note: June cried out to her mother when she died as well). He received the last rites from a Catholic priest, which included a confessional. George reported Rudy seemed pleased to have had the session.

Two Christian funerals were held for Rudy, slightly bending Catholic rules as he did not meet certain requirements (such as having been married and divorced without the consent of the church). On his crypt marker is a cross, whose decision to place it there is unknown. Its possible Rudy was one such Spiritualist who mingled Christian overtones. Yet Natacha always leaned towards ancient worlds, so this is hard to discern. In this 'Spiritual Text' she has Rudy's soul blasting the Church for the most part.

With the factual bases covered, I feel something should still be said on the more elusive angle, that of belief. In her last chapter in Recollections, Natacha asks that those who are ready to 'accept the truth' read forward and those who are not at least go forward with respect. I think that is a perfectly reasonable request. As with most everything else in this book it seems biographers and such have mistaken her words, twisting them to make her more villain-like or look down right kooky. A lot of books like to cite the 'message' about the Opera and meeting other movie stars to show just how 'out there' she was.

Frankly, from a Spiritual or New Age-y point, nothing in the following section is that outlandish. Words, ideas, and things described by 'Rudy' match with what other such new age faiths have long proclaimed (particularly the astral travel descriptions and karmic undertones). Again I would like to reiterate no one can prove a spiritual belief or religion, nor should they present such things as fact. Based on these writings I do think Natacha was quite sincere. And considering she would go on to spend 20 years of her life becoming an Egyptologist of some renowned well...I think some respect for her in this sense is due. New Agers, Pagans, Psychics, kookies, fans, and the like seem to have no idea just exactly what she was up to. From a New Age spiritual point, this is a fascinating text, and I hope the people who would like to learn about it will find it, without further harming Rudy's legacy.

My own personal beliefs are my own and not something I wish to broadcast to the world, but I will say this. I find the same topics Natacha, June, and Rudy did quite fascinating. While I don't believe every self proclaimed psychic, New Ager, or 'medium' should be given blind faith, I do believe there are people in this world who really do have such gifts. But I also think for the most part those people shouldn't use such gifts for personal gain, or to promote an agenda like so many people, particularly those associated with the Valentino Memorial Service and Guild, do. Those who use such things for personal gain probably hold no gifts at all. People who really hold such gifts know how to really use them...not to hock some cheap book or agenda.

Now I know the above paragraph might sound contradictory to this whole section, let alone the whole idea behind Natacha's writings. My feelings of the following section are based on a historical and spiritual viewpoint. I think some of the stuff in here just might be as realistic as any other belief. For those familiar with such teachings they will find this stuff fascinating, and feel no need to hold séances to write books to give their viewpoint.

However, I also do think some agenda crept in. Frankly I think all psychic endeavors pose such a danger...no matter how sincere or true someone might be they might come off one sided. As mentioned, Natacha and June had a falling out (see page 300). They were arguably the most important women in Rudy's life not including his dear, deceased mother. June reported seeing Rudy's apparition the moment he died, though her further Spiritual thoughts remain unknown as she died only a year later. In this section 'Rudy' doesn't mention her at all, despite mentioning the likes of Pola Negri and Doris Kenyon. If such séances were pure, I'm sure Natacha wouldn't want to hear about June (who was still alive when this book was written) anyways. Quite obviously most of the text is focused on Natacha and her family, which in such situations is to be expected. What is particularly odd in this respect is in researching June, I've found most of her Spiritual beliefs (announced before this book was written) sync up with what either Natacha or 'Rudy's Soul' believed. The crediting of souls for their creative endeavors, automatic writing, visualization, all are hallmarks of Mathis' beliefs. Towards the end of this section the soul of Rudy goes on about writers and Spiritualism. The techniques he describes matches June's own beliefs to a T. Yet again June is not mentioned at all.

The only other thing I think tainted the text was the bias towards Theosophy and Madame Blavatsky. George, the Medium, was a student of hers. Whether Rudy really lived the afterlife presented here or not, I don't think the blatant insertion of her name everywhere would qualify as 'authentic'. The insertions seem almost jarring to the rest of the text. George Wehner was a bit of a loon himself. By the late 20s his mental health took a turn for the worst. Natacha and her friends would try to hold séances with him, and he would become either violent or suicidal. After he tried to jump out of a very high up apartment window they quit using him. Personally I am not a fan of 'mediums'.

However on the spiritual side of things, I do find very interesting some of the events that occurred on opposite ends of the Ocean, told by two people who did not like each other. As Rudy lay dying Natacha called an emergency séance. The medium said Valentino seemed to think he was there with them, and the messages he was getting made no sense, so the group switched to speaking with Jenny and Blackfeather. No one knew he was going to die at that point, and the preliminary news had been hopeful.

Ullman, on the other side of the Ocean, said during those last few days Valentino was in and out of it, suffering from hallucinations, such as thinking he and Ullman were lost in a forest at one point. From a sort of Spiritualist stand point it does make for some interesting fodder. Natacha also tells the story of his calling for Jenny, something George later confirmed.

Why did Natacha bother to write this half of this book anyways? I think she sincerely believed at the time it was the thing to do, as she describes in the last chapter of Recollections. She didn't need the money, her stepfather's company was on par with what Chanel or Revlon would be today (in fact it stills exists!) She never would take money just to take it, as she described in Chapter 2 of Recollections. She had talent for design and within a year of writing this book she would open a haute couture fashion shop on 5th Avenue in New York. She didn't need fame or recognition; she actually would perform in many plays in the four years following this book. She even wrote her own play, "All that Glitters" about her life with Rudy (and if anyone reading this knows where a copy exists you contact me right now!)

After 1930 she quit speaking of Rudy, and even in her later years would turn away press, particularly when they wanted to talk about him. So no, I don't think she wrote this book, let alone these 'messages' for fame or money. I think she did it out a sincere belief and desire, and probably grief as well.

Whatever your own beliefs, or your own interest in Rudolph Valentino, I hope you find the following interesting. And I also hope particularly for those so inclined, that they remember Natacha's insistence that mourning Rudy's death was holding him to this earth. Whether true or not one will never know, but in the least it's a fruitless endeavor. He could not possibly be alive this very moment (in my own fictional novel, "Conversations with Rodolfo", I only dared let him live until 2005, many people point out that's a heck of a stretch). With the wonderful technology we have there is no way we can possibly forget him. One can buy many books (good and bad) about him, one can buy almost all of his films on VHS or DVD, and one can hop on the internet and enjoy speaking with others about him.

Rudolph Valentino has been lost in the myth, the legend, and the slander by self proclaimed mediums and people 'in the know'. These people know nothing, and even if we just lay in the ground when we're gone, they have still seriously harmed his legacy and those who loved him. Make of this section what you will, but please don't forget the real man behind everything.

> -Hala Pickford
> **The Founding Sheba of**
> **The Rudolph Valentino Society**

PART II:
REVELATIONS

MESSAGE 1

I WANT to tell you how I first met the great spirit who has helped me to find myself in these new surroundings and who is teaching me to understand the realities of being: the spirit of H.P.B. (Helena Petrovna Blavatsky, Founder of the Theosophical Society). Rushing back and forth from New York to you, right after my passing, as I did in some unaccountable subconscious way, and finding the means of reaching you through George – this channel, this medium, or whatever you may call him – must have brought me to the particular attention of his teacher, H.P.B.

It was during the time they were taking my body to the West. I was just beginning to feel the loosening of the public's thought which had been centered upon me, and in a way, I believe, holding me close to the earth. But as newspaper notoriety began to die down and my remains were being piloted to their earthly resting place, I began to feel more alone. The moment the flattering effect of the public's attention was removed, I realized how separated from all these people I was, so far as sight and sound were concerned.

I felt very wretched and lonely. As you well know, Natacha, I have always been easily touched by praise and flattery. The struggles I had gone through, and the obstacles I had overcome, made the pleasure of public attention all the greater.

But now I stood alone. There was no one to praise me. I began to feel bitter that I had been cut off in the very height of my activity. I'm afraid I valued myself pretty highly, for I could not see how things could go on without me. I can laugh about it now, but it seemed a real misfortune to me then.

There was no one to talk about it. I wandered up and down Broadway. It seemed just as real to me then as it had before. But no one took any notice of me; I could hardly comprehend that they could not see me. I was so real and they were so real that it made the realization of my change very difficult.

I grew tired of dodging out of the way of hurrying people who seemed determined to run into me. Once I jolted against a woman who had headed straight into me and she shuddered and grasped her companion's arm, saying, "My, what a cold wind struck me!"

This made me furious. So death had turned me into a cold wind! I would not have it so. I rushed up to a group of actors standing on the corner of Forty-Seventh Street and Broadway near the Palace Theatre. I seized one of the men by the arm and shouted, "I am Rudolph Valentino!" - but he paid no attention and went on laughing and talking.

I felt so helpless and useless, and yes, I felt dead, too. At that moment I did not believe in God, for how could God, who let me succeed in my earth-life be so unjust as to let me fail now?

The injustice of it drove me nearly frantic. Something was very wrong. Here I was, perfectly strong and well only having stepped out of my physical body, not dead, but full of force and life, and standing right on the very corner I had stood on hundreds of times before, and yet not a soul could understand that I was there. Natacha, I do not believe I ever have loved people or yearned for their companionship so much as at that moment.

Life seemed so preposterous. It was incredible to me that I, who had been so admired before, was now so absolutely shut out. Oh, I tell you, life seemed cruel.

And then it dawned upon me what was wrong. These people did not mean to be cruel. They were just as warm-hearted and friendly as I. But THEY DID NOT KNOW. They had never been told the truth. They were only acting in accordance with the way in which they had been taught.

Then I realized that fault was not theirs. Whose was it? Their parents? Was it the fault of society at large? No, that was not it. At last the idea struck me: Who taught society the truths of Life?

The Churches!

They were the ones that were at fault. What was the matter with them? With all of their preaching about the rewards of the next life and eternal salvation, and all the rest of it, of what avail was it if it left me standing there on Broadway being refused recognition? I felt anything but kindly towards the Churches. Here I was, dead to the world, and all because the Churches had inbred in people's consciousness the false idea that spirits cannot reach back through the veil.

My own Church, the Roman Catholic; it understood these facts. The priest who gave me the last sacraments; he knew it would give my soul a peaceful passing. It did. But what sacrament could continue to give you peace when you frantically banged on the doors of people's consciousness and yet not a single door would open? I tell you, Natacha, it is all wrong. There will never be real peace and happiness on the earth until the truth of life and life-everlasting is made clear to the people. The Churches have not been able to wipe out crime and injustice. But the truths of life and life's positive and active continuance will wipe them out. For people will then understand why they were led to do wrong; they will realize the utter futility of wrong. They will see how useless it is to fool themselves and other people. For spirit sees all!

Oh! The thoughts that coursed through my consciousness as I stood on that street corner. I wept with grief and raged with indignation. But all to no avail.

Then suddenly I thought of you and of the cablegrams you had sent me while I lay so ill. I thought of Muzzie's and Uncle Dick's messages, and suddenly someone touched me on the arm.

I turned and looked. A heavily built woman with very kind eyes was standing beside me. I shall never forget her voice, so low, so reassuring, but the vehemency of her language nearly bowled me over. "Hell-fire and damnation," she said, "so this is how the Churches have knocked the wind out of you! Come, there's nothing the matter with the dear old Churches except that they're bat-blind. What you need is a friend. I'll be it – I'm H.P.B." (Mme. Blavatsky).

Natacha, I didn't know what to say I was so surprised. And the initials H.P.B. meant nothing to me. I did not remember ever having heard them before.

But this strange Being only laughed and said "Come." I lost consciousness, for how long I don't know, but suddenly I awoke and found myself standing in the big stone hall of Uncle Dick's château. It was night, and the big chandelier on the stairs was lit.

H.P.B. stood at the top of the stairs and beckoned.

I went up where so often I had gone in my earth-life. She led me into Muzzie's room. And there I saw you and Muzzie sitting, George was sleeping, as I thought, in a big easy chair. "He is in a trance," said H.P.B., "now you will be able to speak to your loved ones"

That, Natacha dearest, is how I first came to communicate with you. And that is how I came into contact with H.P.B.

Some time after this she talked to me about reincarnation and theosophy. She laughed and said she would enjoy seeing certain theosophists turn up their noses at the idea of her bothering with the ghost of a dead motion picture actor. But she added, "If theosophy does not teach love and assistance to every living thing in creation, what in thundering blazes does it teach?" This sounded pretty sensible to me and I said so. But, of course, I do not know much about theosophy or theosophists. When I asked H.P.B. what theosophy meant, she said, "Theosophy is life and how to live it!" That silenced me pretty thoroughly, for it seemed like a rather large order.

The force is weakening. I must leave. Coming again soon. Good night.

RUDY.

MESSAGE 2

I CANNOT now view things in the same old way. Rushing to you after my passing and finding this means of reaching you through George brought me, as I have told you, to the attention H.P.B. (Mme. Blavatsky), as all seem to call her.

What a woman! At first I was afraid of her. The light – the radiance, I suppose I should call it – almost blinded me. Her eyes made me uncomfortable. They seemed to search out my worst points. And all this happened right in Muzzie's room where you were all sitting. George in a trance, and I, with others, waiting my turn to speak. H.P.B. stared at me so hard and her light grew so dazzling – whitish gold, it seemed – that I became embarrassed and was about to turn away when a flash of beautiful green – I think ray would be a better word – a ray of clear bright green shot from her toward me and I heard her voice, very soft and low, calling me "Rudy" and "Little Brother."

Somehow all embarrassment left me and I went at once to her. She put her arms around me and said, "Well, child, you have left that" – and pointed to the walls of Muzzie's room. A change seemed to have come to my sight, for I saw that the walls, the ceiling, the floor and the furniture all gave off a kind of light, but a light that was drab and dull, a sort of putty-grey and brown.

I was able to see straight through the walls of the château and to look out into the night. The night did not seem dark to me as it used to when I was still in the body. It seemed filled with a luminous glow that somehow lit up between the particles of darkness.

This is difficult to express to you. I can hardly find words to describe thee new sights and sensations. I could see the trees, and the terraces, and the Mediterranean beyond, and all of these things gave off their own kind of light, but so dull and pale in color.

You know how much I have always loved bright colors. You used to say it was the Italian blood in me.

This strange dullness puzzled me. H.P.B. must have read my mind, for she said, "You are seeing the dullness of the earth plane – the pale reflection of loftier and more brilliant spheres." All fear left me.

163

I began to love this strange woman. Suddenly as I looked at her I saw that she became double – or sort of turned into two personalities – maybe that is not the way to express it – but at any rate she appeared in two bodies at the same time. One stood a little behind the other. The one I had seen first was young-looking and very beautiful, so beautiful as to be awe-inspiring. The other was a huge, bulky form, dressed in a shawl and a red petticoat, with a scarf over the head, showing her hair which looked rather crinkly. But the eyes were the same in both – brilliant, piercing and yet very kind.

She must have read my mind again, for I was amazed. The beautiful, slender, young figure turned and pointed to the bulky, aged one, and her voice said, "That is the H.P.B. that the earth-people remember. But I am the H.P.B. of now."

Then behind the bulky form appeared many forms – a long line – one behind another, and yet all seeming to dove-tail or merge with each other in an unexplainable way. H.P.B. laughed and again spoke. "Those are my former selves. A damned lot of trouble they have made me too. But now they are all chained together and come and go as I order them. Like this!"

She waved her right arm in a sweeping gesture and instantly all these forms were swept into – what shall I say – well, out of sight.

The one that had stood right back of the bulky form had been a man, dark-skinned like a Hindu. "Da, da!" (Yes, yes!) she said, turning in a kind of flash upon me, "that was the shell of the body of the man through which my spirit expressed itself before I came to earth as the 'Old Lady.'"

Ever since that time, Natacha – that meeting with Muzzie, you and George – H.P.B has helped me. Sometimes she has sworn at me soundly, and I have been alarmed that perhaps she would leave me. But always at the end of her scolding her smile has reassured me.

After seeing her former selves appear and disappear in this fascinating manner, I was anxious to see my own former selves and asked her how to do it. But I was nearly knocked over by the gale of words she launched at me, calling me "Stupid," "Fool," "Blind Pig," and other choice things, and winding up by saying, "Poor ignorant darling, can a baby run and leap before it has learned to creep and walk?" So that finished me on that subject for some time to come.

There are so many things to learn that it is pretty confusing at times. I have to let go, it seems, of the old way of looking at things. In the earth-world, I, or we, I think I had better say, look only at the outward appearance of people and things and events. We can't help that, because we only see the outside. But here we see the outside and the inside as well. It is really very interesting, for the inside lying within the outer shell is always more bright and more active than the outside. It makes me think of the hidden fires of Vesuvius. In this way, when I now look at earth-people, I see through the body and surface personality and look right at the real self inside. Sometimes this is duller even than the body. Again it is much more brilliant and beautiful.

The visual aspect of things I have learned and believe I understand pretty well, but the interpretation of them is still something beyond my grasp. But I will learn. H.P.B. says so. And you know, Natacha, that I always did accomplish what I set out to do, even if it did take some time.

It is strange, but since I am in this new plane of life I do not feel hurried or rushed any more. I used to always feel when I wanted to do anything that I had to hurry up, that there might not be time enough. But here it is different. Here, I seem to know somehow that there will be time enough and that all I need to do is to go steadily ahead.

Once in awhile, when I am with you or Muzzie, I feel a little anxious over results, and then the voice of H.P.B calls down to me from somewhere, "Steady, darling, steady!" Her voice often sounds close to my ear, even when my eyes do not see her, nor my sense feel her presence.

Where is she, that she is able to know what I am doing and to answer my thoughts when she is invisible? Another thing for me to learn in time.

This invisible guidance does not frighten me now. You remember the impressions I used to get so often? The thoughts that people were thinking of me? And how it used to startle me? But no more. The most unusual occurrences now seem perfectly usual. The weirdest happenings now seem perfectly natural.

So much love I have never seen before. Everyone seems to beam with it. Caruso, whom as you remember I always admired so, comes to me or I go to him. When I asked him about it, he laughed and said, "Well, mio figlio, what does it matter? Are we not together?"

He does not look just as he used to either. He looks more like his music sounded, if you can imagine what I mean. You see, there do not seem to be the right kind of words to tell these things with understanding. But I am doing the best I can and trust to your own keen insight. You used to get thoughts quickly. I hope you do now.

So this is what people call "being dead!" Natacha, they don't know what they are talking about. They are so cramped up in

165

their little bodies, so wound up in their own ideas of self-sufficiency, so looking down. How different the real truth is.

Why don't the Churches tell us the truth? Why don't the Jesuit Fathers explain the loveliness of life? They know all about it, but they seem to be afraid to come right out with it.

I have such a wonderful sense of freedom now. And no fear. I feel as if I could accomplish anything if I could just know how to go about it. Well, of course, people on the earth feel that way too, but there they always have the sense of great obstacles. I know I only have to be shown the way and then start out to accomplish it. On account of this I am sure I shall be able to do good work in awhile. If I learned to be a good actor when on earth, why can't I be a good helper after I learn? I will.

I do not walk up and down Broadway any more. There is no use in it. Nobody knows I am there. And it is too dull for me to be happy there.

I sometimes find myself in theatres where my pictures are still being shown. But somehow they do not seem as real to me as they used to. I do not feel so stirred when an audience is moved by my acting or the acting of others. Something about the earth is growing fainter.

The world seems to be fading out of my life picture.

People who have not been in some way close to me, or who have not really loved me, are now blurred and dim and indistinct to my consciousness. And still I love the earth and its people. I think my ties with the earth are gradually being severed.

I cannot hold the force any longer. Good night, Natacha dear. Do not forget me. Give my love to Muzzie, Uncle Dick, and Aunt Tessie. I feel that all will be well with Aunt Tessie. She was like Gabriella, my own dear mother, and if she comforted me so why should I not provide for her earthly comfort? Who has the right to change my mind after I have gone? I did what I did with my earthly earnings as I felt to be the fairest way. Alberto, Maria and Auntie were the nearest to me then. They were my little family. Why should they not share and share alike? I hope God will let my way be seen to be the fair way. Good night. I shall come again soon.

Rudy.

MESSAGE 3

WHILE I was very ill, but before it was known for certain that I was to pass over, I suddenly saw "Jenny." I was so surprised that I think I called out her name. It was only for a moment that I saw her. She stood before me in a glow of rose-colored light. She looked at me and smiled – just as she used to in her earth-days when she knew I needed encouragement – and held out her arms.

Her smile seemed to voice the idea, "Do not worry," I did not hear her speak. This vision was all over in a second. But I knew then, Natacha, that I was to go. Deep inside I felt my earthly days to be over. It frightened me. I did not want to go. I had a strange sensation as of sinking out of everything.

The world seemed dearer and brighter than ever it had before. I thought of my work and how I loved it. I thought of my home, of my things, and of my pets. Rapidly, one thought after another rushed in a tumult through my brain. The thought of cars, travel, yachts, clothes and money. All these material things seemed doubly valuable to me now.

The feeling that suddenly these things were about to be swept away from me or I away from them, appalled me. My body screamed deadly heavy and at the same time something within me felt very light, as if I was about to be lifted.

Time began to seem very important. Something unknown seemed looming up before me. There was a dreadful sense of immensity all around me which startled my very soul.

I began to think of hundreds of things I had intended to do – important things, trivial things. Even letters that I had intended to write swept across my consciousness. But the fleeting, though intensely clear, vision of "Jenny" had in some way pushed the power to accomplish these desires far, far away from me. Her strange beautiful smile, her outstretched arms, and the unearthly light around her, haunted me.

All this time there was a rumbling sound around me and a jolting sensation as of a moving vehicle. I am not sure, but it seemed to me that I heard George Ullman's voice. Dear George Ullman!

The thought of people crowded into my mind. Faces, faces, faces! Faces of those I had seen but a few days before, and the faces of people I had known long ago in the past. I thought of my cheery fellow-workers, of people that relied on me for help, people of all sorts that ran after me for one thing or another.

Maria's face, Alberto's, Ada's, Aunt Tessie's, Schenck's, Muzzie's, yours! Many, many Memories of my father and my mother. Childhood. Italy. School. My first journey to America. My first papers of citizenship. The rush of thoughts drowned my pain.

The most ridiculous experiences even, yet all so vivid, surged through my memory. Follies, pleasures, griefs; everything I had ever done seemed to come from somewhere and arise to the surface. It made me dizzy. I lost consciousness.

When I came to, the operation had been performed. Everybody smiled encouragingly at me. I had to keep quiet, although I felt as if I had so much to say – so much!

But all through these last days, although at times I felt stronger, a weight of dread lay on my heart. I felt that if I could only get up and begin doing many things I had neglected I might lose this dread. Of course they would not let me get up. Your message was near and comforted me.

I had a remarkable feeling that I might soon see you – that at any moment you might walk into the room. H.P.B. has since told me that this was because I was so soon to go to you instead.

Then I had difficulty breathing and I knew that all was drawing to an end. I was dreadfully frightened. It was too sudden for me to understand it. I don't believe I was actually afraid to die, Natacha; that I began to know then that I was changing. I could feel it taking place in my body and my mind. Something seemed to be dropping away. There was at times a straining sensation, as if some part of my being were tearing itself loose.

I thought of what would happen to my body afterwards – funeral, cremation, the ground. This gave me a sense of horror.

Then the priest came. He seemed like a light in the dark. I turned to him with all my fear, my horror, my uncertainty. My childhood again emerged. Dim cathedral aisles swam before my eyes. The last sacraments!

After the simple ceremony was over, I felt already away from the earth. My mental attitude was changed. The Church, like a strong, friendly hand, was holding me. I would not be alone. Fear left me. Faces about me grew dim. Silence. Darkness. Unconsciousness.

I do not know how long this lasted. Just as if awakening from a long, deep sleep. I opened my eyes, experiencing at the same moment a feeling as of being rapidly drawn upward – then wonderful bluish light – then Black Feather; Jenny; and Gabriella, my mother!

I was dead!
I was alive!
This, Natacha, is the remembrance of my passing.

Rudy.

MESSAGE 4

BECAUSE I knew something about life after death before I came over, it has not taken me so long to find myself. That is, to acclimate myself to these new conditions. My automatic writings that you enjoyed so much, Natacha, taught us a great deal. You remember the writings given from the spirits of Jenny, Meselope, Black Feather, Oscar and many others.

We did not always pay as much attention to them as we should have. It was so easy just to find them interesting. It is difficult to put real help and advice into our daily lives, isn't it?

But since I have come over, the memory of these writings has served to put me into closer touch with life as it really is, and not the false aspect often given out by people who know little or nothing about it. And my natural powers of observation have helped me to progress quicker than if I were slower in that respect.

I find that our powers in the body are about the same, but heightened to a considerable degree when we are freed from it. I am now the same old Rudy you knew before, only now I am a Rudy heightened in perceptive faculty. And I seem to feel emotions more keenly too. Spirits tell me that is because I am still in my astral desire body.

The earth-body itself does not feel, being only a material covering or shell for the astral body which does feel. I am so glad to be able to tell you this, so that when you have sort of a pain, you will know it is not in your earth-body, but in your astral body.

Spirits have shown me how easily the astral body can be vitalized by currents of vitality. They say these vitalizing currents are the life emanations of God. When the astral body is cut off from this supply, it cries out in pain, which is really a warning to you to try to bring it into contact again with the currents of healing.

When this is done the cause of pain is of course removed and the pain ceases. H.P.B. has shown me how this astral body often withdraws itself from the physical body. This happens to people who are in deep sleep.

At night I have seen your astral body emerge from the physical, and I have then been able to get very close to your consciousness and to talk to you. You have sometimes remembered this vaguely upon awakening and thought it to be only a dream. But it was no dream. It was the living reality.

When George goes into a trance, his astral body comes out. In the earth-life when this happens, the astral body is connected to the physical body by a shining kind of cord which seems to be attached to the head. I do not yet understand just how this is, but this is what I have myself seen.

Spirits have also told me that when an anesthetic is given, the astral body emerges, and that is why there is no longer any sensation left in the physical body. This is all interesting to me. When people on earth are able to heal others by putting their hands upon them, it is because they are simply allowing the vital currents to flow through them into the devitalized body of a part.

I learned a lot of this at some lectures I attended, Natacha, you would love the lectures here. There are places they call "centres." To me they look like temples. They are white and very lofty and beautiful. I thought they were of stone but the spirit of George's guide, Henry Watts, told me that they were constructed of the white thought-force of truth and faith.

Everything seems to be made of one or another kind of thought-force. This thought-substance, it seems, is far more solid and enduring than the stones or metals of the earth-world. This is hard to realize. It does not look at all as one would suppose thought-force ought to look. I always imagined it to be a misty, cloud-like sort of thing, and here it is more solid and colorful than the solid objects of earth. Life is truly amazing, and I love it more and more.

I have seen some lovely houses here. Some like little villas and others much more imposing and magnificent. These, it seems, belong to people who were quite humble in the earth-life, even poor. But they were people who had not denied shelter to those who needed it. They had divided their meals with those who were hungry. And on account of their generosity, they have found these places built for them out of the thought-substance of their actions.

It seems very thrilling to me, and I could not keep back the tears when I realized how this was done. The houses are built by the spirits who have learned to mold this thought-force. They are always built just as the people to live in them would like to have them. The spirit builders know how to do this by looking into people's unconsciousness where, it seems, the mental pictures of all they love and desire are stored.

Some of the houses are only partly built, as enough thought-substance has not yet been sent over from unselfish actions. There are also large places, like various kinds of hotels, where people who have no such homes are kept for a while. These are the selfish, uncharitable ones who have not shared. They are people who have denied assistance to those who were in need.

I knew lots of people like that, and now I am sorry for them. These people are talked to, but not in a preachy sort of way, and are taken to see plays showing up such subjects.

There is even a way of showing them picture-like flashes of their own past actions. This is the nearest thing to a motion picture that I have seen. But it is not like that. It is all done by thought-processes. H.P.B. says it is the instructive incidents in a soul's past brought forward and out of the astral-light.

This is all done in the hope that people will realize their mistakes and start to change their attitudes of thought. If they do desire to change, work is at once given to them. There is plenty of work everywhere. They are given what they are most adapted to. In that way they lose sight of self in seeing others being helped, and so begin to form the thought-substance that will build their homes.

If they do not desire to change, but hang to their old ideas stubbornly, they are turned out to wander alone. No one feels at all sorry for them. This surprised me very much at first. But how can you change their minds to begin to earn all they desire? They are fools to say the least.

I am told that they do not wander around very long. The supreme indifference by which they are met soon brings them to their senses.

I have seen some very beautiful houses that belong to people who were wealthy upon the earth. But they were people who never failed to help others. They shared. They realized what their wealth was for.

At first, when I heard about all this, I began to think it was wrong to try to get rich in earth-life. But H.P.B. tells me this is not so. She says it is right for people to be rich if they do good with their riches. She says they have at some time earned the right to possess those riches and that they are being tested. What they possess in the future seems to depend upon what use they make of what they possess in the present.

So you see, life after all seems pretty just, doesn't it? Learn these truths now, Natacha dear, and teach them to your friends. Do not wait till the time of your coming over here.

H.P.B. says it is not true generosity to give recklessly however. Thought and common sense must be used always. Only the really needy should be reached. And not too much help should be given at once. That would make weak people weaker. The best help, she says, is the kind that helps people to help themselves. In that way they grow stronger and more reliant.

173

I asked her about imposters. You know, Natacha, how often I was approached by them. H.P.B.'s answer was, "If I had not the vision to distinguish true from false, I would rather give aid to an imposter than lose the chance of helping one who might really be needy."

Henry Watts says that all souls need some kind of help. We must share whatever we have, whether it be possessions or knowledge. So this is what makes that thought-force substance of which the homes are built. I wish I had known this in my earth-life. I would have done many things differently. But you can depend on it now that I am going to try to put what I learn into action. I want to progress.

I would like to become a guide. But friends of my profession whom I have met here tell me I had better stick to the theatre.

It turns out that the unusual magnetism I possessed when appearing on the screen was due to the fact that I have been an actor in previous lives.

I wish I knew what those lives were and who I was. I am told that an account of all one's experiences are indelibly stamped on the Great Records and can be reviewed in the Astral Light. But one cannot do this until he has learned how or earned the right. This is another thing I am anxious to learn. You see, there are a good many things that make life fascinating.

My friends have taken me to see the theatres. They are enormous and very, very beautiful. They are also built of thought-substance, but of that thought-substance which comes from true poets ideals. You cannot imagine how wondrous in form and color these theatres are.

In these theatres many thousands of spectators are enabled to watch the performances. The plays are great dramas of the soul. For these theatres the writers create for the joy of creating, and not for the need of money. So, of course, marvelous plays are to be seen.

All the great actors act in them. But there is a strange difference in the acting here and the acting of earth. On the earth plane a clever artists can portray any part given him by a manager.

Not so here. There is no more cleverness here. All is sincerity.

No artist here can portray a single emotion that his soul is not capable of expressing in reality. There is no imitation. There is no assuming. All is real. All is genuine. All is true.

An actress cannot play a role of noble quality unless she has truly developed that noble quality in her own soul. There is no sham here.

A man cannot portray a king unless he is majestic in character or soul. On earth the Passion Play comes the nearest to this sincere expression.

Artists are not allowed to play evil roles unless the evil to be portrayed has been overcome by the artists themselves in some former life-experience. Evil is only portrayed to serve a purpose, to heighten the effects of the good.

There is no scenery on the stage in the sense that there is scenery in the earth-world theatres. The mood and purpose of the play create a thought-substance reflecting it and this substance, colored accordingly, forms a great and perfectly natural background for the performance.

And the actors, according to the emotions being expressed, give off thought-forms, brilliant or sombre, according to the particular emotion. These thought-forms, playing against the background of the mood, form a marvelous symphony of color.

No words are actually spoken, as upon the earth. The ideas are all expressed in thought, and as ideas are universal, all earth-plane languages merge into one in this after-life. So all the spectators, no matter what their language on earth may have been, understand fluently the thought-language of the drama.

Oh, Natacha, I know you would love it.

Yes, I feel I do belong to the theatre, and I shall be so happy when they let me begin to play, even if the parts they give me at first are small. I am told there is no jealousy among the artists as there is in the earth-world. There cannot be. Everyone knows he can only play what he is fitted by soul-experience to play. Here, no one can step in and play another's part, for there are no two emotions alike. Life is too many-sided for that. All work together in harmony, intent only upon the purpose of the drama and of the service it will give to the spectators.

The force is gone. I cannot communicate any longer. I have more to say on this and will continue another time.

Rudy.

175

Enrico Caruso

MESSAGE 5

I HAVE been taken to hear some wonderful operas. You remember how much I loved music.

The operas are not given in theatres as in the earth-plane, but in immense and very wonderful temples. Music here is sacred and is always listened to in reverence. Do not let this alarm you, Natacha. When you hear the kind of music it is, you will understand. You have no music like it on the earth-world.

I would not be able to tell you all this about if it were not for the fact that Caruso[*] had explained it to me. It is he who took me to listen to the opera. He also took me all over the temple. Caruso sings here very often, as do all the many singers who have come over.

Enrico says that the great composers here know that life itself is music. They have learned to strike the keynote of many vibrations. Of course they have not mastered them all, but they are constantly studying to do so. Since everything is vibration, you can see what a study it is.

In this way, Caruso says, real and true music is created. Music that mirrors every emotion the human entity is capable of expressing. Also the multitudinous sounds of the nature world. And the unearthly music of the planets motion.

In the earth-plane the number of keys is very limited, there being only twenty-four scales, Caruso says. But here, composers have discovered that the number is unlimited. There are many keys as there are different vibrations. That is why music is such a vast and inexhaustible subject.

Earth-plane ears could not define those keys of which I speak. Only the inner ear, the psychic ear – the soul's true ear – is fine enough to catch these sounds.

But, Natacha, music composed in these keys is so exquisitely sublime that it lifts the listening soul to the very height of ecstasy. Caruso says that if earth-plane ears could hear it, the intense vibration effect upon the nervous stem would be so great as to shatter it.

[*]Enrico Caruso was an extremely popular Italian Opera singer, and according to some, one of the greatest of all time. After taking ill he was examined by an unsanitary doctor and like Rudy died of peritonitis in 1921. He was 48.

177

Music here is not used only to please the senses or to appeal to the intellect; it has far higher purposes. H.P.B. says it is the idealized soul of vibration and therefore has unlimited power for good or for bad, depending upon how it is directed.

It is used to harmonize large bodies of people. It is used to key them to a higher pitch so that in this way they are lifted to a higher plane temporarily for purposes of instruction.

Certain planets are also communicated with by means of this kind of music.

I asked H.P.B. about this and she explained it, but I do not think I can give it to you as clearly as she did to me. But it seems that each planet has its particular keynote or scale, and that everything on that planet has a keynote that is in relationship with the main scale. I hope I am saying this so you will understand. My language may not be technical enough, but I am doing my best.

The music by which the North Star is reached is peculiarly magnetic in attractive quality and rather metallic in tone. There are planetary spirits, you know, and H.P.B. says those of the North Star are adepts in guidance. That is why in the earth-world it has been used as a focus-point for adventurous travelers from time immemorial. All compasses point toward it. She says if people who are confused and lost on the way, as it were, would only collect themselves and become calm enough to turn to the spirits of the North Star, their confusion would cease and they would find guidance. Whenever you lose your way, Natacha, in the mazes of life, turn to find the right direction from the vibrations of the North Star. She calls this star Isis. It affects other worlds than the earth-world.

The music of Venus is glowing and vibrant with vital force, says H.P.B. I can't remember what she said about Mercury, but the music of Saturn and Uranus was described as exotic and hypnotic and could be used for evil if people knew how. Neptune's music, she said, is so peculiar that earth-people would never comprehend it. It would sound to them either like a thunderous roar or else like a faint twinkling of a wavelet against a wavelet.

The music of the Moon is calm, but compelling. It acts, she says, mesmerically upon all fluids. Composers who are able to tap inspiration from the Moon vibration are always able to sway and win their listeners by their creations. Such inspiration is hauntingly beautiful, yet strangely pale and metallic in coloring.

The Sun music, H.P.B. explained, is – well, here are her words, "a drenching dew of Heaven's melody, life-giving, sustaining, creating." It is the music of eternal creation, of joy unlimited. Every

178

soul echoes it, she says, but earth-souls are deafened by its tremendous harmonies and do not realize that it is the symphony of their life.

There are other planets, the music of which she described, but I could not retain all this learning at one time. The greatest of all planetary music, she said emphatically, was that of Isis, the magnetic Star of the North.

Guardian spirits of certain souls in the earth-world often use music to quell storms and to avert disasters when it does not interfere with Karmic laws. You know there are stories and legends of sailors hearing strange music in the midst of storms and of the waters being mysteriously clamed. These stories are all founded on psychic facts.

Certain healings are also affected by it. Florence Nightingale, the well-remembered nurse of your world, told me this. She says that very often patients lying near death's door hear, as in a dream, glorious voices, or ethereal music, and are soon after restored to health and earth-life. And how often, she says, does the departing soul hear this wondrous music of the spheres as it leaves the body and is received beyond the veil?

Oh Natacha, cara mia, that veil is not away, nor is it so thick as earth-people like to believe.

The operas are given as dramas are. Only the scenic display of color is far greater. You, with your earthly conceptions, cannot begin to conceive the intricate beauty and glory of this color play. Music seems to show itself in colors more vivid and more piercingly bright than do the thought-forms.

Not long ago – I think that is how to say it, for I seem to have lost track of time here – I heard Caruso in an opera called *The Journey of the Soul*. When I say I heard Caruso in it, I say so because he seems nearer to me than others, but I heard many great singers in it. There were great choruses visible and invisible. At one time the music arose to such a height of grander that other planes were contacted and we heard the answering choruses from those planes.

That is one of the most remarkable things I have learned about music here – how it does not seem to be just a finished thing of itself as an opera in the earth-world is. Here, music links with other music in other planes. Of course, I cannot begin to understand how or why this is, but it is so.

Natacha, I have never heard anything like this opera in all my experience; you see, I do not say "in all my life" any more. My whole soul wept for joy. Caruso's voice soared out to us like the tones of some great organ, and the colors that poured from his aura while he sang were infinite in variety – brilliant shades of gold and

179

many tones of violet and purple. There were flashes of silver, too, at times and a color I have never seen before – a kind of color between silver and copper, with a pale green, such as you see in certain metals, mixed in with it. There are so many colors here that we cannot see in the earth-life.

You above all people would be thrilled at all this color. At one time during the opera I suddenly lost all sense of sight or sound or feeling. The prismatic display disappeared, I no longer heard the music, and I was no longer swayed by the emotion. I became frightened and turned to H.P.B. who sat beside me. She laughed and said, "Little fool, it is simply that your soul has not progressed enough yet to be able to comprehend this part of the opera. These colors are beyond your present powers of visualization. This music is in too high a rate of vibration for your soul to feet. Have patience. Learn to wait and grow."

Wasn't that curious. What would I do without H.P.B.? There must be something good in me to have attracted her as a helper. I always seem to be able to understand her words, and they are indelibly stamped on my memory. I do not forget the things she says.

This is all I can tell you about music, for it is all I have learned. I am so anxious to study and learn. Are you pleased that I am doing so?

Before I leave I want to tell you that after the opera I was so excited, I wanted to bring you in your astral body, while you slept, to experience one, too. I asked the spirit of Henry Watts about it, but he said that I must not attempt it. To do so took great experience, and, of course, I am so new here yet. He said if I tried I might do you great harm.

But all the same I wish you could hear and see one. It is really worth dying just to experience this indescribable beauty. I still love beauty just as much as I did on earth.

Buona notte, for the present. I will come again soon; I feel so happy, so fortune, to be able to reach you again, and you, carissima, know why.

MESSAGE 6

IT seems so strange to me now, as I look back on my earth-life, how blind to realities we are on the verge of truths and yet in our blindness pass them by. If only our inner vision were more developed. There would then be no misunderstandings, ridiculous and foolish as they always are when looked back upon, such as yours and mine were.

Had we that keener vision, we would see that such petty difficulties are only like winter frost on a window-pane. Frost that would melt at the first warm breath of a word of love.

But no. We do not wait to even try to see. We act at once, impetuously and without reason. Our anger – muddy-red, and blinding and bewildering – suffuses our facilities, clogs our perceptive channels, and altogether drags us downward. H.P.B. has explained this so well to me, because at first I was quite confused as I looked back upon our differences and our parting.

Now it is all much clearer to me. She says that when this red cloud of anger surges over us it attracts, through appearing in our aura, the attention of destructive entities, both human and elemental. This muddy color is to them an invitation to advance. They swarm about us, and through our consciousness. Their delight in destruction, and their intense desire to drag down other souls to their own level, is so great that our anger is intensified. We finally, when we give in to anger repeatedly, fall under their dominion entirely. These entities do not let go easily. Their method of victimizing is poisonously patient.

You and I were both headstrong and prone to rapid anger, and H.P.B. has shown me how we both attracted destructive forces that ended our earth-plane union disastrously – but now we know that that was only frost upon the windows of our soul. The unclouded vision of my spirit has melted that now.

It is so, too, with people whom I did not like very much when in the earth-life. Now, as I look at them and see beneath their surfaces, I see a great deal in them to love. They would, no doubt, laugh if I told them this, but ignorant laughter never changes truth. Does it? It is very easy to scoff. But truth remains truth all the same. If we insist upon not learning it in our earthly existence, we shall most certainly learn it here. We could not avoid learning it even if we wished, as our eyes become clear-seeing and these verities stand out most startling.

Thank Heaven I was always adaptable to my surroundings. This faculty stands me in good stead here. H.P.B. says it is on account of this that I am acquiring knowledge of this plane so rapidly. She says adaptability is the sense of unity and leads eventually to oneness.

This place where I am living is the Astral Plane. But that term is very expansive. When we used to get automatic messages about it, I always thought it was a realm of rather low spirits.

Now I find that while it does take in those misguided spirits, always very close to the earth, still it embraces many progressed souls as well. All these lovely places I have told you of are in it.

It seems to be, as far as I can make out, a place of progression, where many problems are worked out. It is a place where souls are awakened to realities. It is in a sense the purgatory of the Roman Catholics. I used to worry a good deal over purgatory.

Well, here I am in it, and I do not find it anything other than interesting. Of course, if I were stubborn and clinging to old desires and prejudices and jealousies and quarrels, I should most likely find it a pretty lonely place. There are the lonely ones here, the discouraged ones, and the evil ones too. But help, when sought, is ever present. How thankful I am to know this!

It is strange how people in the earth-world like to say that communications are possible, but only from the ignorant, evil or misguided spirits. Being the nearest to earth does not in any way make them the nearest to humanity at large. In fact, the guides tell me that it separates them more completely. They are near only to people who attract them and who are somewhere in their natures of like caliber.

But there are exceptions. Under certain conditions these souls are allowed to communicate for purposes of gaining deliverance for themselves. At other times to serve as illustrations to certain lessons the guides are giving.

Natacha dear, if such undeveloped souls are in any manner able to communicate or appear to people of the earth, does it not stand to reason that more advanced souls – souls that were helpers and teachers in the earth-life – would, with their keener intelligence, the sooner find the way to communicate their knowledge of this after-life?

Why am I striving to communicate to you? Because I love you. And I love the people of the earth. If my new learning, that I am gaining every minute, hour and day, every atom of time, is of profit to you, it may be of profit to others. And so I am making haste to give it to you and to that world.

How fortunate I am to have so well-trained and facile an instrument to come through. Of course, Natacha, I am helped to do so by several spirits. Sometimes it is Annie, the mother of the medium who assists me to hold myself in the medium's vibration. Sometimes it is Henry Watts, or Ami, or Alestes, or U.K., and often it is H.P.B. herself.

You see, it is this way. Being now in the life of the spirit. I am vibrating at a much more rapid rate than when in a physical body. I could come to you, or Muzzie, or Uncle Dick, or Aunt Tessie, and speak all day, and yet you would not hear me. Your vibration is so much slower. And you can only sense things in your own vibrations.

But mediums are vastly different. Thank God for the power that lets such peculiar physical organisms exist! They are so constituted as to possess variable rates of vibration. When a medium is to be used, he is put in working order by special guides who have made a study of this. White Cloud, the old Ojibway Indian, is the guide who does this for George.

Now I will tell you exactly how I communicate with you, Natacha.

You decide to have a séance. You and Muzzie, Aunt Tessie and Uncle Dick. You are all seated in your chairs in a circle, George in his easy chair – we call it the Receiving Station. George relaxes, and, making his mind a blank (I don't know any better way to express it), leaves the body. His mother takes charge of his soul in its astral body and takes care of the astral cord, for it is the connecting link between spirit and matter. His mother is the best one to do this service as she is nearest to him in vibrational key. In a way, it is fortunate for George's psychic work that his mother has passed to the life of the spirit.

White Cloud takes charges always of the sleeping physical body, which is limp and empty now. This body is now vibrating much more rapidly than in normal activity. The blood is drawn magnetically inward around the nerve centres and spinal cord and brain. The body is now giving out certain musical sounds; if you could but hear them!

Sometimes there is not enough magnetism in the medium's body to accomplish the entrance of a spirit, so a surplus is drawn from the sitters; from Muzzie, Aunt Tessie, Uncle Dick and you. Other guides do that. Henry Watts, or Ami, or Black Feather. When enough magnetism is obtained, we, by means of it, are one at a time drawn into the physical organism of the medium, animate it – often clumsily at first – and speak to you as best we can.

184

At first I could not learn to enter the body very well and could only get in a word or two. That was because I was told to focus my mind upon lowering my vibrations to the rate of the medium's. This is done through sound. The sound I spoke of, coming from the medium's body, is the pitch we have to key our vibration to. We sing in our mind the same tone, as it were. I hope I am making this clear. I am trying my best to do so.

But I found this extremely hard to do. When I started to speak to you, I would forget to keep the vibration-note in mind and immediately up would go my vibration and I would find myself put out of George's body. Then White Cloud would help me to be drawn in again by the attraction of the magnetic current. I could hear you all saying, "Oh, don't go, Rudy, come back and talk to us!"

You can see that it takes practice to be able to enter a body, stay there, and speak clearly and fluently to our loved ones. That is why with many mediums, Henry Watts explains, the messages are sometimes so trifling and incoherent. But George's vibration is unusually steady most of the times, and that is why we can control him so long at a time and speak so definitely and clearly through him.

Now about names, Natacha dear. You, and others, have remarked how often spirits are ale to give their names clearly through George's mediumship. And when you went to many other mediums you got very few names. The reason for this, I find, has to do with sound also.

Our given name is the name that belongs to us inherently. At any rate, the name that identifies us, whether it was a baptismal name or a name assumed, is the part of the full name that represents us. Now it seems that this name, in some way as yet unexplained to me, is a power – a vibrational power. And whenever it is thought of or called into being, it sounds its individual keynote.

So when, during communication, we are keeping our mind on the vibration-rate-tone, in order to stay in the body and attempt to give our name to you, the keynote of the name sounds. This, confusing with the vibration-rate-tone, upsets our concentration and sometimes dislodges us entirely from the body, or causes us to mumble, or to give the name indistinctly. It is hard to hold two sounds in the mind simultaneously. Try it and see. And the moment you let go of the medium's vibration-rate-tone, which keys you to him, up bobs your own vibration and you have let go of the control.

I am afraid I have repeated a lot in explaining this. But as it appears rather complicated, I cannot seem to help it.

With a medium like George, whose vibration is so generally steady, it is much easier to hold the tone, as his tone is not so constantly wabbling up and down as in the case of many.

185

At the beginning, when I could control in this way hardly at all, I would give up trying and would tell White Cloud what to say to you for me. Spirits coming to a particular medium for the first time are seldom able to control, unless they have had experience in coming through other mediums. The method of control is practically the same with all mediums, I am told. Although I have not tried any number as yet.

I am having the time of my life learning all these ways and means. Life-existence is the most fascinating study. I am filled with the joy of it. I have much more to tell you, but the force is growing less now, and I must let up on my control.

I will soon come again.

Rudy.

MESSAGE 7

ONE thing that pleases me beyond everything is that I find a nature-world here, just as in the earth-world. Only here it is more radiant – I think this is the world nearest to what I mean – anyway, far more beautiful. There are plains, mountains, rivers and lakes; trees, flowers and birds.

The trees seem greater in height, and their lofty branches are heavier with foliage and of a green far clearer and bright than on earth. The flowers are intensely brilliant. They do not seem composed of the firm petals we are used to in the earth-life. They seem to be, instead, forms of living color, vibrating, or constantly glowing, as it were. This is hard for me to describe.

H.P.B. says I am still so new to this change of dimension that I keep comparing things in the old way. These glowing color-forms are the souls of the flowers; their bodies were left on earth to decompose into mold.

I notice a much clearer and stronger fragrance with these soul-flowers. H.P.B. has also told me that the perfume of flowers in the earth-plane consists of the effect of the flowers' auras on your olfactory nerve-centers. She says that this fragrance – these various odors – are in themselves color emanations. The mortal eye is not developed enough to see them, but the sense of smell catches the vibration. So you see, Natacha, it all comes back to vibration.

H.P.B. also says that if people's noses were as dull as their eyes, scientists would probably swear up and down that flowers gave forth no odors! She says that every flower gives out some kind of fragrance, because souls of any kind whatsoever possesses auras. But some of these perfumes are too delicate for even the sense of smell to detect. People therefore claim such flowers to be odorless.

H.P.B. told me that mediumistic eyes often see these perfume vibrations, and some people, she explained, are so sensitive that they are able to feel these flower vibrations

This idea seems to make sound, color, taste, feeling and odor to be simply different effects of the same cause; different degrees of vibration. At least, that is how I have figured it out so far.

I asked H.P.B. if that didn't reduce life to just different expressions of the same thing. She smiled and said, "Yes, dear child, and that thing if God; and God is Love; and Love is expression; and expression is creation; and creation is truth; and truth is nine multiplied by nine indefinitely, which reaches back to God again. And so the circle of life is complete." I guess she thinks I ask an awful lot of questions, but she always takes the trouble to answer me.

There seems to be every variety of flowers that you have on earth blooming here, and many others I have never seen before. The beauty of these astral flowers is beyond my powers of description. Many of them are geometric in form and color effect, and some are very complicated in structure. There are such quantities of these curious astral flowers, new to me, that I have only learned to know a few of them.

There is a kind whose blossoms twist upward in a spiral, the top cluster ending in a point. These are of every huge that a prism is capable of giving off. They are called "Flames of the Soul."

Another extremely interesting kind is popularly called "Heart-beats," but H.P.B. says they are the real "Immortals." They are very delicate and have but one pendent heart-shaped blossom of glowing white light. A current of red life-force is continuously coursing through the center of the semi-transparent blossom, pulsating like a ruby heart-beat.

These flowers are so sensitive in reacting to conditions or vibrations to which they have been keyed, that spirits use them as a kind of barometer by which they gauge the health of their earth-friends and the state of affairs around them. It is a most curious plant. I have not seen a house here that does not have them blooming in the garden.

One can see many spirits going earthward carrying these beautiful plants. They take them to earth and leave them for awhile in the houses of their loves ones. The "Beating-heart" flowers, in some way, become tuned to the true keynote of the vibration of the earth-personality, through absorbing the auric emanations. And they retain this vibrational pitch until the earth-death of the person to whose vibrations they have become tuned.

Later, the spirits take back these flowers to their own homes in the astral plane, and by noting the pulsation of the red life-force within the transparent white flower, can tell exactly the condition of the earth-person it is keyed to; whether he is calm or agitated; well or ill; and even when he is going to die.

Wallace Reid

Spirits seem to be very happy when a "Beating-heart" flower shows them the coming death of a relative or friend. They all get together in a meeting – something like our parties of the earth-world – with singing and dancing. They are all so pleased that another soul is coming into the realness of life.

Do not be surprised that I say there is dancing over here. Everyone dances. But not exactly in the way of the earth. It is mostly symbolic, and is the expression in action of one's higher emotions. I can well imagine some of our friends, Natacha, thinking this is rather highbrow, but let me tell you, it is not so. The music is so wonderful that everyone is caught by it and just lets go and expresses himself in rhythm. You will enjoy it when you come over because you are a natural dancer.

High souls like to tell you there is no jazz here, but that is not quite true. There is. But you have to know where to find it.

Wally Reid* has told me all about it and he even took me to see it. You will find this kind of dancing on the lower astral plane. That part of the astral world, you know, dovetails into the earth. So all that sort of thing is quite near to you. I will tell you more about these people another time.

You will be pleased to hear that I have met Vernon Castle** again. He is just the same charming fellow. He has told me a good deal about dancing too.

Vernon says that for the people still on earth, dancing is very excellent. He explained to me how dancing sets in motion, within the physical body, currents of nerve-force that go spiraling up the spinal cord until they reach two glands in the brain called pituary and pineal. These glands are great psychic centers.

Vernon told me that the lower forms of dancing are not good, and because of attracting deteriorating entities, hinder the soul's progress. They stir lower desires and allow the wrong kind of elementals (nature spirits) and sensual human spirits to use a hypnotic influence upon the mind. It seems these spirits have a way of merging themselves into the physical bodies they contact by these means, and are then able since more to experience sensation.

---

*Wallace Reid was a silent film actor, a sort of 'Great Lover' before Valentino's own stardom. Injured performing his own stunts, Reid became addicted to morphine at the height of his fame. The addiction destroyed him despite many attempts to get clean (the concept of rehab did not really exist during this time) and he died at the age of 31 in 1923.

**Vernon Castle was one half of a wildly popular dance team, dancing with his wife Irene Castle. At the height of their popularity Vernon joined the war effort as a pilot. He survived battle and was awarded the Croix de Guerre for his efforts. He died after crashing during a training exercise in Texas in 1918. He was 30.

The study of these facts is most fascinating to me, and it throws light on many things that puzzled me during my earth-life. I now understand the causes for the actions of certain people I used to meet and whom, I am afraid, I was too ready to condemn.

Now I know why they threw their life chances to the winds – because of allowing themselves to be controlled by entities through their lower desires – and I am very sorry for them.

Dear, wild, old Hollywood – the scene of my struggles and my triumphs – what a place it is of undeveloped souls. There are wonderful souls there. There are broken souls there. And there are many souls that might be great were they not being suffocated by the intense materialism of that artificial life.

With the knowledge I now have of life, gained by my clearer perceptions and the help of my teachers, I would not care to return to the life of Hollywood.

Life there is superficial and a sham, and such conditions are not lasting. I always did love the out-of-doors and Nature, and that, I think, is what sustained me through it all. Over here I find that Nature is so very important. People do not realize its importance in their lives. It is important because it is so closely linked to us, to the physical body, and at the same time without inner character. Earth-bodies are composed of the elements of earth, the same currents of force flow through them, and all the beauty that the earth can produce is reflected in our inner character.

Oh, Natacha, I want to tell people to go out among the trees and flowers and birds. Tell your friends to do so. Look up gladly into the blue ether overhead and realize that greater planes of life are there. Then look around at the gloriousness of Nature and realize that a great plane lies there. Then try to consider how closely joined together are all these planes, like the links of a beautiful chain. The thought of planes linking together will give you the idea of brotherhood.

Never feel sorry when you see trees falling before the woodcutter's axe. H.P.B. says the nature-world gladly serves humanity, and, by so doing, fulfils its mission, destiny, or purpose, and finds its evolution and advancement. Perhaps I do not know just how to say this.

Of course, ruthless destruction, I am told, is waste, and waste is very wrong. Service is quite another matter.

The force is gone. I have more to give another time and will come again.

Rudy.

MESSAGE 8

HERE I meet so many wonderful souls. There is no holding aloof and waiting for introductions. Nothing like that. I find life here to be a true brotherhood. Our likes and longings are met with an understanding response.

If I have admired any particular person for his life and work, that person psychically knows of it without any words to that effect, and extends immediately the hand of fellowship. So you can see that life in these planes beyond earth is on a truer basis than we have known before.

One's innermost thoughts, I have learned, are revealed to anyone in the same degree of development, or higher. For instance, all people here who have attained to the soul-development that I have, and I guess that is very little so far, can read my deepest thoughts. And souls that are more and more advanced than I can not only read these thoughts, but can see the reason for them and underlying cause of them. In this way, you see, there are no secrets. And by this clear-seeing of others can one alone be helped.

It made me very uncomfortable at first, for we all have a foolish sort of pride about our hidden likes and dislikes becoming known. But when I realized that this reading of the character was a fact, I thought it best to act like a sport, and so I gave in at once.

This brought, to my surprise, a feeling of intense relief. It seemed as if a load had dropped away from me. I felt nearer to the truth than ever before, and far nearer to people – real people. I then realized that there was brotherhood, and unity, and protection.

Life on earth would be vastly different, I am sure, if people only knew the actual conditions they were going to face sooner or later, through death. That is why I am anxious to tell these facts as I discover them.

It is interesting to me to see how people here, that is, people who are at all awakened, seem bent only upon trying to unfold their latent spiritual qualities. You see, we have all left behind the things of earth; our business, professions, money, property, and all our worldly pursuits.

We find ourselves absolutely shut away from all this, that is, from continuing with is in the same old way, and discover ourselves

194

standing ready to began an entirely new life, and with what seems, at first, an apparently blank future slate before we pass over, this literally new birth comes to us as a very great shock.

Many people cannot hold up against this shock and surprise. So they, through ignorance, fear and resentment at having been taken from the material world they loved too well, spend all their time haunting their familiar earthly surroundings and become tied, mentally, to the earth. They are in the lower astral plane, out of the world, yet they are still in it through their tenacious clinging to worldly attitudes of thought. These unfortunate people are the earth-bound we used to hear about in our automatic writings.

I am told that some of these souls are so stubborn, so anchored down by the set conviction of their former mode of thinking, that they are actually blinded, and cannot see or realize the possibilities of advancement in the newer world before them. They are unadaptable, obstinate and unprogressive.

They are the ones who, when on the earth-life, were the first to oppose innovations of any sort. And you may be surprised to learn that they are in all walks of life. There are among this type of earth-bound, ministers of the gospel, priests, and religious men of all kinds who have been hidebound to their creeds, superstitions and beliefs. Among them are many fanatics.

There are also kings and queens, and all sorts of people of the ruling classes, who will not let go of the ideas of temporal power. There are countless souls, too, of the humbler classes who are tied by the limited aspect of their thoughts; peasants, who still cannot see more than ten feet before their ploughs; soldiers, who insist upon believing their might is right, in spite of the fact that death has proved otherwise to them. All who are narrow and pinched in the mental outlook, all such, are tied and earth-bound.

The worst of it is, these souls may be bound in this way for years, as you count them, even for centuries. To me, this is a rather appalling aspect.

The best of it is, the very moment such a soul changes his mental attitude, he at once realizes the folly of clinging to limitations. Then, if he has any sense at all, he will let go, turn right-about-face, and so go marching on.

Scientific people of all kinds, I am informed, change their attitudes very readily. They may have been unbending in their views when on earth, but for all that, they were in their own wonderful way, seekers. When the stark realities of a new existence stare them in the face, they are not stupid about it, but immediately regard the matter as a new specimen to be inspected through their microscopes.

I must tell you at first I was somewhat held back by my earthly egotism. I can now look back at it and laugh. H.P.B. has shown me how humorous it appeared to such spirits as watched me, and who tried to help me.

I actually thought the motion-picture industry would be fatally crippled without me. I imagined I was about the greatest actor on earth. After seeing the acting in the theatres over here, I blush in my very soul to think of my conceit.

I was angry, too, when the helpers confronted me with my egotism. I was angry because I was really ashamed to find out that this was true. I know it even appalled you – my colossal egotism – when I expressed my opinions, through the medium at the château, upon my highly esteemed self. But Uncle Dick and Arthur Forrest and Mrs. Cora Brown-Potter, too, were all wonderful about it. None of them laughed at me. They even coincided in my views of how great an actor I thought I was.

But that is because Arthur and Cora are artists, and Uncle Dick wanted to say the sporting thing. They all knew well enough that there is always someone ready to go right on with any work that is left behind. I know it now, too.

People, people, people! They are what really count. I love them more and more as I come to know them in a spiritual way. What is life? Nothing but an infinite sea, and the drops in that sea are people.

Life seems so tremendously beautiful to me now – so full – so real – so joyous. I am in a world of artists: actors, musicians, writers, painters, sculptors, architects – yes, and even landscape gardeners. How did I ever miss becoming a landscape gardener, when that was what was hoped for me at first? Because the experience gained in past lives as an actor (I have found this out about myself) was somewhere stored up in my consciousness and had to express itself again in order to overcome some obstacle still left undefeated.

I am so happy in this artist-world that I have asked H.P.B. if this is not heaven. She seemed to look right through me for a few moments, then her calm eyes deepened into a genial smile. "If you and your artist friends find happiness and contentment here," she said, "then you are in the heaven for artists. But remember, little mountain-climber" –that is what she called me– "remember that the farmers find also a heaven for farmers; the red Indians, a Happy-hunting-ground; and the Buddhists, their Nirvana."

This statement, as so many of Mme. Blavatsky's are, seemed to me to be designed to make me think. So I thought it over for awhile and came to the conclusion that perhaps I was getting so enthusiastic with my surroundings and friends that I was in danger of becoming contented enough not to care to look further. I told this to H.P.B., and she answered, "You are thinking and learning. Yes, contentment to remain in one place causes blindness. Life eternal is a ladder. Climb!"

I have met Luther Burbank.* He looked so young and sort of radiant that I could hardly believe it when I was told it was he. He came right over to me, because he understood at once how much I had always admired his work with flowers and fruit. He told me that he was not amazed to find a nature-world over here, that he had fully expected as much. He said that no one could work with the miracles of nature and not come to realize that an after-life of progression existed. Burbank, or Luther, as he asked me to call him (everyone seems to be called by their baptismal or nicknames here) is studying plant-life just the same as ever, but with the heightened sight that death brings with the assistance of spirits here, who have a greater knowledge than he.

Luther Burbank told me how surprised he was to find no insects here. If there are flowers here, I asked him, why are there no insects? He explained that most insects are of a low order in the evolutionary scale of life, and they upon death, immediately reincarnate into similar forms in order to enlarge by much experience their intelligence. Insects, he said, possessing already a high type of intelligence, such as ants and bees, are ready upon their death to reincarnate into a higher form of life. So this is the fascinating working-out of evolution. I understand much better now.

When I expressed my delight over this to Mr. Burbank, he smiled and answered, "Well, you and I are now standing on the threshold of knowledge, on the verge of realization; a vista has been opened up to us of the enormity of life, and we are for the moment overwhelmed by its sublimity."

I asked him if he would care to visit the earth again very much. He said he most decidedly would; that he was interested in his students there and in their continuance of his work, and that as soon as he learned new wonders of life's laws, he intended projecting into the minds of such workers, as would be receptive to his influence the results of his labors. "I will inspire them with my discoveries, and so help the world," he said.

---

*Luther Burbank was a pioneering agricultural scientist (his work includes the Burbank potato, which most potato chips are made of). He died shortly before Rudy, of a heart attack in April 1926. He was 77.

So you see, this is one of the reasons why disembodied souls return to the earth; to help humanity learn more readily the lessons that will most advance it spiritually.

John Burroughs*, too, I have seen. He is also active in studying the nature-world. He is often working near and with Mr. Burbank. They link up quite naturally, I have discovered, with other naturalists who have gone on before – Audubon and others – just as I am linking up with artists. Like attracts like, and in this way life goes on in circles, and every circle, no matter how individual, connects up with others. This is what communicating spirits call the "Chain of Life." They like to express themselves symbolically, H.P.B. says, because symbolism is the true language of the soul, but I am urged by her and others to tell the facts as I learn them as plainly as I can. They say that earth people become confused and often lose the spirit of the communications when too symbolic or technical language is used. Of course, my helpers explain much of these truths to me before I reach you, and then I tell it in my own way, as best I can.

The force is gone now, I will go on with this another time. Good night.

Rudy.

---

*John Burroughs was one of the first conservationists, and was widely known as an all around nature man. His writings were very popular around the time he passed. He died in 1921 at the age of 83.

MESSAGE 9

I HAVE seen Harold Lockwood*. It has made me very happy to have met him, as he has greatly developed spiritually. I am sure he will be a help to me. He always was serious minded in his earth-life. He is naturally interested in helping the people of his profession to find themselves, so to speak, when they arrive over here.

Harold says that all actors are very child-like in nature, and that their naïve way of looking at life makes them unusually susceptible to influences good or bad. Their arrival into the astral plane is a very critical time for them, he says. Being usually given over to worldly pleasures and light-hearted fun, they are apt to fall prey to the temptations and allurements of the lower astral plane.

I admit, myself, Natacha, that I have found it very fascinating to visit and watch this particular phase of astral life. In it, the material illusions of joy are erroneously magnified; out of all proportion.

But so stimulating are these false illusions, empty as shining bubbles, that the participators in them are so tormented by their sharpened appetites, that they rush madly back to earth to gratify themselves through mediumistic people.

This lower astral plane is a glittering, but false paradise, if I may use that expression. A place, more brilliant in its highlights than Broadway's whitest glare; a place more sombre and ghastly in its shadows than the darkest dives of Limehouse.

And the ensnaring part of it is that everything seems so actual and real. From this plane, Harold Lockwood says, come all the stories from spirits about tobacco, food, shops, and all the rest of it, because these spirits cling too closely to the world to get away from those mundane ideas.

The buildings here are not as I have described those of the higher astral plane. You remember I said those were built of thought-force. Well, these in the lower astral are of thought-force too, but of a much coarser quality.

---

*Harold Lockwood was one of the first romantic screen idols, usually paired with May Allison. He died from the Spanish flu in 1918. He was 31.

Olive Thomas

There is nothing inspired or ethereally beautiful about them. They look almost identical with the buildings of the earth-plane, only they are more high-keyed – in some way more subtle – I think I should say.

There are places there like jazz palaces and night clubs. People who loved such places in the earth-life frequent them. It is sad to see so many souls earth-bound to such ideas.

Here, to the illusive happiness of this plane, Harold Lockwood, Wally Reid, and Olive Thomas* took me with them to visit. You must understand, Natacha, that while we cannot ascend into higher vibrations than we have attained to, we can, at will, descend into lower, to visit, commune, or to help.

There was music – jazz - and a great deal of dancing, good and bad. There was no restraint whatever. People did exactly as they chose. Some sang at the top of their voices. Some shrieked madly. Some flung themselves into the most grotesque postures – sort of solo dances, one might call them. Others told all kinds of stories of drinking and of various vices, for the purpose, I was informed, of exciting their desires.

Whenever people reached what appeared to be the height of their wildest frenzy, they trooped off, in great mists of dull red color, brown, and reddish orange, earthward, to gratify through human beings their frantic desires. Having no longer physical bodies of their own, they are forced to use the bodies of others still living upon earth. H.P.B. has told me that earth-people reached and attacked by these earth-bound souls find their own desires and appetites, quite unaccountably to them, literally sweeping them off their feet.

She says their sensations are greatly magnified as they enjoy not only their own but the added sensations of the influencing entities. Now I can understand the realer reason for perverts of all kinds – habitual drunkards, drug addicts and degenerate persons; all of them, weak, evilly controlled people.

Harold said that they would come to see the emptiness of it all sooner or later. There are millions of spirits watching and waiting to help their millions of friends who are earth-bound and deluded.

---

*Olive Thomas was a popular film actress in the 1910s (she would go on to be the first official flapper in 1920). She married Jack Pickford (a friend of Rudy's) and the two had an on and off again styled stormy relationship which may or may not have involved drugs, adultery, and alcohol to an extreme extent. On their second honeymoon, after a wild night of partying, Olive accidentally mistook a bottle of Mercury Bichloride for a bottle of sleeping potion and accidentally poisoned herself. She died in the hospital soon after in 1920 at the age of 25. Mae Murray claimed Olive was with her the night she first met Rudy. Reportedly when asked who he was, Olive replied, "He dances at Maxim's, I think. Damned beautiful isn't he?" Olive was the first modern celebrity to die in a public way similar to Rudy, John Bunny was the first.

Many people here, and probably many of earth, who do not quite understand these truths, have wondered at my rapid progress spiritually since my passing over. They do not take into consideration that here time means absolutely nothing, and that great progression may come to one in a single revealing flash of realization.

Many spirits who wonder at my progress have themselves tried to communicate with their earth friends and were but barely able to reach them, and entirely unable to explain anything of this life to them. These people seem at a loss to account for the fact that I, so recently come among them, can so easily go back to the earth and give the truths as I learn them

They do not know that I am able to do this because in my earth-life I was a natural medium and more than a little developed in my mediumship, and also that I already knew before death considerable about communication with spirits. I am so glad now that I did know these things. Otherwise, Natacha, I could not so soon have reached you, and through you, others.

Harold Lockwood was also very mediumistic in his earth-life, and his knowledge of the beyond has helped him immensely, he says, to a more rapid progression. Then, too, we have both been fortunate to have such enlightened helpers. And it is lucky that I have had so clear a medium to express myself through.

Harold says he has often come through mediums in the earth-plane. He says that Virginia Pearson is a medium, and he often visits her.

I find that Pola (Negri) is a mediumistic if she only knew it. She gets very clear first impressions of people and conditions, but she seldom follows them. I am sure she felt my presence when she viewed my remains, for I went up to her and shook her by the arm and shouted into her ear that I was not dead, and that I was very sorry for her grief. But she could not hear me. Yes, Pola is psychic. That is why she is so temperamental – so impressionistic. I wish she understood.

So many people are psychic, more or less. Nearly everybody. Charlie (Chaplin) is too. He knows it, but would smile if I told him so. He is exceedingly impressionistic and inspirational in his way of working.

Doris Kenyon is another naturally mediumistic person. Not that she actually sees spirits, but she is able to hear them with her inner psychic ear. That is why she is able to receive writings from them. I do not mean that she has not talent of her own for writing; she has; but certain spirits are able to inspire her. Ella Wheeler Wilcox says she goes to her.

But there is one person I know who can hardly be called psychic, and that is Jimmy (Quirk)*.

During the time my body lay on view in New York, I went to his office several times. I always liked Jimmy and I tried to make him realize I was still alive. I touched him. I thumped on his desk. I shouted in his ear. But Jimmy could not seem to hear. He is too surrounded by a wall of the hard-and-fast facts of everyday life to be easily reached psychically. Yet Jimmy's impressions of people are usually right. Somewhere within his complex lingers that psychic spark which, under certain conditions, might be fanned into a flame.

As we left the bright illusion-world, we passed through some gruesome aspects of life. I was glad that I was with my friends. Black forms jostled us, or rushed by muttering fearfully to themselves, some moaning. Many were weeping and crying aloud. To have seen and heard this misery is the worst thing I have ever experienced.

I wanted to put an end to it. I wanted to tell these souls of the lovely higher astral plane where I am living. It seemed so unjust for these souls to be doomed.

Just as my desire to help them surged like a wave through my whole being, a dark form brushed against me and two arms were thrown around me. A voice called, "Rudy, Rudy!" I stared at the form. Its contact with me seemed to cause it to become faintly illuminated. The shock of recognition which followed caused my whole soul to tremble.

It was the spirit of Bobby Harron**!

---

*Quirk was an editor for Photoplay, a popular movie magazine in its day. He had been kind to Valentino in life, remarking that Rudy seemed as happy with his fame as a 'little boy is being kissed by a bunch of fat aunts'. Quirk was also the one who spread the rumor that Rudy was not really in his casket for the viewing, but a wax dummy instead. There has never been any evidence to support that claim.

**Bobby Harron grew up in film, acting as a messenger (and/or prop boy) for the Biograph Company at a young age. At the age of 14, D.W. Griffith decided to try him in front of the camera. Harron would go on to become a popular teenage leading man, usually acting opposite of Dorothy Gish who he was said to have dated for awhile. By 1920 both Dorothy and Griffith had replaced him, causing him to fall into a severe depression. As "Way Down East" (the film Griffith had passed him over in) premiered, Bobby shot himself. He died at the age of 27. A ridiculous story was made to cover up his death, claiming the gun had been in his pocket due to a good deed and accidentally discharged. His medical records and death certificate irrefutably dispute that version.

Bobby clung to me as if never to let go again. He seemed frightened and panic-stricken. He gasped like one who had been suffocating. "Give me light! Give me light!!" he kept exclaiming, just as a person on earth would cry out for air.

I did not know what to do. Harold, Wally, and Olive Thomas gathered around him. "You are safe now," said Harold. "We have been looking for you. You have asked for light and now we can give it to you."

It was some time before Bobby could calm his excitement. "I went too soon. I went too soon!" he repeated over and over again, speaking of his sudden death.

This touched me so I could not refrain from weeping. But my emotion was that of joy. I was so pleased to have had a share in the rescue. This is the first time that such an occurrence has come my way.

When Bobby grew quiet, he told us that ever since his too sudden passing out, he had been in, what seemed to him, constant darkness. "But now you will be with us in the light," Harold Lockwood assured him.

Olive Thomas told me that she had had almost the same experience. "No one," she said, "who has not gone through it can begin to realize the awfulness of it."

There are many spirits who do nothing else but rescue these earth-bound people. It is their chosen work. I thought I would like to do it, but I have not been over here long enough for that sort of thing yet, Harold tells me.

During the great storms that swept over Florida and over the sea, I saw many rescuers working with the souls of people who had perished and who did not understand the new conditions of the life before them. People who come over so suddenly from these catastrophes or accidents often do not believe they have left their bodies and the world. They feel that something terrible has happened, but they cannot tell just what.

During these great storms I heard strange sounds in the ether, or atmosphere, or whatever you call it. If you heard them in the earth-world you would probably think they were great bells toiling. I asked Henry Watts, a guide of the medium's, what those sounds were. He said they were astral signals, announcing the coming over of souls from some big earth disaster.

The force is gone. I can't speak any longer. Good night, I will come again soon.

Rudy

MESSAGE 10

I WANT to talk to you, Natacha, about my acting. I have learned more about it since coming here than I ever knew before. I can now look back with a new understanding upon certain incidents that used to perplex me.

This understanding comes from talks which I have had with Charles Frohman* and Clyde Fitch**. These men know the psychic truths about acting and writing. Both men are still vitally interested in the theatre and in writing for it. They are also interested in inspiring earth-people to write for it. Their knowledge of the subject has helped me greatly.

Mr. Fitch says that the characters in a novel or play become, as the writer's mind evolves them, real, living entities! The writer, according to the degree of his powers of visualization, holds the form of his characters so concentratedly in mind, that a real mental body for them is formed. Into this mental body the force of his creative faculties pours the emotional qualities necessary to endow it with an individuality. In this way a distinct personality is built up.

The building up of this body-form, held so strongly in the writer's mind, begins to attract to itself astral substances, and it also absorbs from the writer himself ectoplasm and auric emanations. This is all rather hard for me to say, but H.P.B. is helping me and I hope I am giving it to you in an understandable way.

In this way an astral envelope is gradually formed. The writer's thought-entity enters it, and finally the creation detaches itself from his brain, and goes on living an independent, though limited existence.

---

*Charles Frohman was an extremely successful theatrical producer and talent scout. By the time of his death he had produced more than 700 shows. He died in the sinking of the RMS Lusitania in May 1915 (an act that brought the US into World War One). He was 59.
**Clyde Fitch was a playwright who wrote over 60 plays, including Beau Brummel. He was a friend of one of Natacha's step-aunts, Elsie de Wolfe. He took ill with appendicitis and refusing surgery, eventually died of blood poisoning in 1909. He was 44.

So you can see, Natacha, that these character creations of an author are in all truth his brainchildren, who have been conceived, gestated, and born. That is a true creation, H.P.B. says, and she told me that this is the way the Power called God creates offspring; through thought.

Clyde Fitch went on to explain to me how very often writers dreaded getting at the job of producing characterizations. And now I see this to be the reason for it; they dread the labor and birth of their astrally materialized creations.

H.P.B. explained that these mind creations are limited in the scope of their activities to the degree of development to which the writer has brought them. They possess souls, inasmuch as they have within them a spark thrown off from the soul-fire of their author, who himself is but a much more highly developed spark thrown off from the fire of God. These thought-entities are entirely without previous experience, being able to express only the part laid out for them in the story by the writer, and what independent thought-action they may possess is also constricted to that circle.

When such a thought-character becomes known to the reading world, talked about, thought over, hated or loved, it may continue to exist as an independent entity for years; for as long as human interest may feed it, and thus keep it alive. But when thought-characters are unimportant and unaccepted or soon forgotten by the world, their existence is a short one. They fade out, as it were, and are dematerialized and reabsorbed into the great plane of ideas.

H.P.B. says the stronger among these thought-entities sometimes manifest in a séance, when people who might attract them are present, and they are even able to speak through the medium. They can readily be detected, however, as they usually appear with an artificial ring to their vague utterances. Often they express themselves in a line or two of dramatic intensity borrowed from the story-world to which they belong.

Clairvoyant eyes can sometimes see them. On account of this, they may sometimes be confused with real spirits. They usually look to be smaller or else much larger than genuine spirits. They become enlarged in form and power by the public thought-force of many years being focused upon them.

Now I will show you how this curious race of thought-beings (for there is a whole race of them) connects with my acting. I say "my" acting, because I take myself as an example, knowing my own experience better than that of others.

Whenever I used to read over a script that interested me, I began to concentrate my whole attention upon the character I was to portray. The first reading or two never seemed to do more than awaken within me a responsive interest in the role. The reading of the part was only like getting a more or less hazy outline of the possibilities the characterization afforded.

But it was when I was away from the script, when I was by myself, sometimes during the day, more often at night, that the stranger side of acting presented itself to me. Once I had read the part I was to play I could think of nothing else. What I then took to be a mental vision of how the character should look (but what I now know to have been a clairvoyant view, through my mediumistic powers, of the thought-entity created by the writer of the story) haunted me day and night. I could not free myself from it, nor did I want to for the sake of the work, even though I was then ignorant of the true conditions of the matter.

Clyde Fitch says that actors who are only slightly mediumistic easily throw off the influence of the thought-entity when they are not actually working the part. But you see, I was a real medium by nature, and instead of being able to shake off the control of the entity, I fell more and more under its compelling spell as my interest in it grew.

Clinging tenaciously to my super-sensitive responsiveness, the thought-entity quickly merged itself into my very being, where for the time it became life of my life and dominated entirely my actions. It was my gift of impressionable negativeness being controlled by the living, acting, character-entity as it worked out its life-mission it its little world of the story.

For the duration of the entity's control, my own individuality slumbered. I know that often it surprised you to find me carrying out the details of a characterization when away from the studio, in the quietness of our home life. But that curious faculty – gift – of mediumship was what made me as good an actor as I was.

Another psychic phase of acting is this. Sometimes certain spirits go to a writer and project the picture of themselves into his brain, so that he works them almost subconsciously into his story. Mr. Fitch says this only happens when the play or novel is important enough to cause the spirits to feel it really worth while to reach earth-humanity in this way. These writings are those with some great message to the world.

Charles Frohman says that all writers are mediums; that is, all writers who give any kind of a message in their work. Their concentration makes them a centre of magnetic force which facilities spirits to project any help they may have to offer the writer of the world.

Actors are often inspired while playing by the very spirit who impressed the part upon the writer. When the actor is really mediumistic, as all great actors are whether they know it or not, the spirit may actually play the part through him.

Sarah Bernhardt* has told me that this was often the case with her, and that she knew it. Duse**, too, says she was very sensitive to such influences, and that that was the reason for her ability to play tremendous roles when she wandered about Italy as a mere child.

Life, Natacha, holds many truths that seem like wonders until we come to understand them. Then they appear to be what they really are, perfectly naturally occurrences.

Charlie Frohman says this element of mediumship in me would have developed as time went on into a much keener sense of receptivity, until I should have become such a responsive instrument to these impelling entities that I should have been able to portray with ease really great roles. But that happiness, for some good reason, never fear, has been denied to me in this last earth-incarnation. Another time perhaps.

Here, with enlightened knowledge, with understanding of the true facts, and with such intelligent helpers and advisors around me, I know I shall be able to forge ahead with the beautiful art which means more to me than life itself, somehow. Oh, I am so glad that does not rob us of the power to go on and on. How dreadful it would be to really have to lie cold and lifeless in a grave, until some far-off judgment day summoned us to life again. By that time, I am sure, I should have forgotten all I ever knew about acting!

Now, in the midst of this glory of onliving, in this heaven of work-continuance, I see how those teachings of my childhood were utterly preposterous.

Oh, Natacha! Think of it – life – sweet, loving, helpful and friendly, progressive and continuing on for ever – it is not magnificent? Is it not God? To me it is like the greatest burst of melody one could imagine.

Cara mia, the force is waning. I must let go of the medium and slip away. I will come again soon. *Buona notte.*

Rudy.

---

*Sarah Bernhardt was one of the most famous stage actresses of her day. She eventually tried her hand at film, though her style of acting did not take. She died of complications from kidney disease at the age of 78 in 1923.
**Eleonora Duse was an Italian stage (and occasional film) actress who rivaled Bernhardt in greatness. She died at the age of 65 in 1924 from pneumonia.

MESSAGE 11

IT may surprise you to know that I have met Curley over here. You remember, he was the animal trainer. I was very glad to see him, and he certainly seemed pleased at meeting me.

A curious thing about Curley is that I cannot look at him without seeing his aura. There is a lot of red in it, and orange. I do not see everyone's aura, but Curely's is so vibrant that it becomes outstanding. When I spoke to him about it he did not seem to understand. He said that if there were colors around him he did not know it, and so far as he knew, no one else had ever seen them before.

Of course, we talked about animals. Curley knows more about them now than he ever did in his earth-life, as his vision is not so limited in this plane. He is not in the higher astral plane, but he is not earth-bound.

Curley feels if he had only known more about psychic influence before he died, he would have had much better results with animals. He has been shown by his "helpers" that it was detrimental to his own development to have to resort at times to harsh methods.

But this did not really hold Curley back, because in his heart he was not unkind. He always had tried kindness until he saw that an animal was too vicious to respond. I asked him if he thought it was a wise thing to try and train wild animals. According to his "helpers" it is not, unless kind methods only can be employed.

Curley is now studying animals from a psychic viewpoint, which shows them up in an altogether different light. He finds them far more open to astral influences than is man. Truly psychic people often tap planes beyond the astral, and so pass it by.

But animals and also primitive people are close to the currents of the earth and of the lower astral plane. Curley has learned that the earth is filled with magnetism, and the atmosphere with electricity. He notices that animals respond to these forces more readily than most human beings.

He divides the animal world (leaving man out of it as a distinctly different type of being, although using an animal-like body) into these divisions; reptiles (including fish and insects), mammals and fowl.

The reptiles, according to Curley, draw their motive power from the magnetism to the earth when it is warmed by the friction of the rays of the sun. That is why they are either legless or else have but very short legs. Nature requires them to lie flat against the earth a large part of the time, in order to absorb and sustain currents. Food is taken much less frequently by reptiles than by mammals, because it only provides sustenance for their bodily growth; they do not depend on it for motive power. Snakes, especially, are often more active after a long fast.

In winter, when the magnetic forces are less active and the electric currents more powerful, reptiles become unable to absorb enough earth-magnetism to remain active, and so lie dormant until the forces are renewed. Psychically, winter seems to be a sort of recharging time.

Not only reptiles, but also some of the animals – for instance, bears and woodchucks – go into this trance-like winter sleep. Curley finds such animals as do so to be almost non-meat-eating. Creatures that hibernate crawl into caves or holes, deep in the earth as possible, where what magnetism they are able to contact keeps them charged with the vital currents of life.

This is all most interesting to me. Curley does not tell it to me in technical terms, and I would not understand it if he did. So I am telling it to you in the same simple way, trusting I am making it understandable to all.

Curley says insects and lizards draw their magnetism from plants and trees, which are always highly charged. He says that is why wet trees are so often struck by lightening. He thinks from what he has learned in the astral plane that many insects are much more highly evolved than reptiles and many mammals.

I asked John Burroughs about this too. He is a dear friend of the medium's mother, and it was she who first brought me into contact with him. Mr. Burroughs laughed and said that the trouble with science was that under it everything was too strictly classified; too mechanically, too materialistically labeled. It all comes down to a matter of viewpoint, he explained. A scientist either looks at things through materialistic eyes or through psychic eyes.

If he uses the former method, he accounts for only what actually appears to lie before him. He forgets, too, that before the invention of the microscope he neither saw nor believed many of the things that he does now. Men do not like to believe what they do not see until some instrument is invented to make what was invisible, visible. He forgets also, with all his eyes and microscopes do see, the main thing still remains unseen – the very force binding the atoms of the specimen together; the vitality which animates it – the life-current. The most important thing of all ; the power which has produced whatever visible, tangible, material proofs his physical eyes may see, that power itself remains unrevealed to material eyes.

Greater than must be the unseen than the seen.

With material eyes we view the effect, but the cause is only perceived psychically. So the materialist is baulked at the very beginning, but he is usually too pig-headed to admit it.

When the scientist has learned the psychic truth of these matters, he realizes that true classification depends upon the degree of development to which the specimens have attained. For instance, some insects are more intelligent than many men. Ants, bees, wasps – are they not more intelligent in their group work, in their industry, than many men from the lower walks of humanity en masse?

Among animals, how many there are, especially dogs, whose loving loyalty, faithfulness and courage have gone far beyond those qualities in certain human beings. What number of horses there have been whose fine intelligence has saved many a human life, when conditions prevented that human intelligence from seeing its way.

And to think there are people so callow, so stupid, as to say these creatures have no souls. They have souls. Death has taught me, Natacha, that everything created by God – all things, animate or seemingly inanimate – are possessed of souls. But they are all in different stages of evolution.

It is, of course, a great deal of joy to me to learn that animals live on. John Burroughs explained that intelligent animals and birds often remain in the astral plane for considerable time before reincarnating. Some teachers claim, he said, that animal life at the change called death merges back into what is called the animal group-soul. But Mr. Burroughs says that is only true of unevolved animal life.

Animals, absorbing through close association with man more or less of his intelligence, step out from the mass of animal life and become individualized. These, at death, are not absorbed into the animal group-soul, but go on independently, progressing through many incarnations, up the gradual scale of life.

Such animals, with their beginning of soul development, often have keen sight of things in the astral. Dogs, cats, parrots, horses and elephants often clairvoyantly see spirits. And spirits often able to influence animals accomplish seeming miracles. What power is it that guides a horse ride through the blinding terror of a blizzard? It is the guiding hand of the rider's guardian spirit leading the psychic horse onward to safety.

Why do dogs so often howl before the death of some member of a family? Is it just coincidence? No. It is because the dog's psychic faculties sense the subtle change that is commencing in the physical organism of the person who nears the hour of change; and that change, the mysterious loosening of spirit from body, gives off a peculiar vibration which startles and alarms the dog.

Henry Watts says this death-vibration may be seen as a color; a mauve-grey. It may also be heard as a sound; a continuous, low, sighing whistle. And it may be smelled as an uncannily permeating odor.

There are so many things to learn about life. I am only touching on the verge of them. This is all I have learned about animals so far, but as time goes on and I learn more, I hope to be able to come back and share my knowledge with you, Natacha, and with others.

Now let me tell you about "Sheik." One of the first things I saw after I had passed over was this dear old police dog. You know how much he loved me and how he always pined for me whenever I left him.

You also know how I did leave him and how, on account of home-sickness for me, the poor fellow died. I am truly so sorry for that. I know it was very wrong of me, leaving poor "Sheik" to pine away, when with a little extra trouble I might have taken him with me. I have certainly found out here, where so many belated lessons are learned, how wrong it was. I have also found out that there are unwritten laws governing every one of our actions, good or bad.

I was feeling pretty lonely, and not yet used to my new surroundings, when as if to bid me welcome, I saw the quizzical eyes, the pointed ears and the wagging tail of "Sheik." I was overjoyed. He seemed a friend in need. But just as I rushed up to put my arms around him, he disappeared, and I was left alone. I felt as if I had been struck. Then it dawned upon me that perhaps this was the way poor "Sheik" had felt when I left him behind.

I felt a touch on my arm. Turning round I saw H.P.B. standing beside me. Her eyes seemed to burn right through me.

"What does it mean?" I asked her.

H.P.B. replied something like this – "One of Life's lessons, my boy. You neglected that dog and he died for love of you. Because of this you will not be able to have him with you again until you have earned the right. It is the law of karma."

I felt awfully ashamed. But I hope soon to be able to have him again. One consolation is that I know Curley is keeping "Sheik" for me.

I thought you might be glad to know this about "Sheik." Remember, Natacha, if we attach animals to ourselves, we owe a responsibility to them. We are their guardian spirits.

The force is weakening. I must go. Good night, Natacha, good night.

Rudy.

PART III:
REDISCOVERING

The Legacy of Rudolph Valentino

Every year since his death on August 23rd 1926, albeit 3 hours late, a random assortment of psychics, quacks, the self indulgent, fans, admirers, and the curious gather at the Hollywood Forever Cemetery in Hollywood, CA to mark the anniversary of the death of the great silent film idol Rudolph Valentino.

Dying unexpectedly at the height of his fame, Valentino has lived on in a sort of infamy much like James Dean, Marilyn Monroe, and Elvis. Many people these days have never seen a silent film, and many do not even know his face. But they definitely know his name.

Ever since Valentino's untimely death, his life and his work has long been overshadowed by his demise. The fascination of his death does not stop at mourning someone lost at the age of 31, however. For years after his demise, women would come to his crypt, claiming to be pregnant with his child. George Ullman, his manager, wrote that no less than 32 women put forth such claims in the two years following Rudy's death. The cemetery groundskeeper found these stories so odd and overwhelming he wrote a book about it.

Not content with Immaculate Conception, any number of people, some of whom were in need of mental health care, have claimed Valentino's ghost has either visited them or spoke to them. Numerous women report him haunting random places he might have visited or lived in during his lifetime, usually in bed. One particularly interesting case had a woman claiming Valentino told her what groceries to buy.

Flamboyant gossip monger Kenneth Anger became obsessed with Valentino, spreading numerous pieces of slander in his trashy "Hollywood Babylon". By his own admittance, one of Anger's favorite hangouts was Valentino's mausoleum, particularly when he was young. To this day, Hollywood Forever Cemetery can promote any event simply by mentioning Valentino is buried there. In an interesting sort of way, they project films every summer on the mausoleum where he is interred (an event people from outside of Los Angeles don't seem to understand, though Angelinos absolutely adore it). People, however, do not realize that he is on the other side of the building.

217

The cemetery eagerly sells maps for an exuberant price… admittedly it'd be hard to find your way around without one. A visit to Rudy's crypt usually reveals all sorts of flowers and lipstick prints on his headstone. Once, while laying flowers for another star, I heard the father of a family in full tourist regalia ask his children excitedly, "Should we go see Valentino next?" as if it was similar to riding Space Mountain at Disney World. While I'm not for a full on Lady in Black affair, I do find it sad people find him a curiosity, not a human…not even an actor.

After Valentino's death, a Memorial Guild was created in his name. Originally meant to provide charity to children's hospitals, somewhere along the line it was commandeered for another purpose. Self proclaimed medium, Leslie Flynt, became president of the guild. While amassing a huge collection of Valentino memorabilia, he also claimed to speak to Valentino from the dead, recording hours of long séances supposedly with his spirit. When Flynt died in the 1990s, the Guild died with him. Possibly the only good thing they ever did was save the small fragments of The Young Rajah, a mostly lost film.

It seems as the years passed, Valentino the man faded and Valentino the legendary spirit took over. People drawn to the occult and the afterlife were obsessed with him.

While there is nothing wrong with such beliefs in and of themselves, what particularly bothers me about The Valentino Memorial Service and those associated with it (and other such goings ons and claims) is their constant focus on only THEIR viewpoint of things. Never once in 80 years have they celebrated his life. In fact current kookies affiliated with these goings on, once asked me, "What's wrong with celebrating his death?"

What's wrong with it is all spiritual beliefs and good taste aside, it's just obnoxious (for more on Spiritual thoughts and ramifications including Natacha's own please see page 147). Rudolph Valentino was arguably one of the greatest actors of all time, and we are very lucky to have a solid body of his work available to view.

In addition, these types like to try and mold Valentino to some sort of perverse vision of their own, usually presented as 'factual' and/or 'sensational' when indeed it is nothing more than a fantasy. In the mildly annoying camp are those trying to turn him into some Great Lover type, as if he were really the Sheik when off screen. According to these types, he slept with every woman ever, and now haunts every woman's bedroom he can find.

On the other, more harmful side, are those who wish to claim him as homosexual or bisexual, despite the fact that no such factual evidence (or anecdotal even) exists. During Rudy's lifetime no such assertions were made (certain yellow journalists would call his costuming effeminate, as at the time a man wearing baggy pants or a wristwatch was seen as feminine. But no one ever questioned his relationship with Natacha or Pola). In fact most people now just believe these rumors have 'always been' when in fact they were started by such damaging self proclaimed important people.

In the 1960s a slew of trashy and sensationalist books were released, touted as 'biographies'. To make matters worse, this was the era of "Hollywood Babylon" which would infamously slander Rudy's name and legacy to this very day (not one word in that book is true about anyone. Literally not a word.)

This was the decade that the final silent film stars were dying off, leaving their loved ones to deal with such hateful fodder. Clara Bow's sons wished to sue Anger, but were unsure what recourse they had. Valentino's brother Alberto was still alive and living in the States. He successfully sued the 1950s movie, as did Alice Terry. The Valentino family also tried to sue the trashy 1970s movie, but lost as the Judge felt they didn't have a right to recourse. Natacha and Nita Naldi lived until the mid 60s, but both were in very poor health for the final decade of their life and likely were unable to be in a position to speak out. Nita was an alcoholic, and Natacha was so ill she suffered from dementia at times.

Worst of all, not only have these kookies come to represent the world of Rudolph Valentino, but the things they have made up have infiltrated every film site and book one can imagine. Wikipedia and IMDB were rife with such inaccuracies until the Rudolph Valentino Society cleaned them (and that was quite a battle). Many websites and books take Hollywood Babylon, or Dream of Desire by the Anger wannabe David Bret, as fact. Even when they debunk one thing (such as the dildo) they spread another (such as Natacha being a lesbian). Worst yet, some such sites and books have taken Leslie Flynt and other 'mediums' 'séances' with 'Rudy' and cited them as real words Valentino once spoke, assumedly when he was alive.

It has gotten so bad that even the best biographers or sites must resort to saying 'well at the most we can say he was straight, but maybe bisexual'. It's like a terrible compromise, with the kookies gaining a small foothold. Both Dark Lover and The Valentino Mystique take such a road. Both books are wonderfully researched and spend several pages proving with facts and sources how Rudy was straight. Then, as if to not offend anyone, they throw in a 'maybe' directly after. Frankly, it's ridiculous. And surely the proud Italian man would not be pleased.

Valentino had many gay friends and co-workers. His circle was made up of the most liberal and flamboyant characters in Hollywood history, but that doesn't mean he partook himself. In fact, ironically, most of those around him were women such as Alla Nazimova. He did have some supposedly gay friends, though who was exactly what is hotly disputed and since I have yet to see anyone give solid proof any of those men were whichever way I'm not going to speculate here. It's gotten so ridiculous womanizer types like Norman Kerry are constantly painted as gay…despite the fact he ran with the Jack Pickford/Mickey Neilan crowd.

Valentino was a firm believer that people should be treated equally and fairly, infamously speaking out about the terrible portrayal of Arabic people in the first Sheik (he would go on to fix this with Son of the Sheik, though it's still a fantasy film above everything else). It is not my wish to be homophobic or deny history. There were some legitimately gay and bisexual stars in the silent era such as dear Ramon Novarro, Joan Crawford, and Alla Nazimova. But not EVERYONE in Hollywood was gay or a hedonist. If such scandal mongers were to be believed, the 20s was a time one could see Lillian Gish shooting up coke before making out with Dorothy (yes Kenneth Anger alluded to an incestuous relationship in the opening of Hollywood Babylon. Obviously no, it's not true.) People like Kenneth Anger, Neil Botham, Darwin Porter, and David Bret just write out their twisted fantasies, claim they have hidden evidence, and present it as fact. Such people are mentally ill.

I can not even begin to fathom why this has become acceptable to biographers, historians, fans, and the like to throw in a 'well maybe supposedly' on nothing more than a guess or an antiquated piece of obviously debunkable…bunk. If this crowd were to be believed, every person before 1980 was somehow homosexual. Imagine the uproar if one were to claim Ramon Novarro 'might have been straight' or that Rock Hudson was married to a woman so he too must have been straight…

If no other author will say it then I will: Valentino was straight. 100% bonafide straight with no maybes as far as facts or evidence can tell us. Same for Natacha (who is a little more complex, but the research is still secure enough that I will declare that.) Anything else is pure speculation and/or fantasy on behalf of people wanting to hock books or promote their own agendas/wishes.

As for my other complaint, that of the Memorial Service, I can say it is my wish that in my lifetime it be done away with. I think that will come to pass. Rudy will absolutely never be forgotten, but I do believe that even with all the morbid in the world, people would rather remember him for his films and his wonderful life than hocking cheap books in front of his crypt every year. Someone once said to me, "Well at least they kept his name going all these years." I replied I'd rather they had not. I think Rudy's legend would have lived on without them. And if he had indeed fallen into obscurity, at least he would be waiting there without slander and kookies attached to his name. Frankly I think had they never existed, he would have ended up more like Chaplin than Pickford. Not because of a dispute over fame or infamy; but because he was an icon who was the first to pass in such a modern era. I cite this belief with Olive Thomas, who has long been forgotten, though there has been much renewed interest in her these past few years. She too was taken down by the scandal monster that is Kenneth Anger (no she didn't kill herself, and no she didn't die alone draped in a velvet curtain.)

This book was originally written, I do believe, to show Rudy's life. Natacha wrote all these stories that had no particular gossip value. She glossed over the breakdown of their marriage, and still did not give anything particularly juicy in her rant against Hollywood. Instead she included stories about Rudy the man, the sweet little boy who had too many animals and destroyed various machines while dreaming of the castles and expensive cameras he would own.

I hope fans old and new alike will read this book, and come away with an appreciation of Rudy the man and the actor. I hope that for once we can remember his life and his art, not his death and what words mentally ill self proclaimed psychics have put in his mouth.

Hala Pickford
The Founding Sheba of
The Rudolph Valentino Society

221

NATACHA RAMBOVA
BIOGRAPHY AND FILMOGRAPHY

For more information on Natacha Rambova
please see rudolphvalentino.org/ natacha.html

Natacha Rambova never gets the fair shake. Most people don't want to take the time to see why they should or shouldn't like her, and most just assume many things about her. At the very least, she was a fascinating woman who was the love of Rudolph Valentino's life. An amazingly talented designer, she designed some of the most revered sets and costumes in silent film history. Later in life she took up the study of Egyptology, something she had loved since her teenage years. She never spoke about Valentino after the 1920s and passed quietly in 1966. Sadly today she has been relegated to a footnote in a factually lacking history.

Rambova was born Winifred Shaughnessy in Salt Lake City, Utah. [1] Once on a stop during the Minervala Dance tour, the local paper billed her as 'the pigtailed Shaughnessy girl'. She locked herself in her hotel room crying and refused to come out all night. [2] Her father, Michael Shaughnessy, was an Irish Catholic who fought for the Union during the Civil War. Her mother Winifred Kimball, nicknamed 'Muzzie', was a descendant of Mormon Patriarch Heber C. Kimball. [3]

Her father was a businessman who partook in mining interests, but eventually his alcohol and gambling problems became too much for her mother. Muzzie became an interior designer, and moved her daughter to San Francisco. Muzzie married four times (Michael was her second husband), eventually settling on millionaire perfume mogul, Richard Hudnut.

In the 1920s Hudnut was as well known as Max Factor or Chanel. The company still exists today. Rambova was adopted by her stepfather, making her legal name 'Winifred Hudnut'.

Rambova (and later Rudolph Valentino as well) was extremely close to her Aunt, Teresa Werner. Before her marriage to Hudnut, Rambova's mother married Edgar De Wolfe, brother of Elsie De Wolfe, a prominent Interior Designer. With this marriage, her mother became socially successful and wealthy, but tensions grew between her and her daughter. Rambova was rebellious, and mocked her stepfather for being passive. She was sent home from boarding school for 'conduct unbecoming of a lady'. [4] To straighten her daughter out, Muzzie sent Rambova to a strict British boarding school recommended by her Step Aunt. At the boarding school Rambova learned ballet, French, drawing, and studied mythology. [5]

Rambova continued to be rebellious, labeling her step family 'social climbers', calling her boarding school 'pretentious', and continually clashed with her mother and Step Aunt. [6] Rambova withdrew from her schoolmates and kept to herself pursuing her passions. Her Step Aunt loathed art deco, possibly drawing Rambova towards it.

Rambova was gifted at ballet, and trained with Rosita Meuri at the Paris Opera during the summers. [7] She traveled to London frequently to watch other performers; including Pavlova, Nijinsky, and Theodore Kosloff.

Right before World War One broke out, Rambova returned to San Francisco where she clashed with her mother once again, insisting she would pursue ballet as a career. Her family had trained her in ballet as a 'social grace' and were appalled at the thought of it becoming a career.

Aunt Teresa intervened, offering to move with Rambova to New York, where she could study under Kosloff. Rambova, now 17, officially changed her name to 'Natacha Rambova' at this time. At 5'8 she was too tall to be a classical ballerina, but Kosloff continually gave her leading parts. [8] She performed with him in his "Imperial Russian Ballet Company". Around this time Rambova fell for the 32 year old Kosloff (who had a wife and an invalid daughter in Europe) and the pair began a tumultuous love affair. [9] Muzzie was outraged when she found out, and brought charges of statutory rape and kidnapping against Kosloff hoping to have him deported. Rebelling, Rambova fled New York, hiding from her mother in Canada and later England. While in England, she posed as a Governess to Kosloff's wife and child. Muzzie, wanting to bring her daughter home, relented by dropping the charges. She allowed Rambova to keep performing with the company and promised to underwrite the costumes.

Rambova returned and began touring with the Kosloff Company. In addition to dancing she began designing costumes as well. [10] After the tour ended, Kosloff was hired by Cecil B. DeMille to act as well as contribute designs to his films. Rambova joined him, and was dismayed to find herself as part of Kosloff's 'arty harem'. Kosloff had taken several lovers amongst the dancers, who would perform with his company, teach at his studio, and assist him

224

uncredited in his film work. [11] Rambova took to researching historical accuracy for her designs, which Kosloff would then use without giving her credit, stealing her sketches and claiming them as his own. [12]

Through his film work, Kosloff met fellow Russian, Alla Nazimova, and convinced her to use his services for an upcoming film based on "Aphrodite". Nazimova was an eccentric powerhouse actress, one of the most renowned during the 1910s. [13] Usually considered a lesbian (she did occasionally have relationships with men[14]) she would play an interesting role with both of Valentino's wives. However it is likely her role with Rambova was platonic, unlike her role with his first wife, Jean Acker. Acker had been dating both Nazimova and actress Grace Darmond when she met and agreed to marry the unknown Valentino. Valentino apparently didn't know Acker's history. [15] Natacha was not a lesbian, and was noted as saying she despised lesbians, despite having many for friends and co-workers. [16]

Kosloff sent Rambova to show sketches to Nazimova, claiming they were his own when they were actually Rambova's. Nazimova was impressed and when she asked for revisions to some costumes, Rambova took out a pencil and began to make the revisions herself, thus showing she had done the work. Nazimova was surprised, and offered Rambova a position on her production staff as an art director and costume designer. The work would pay up to $5,000 a picture. [17]

Rambova's work had been used in four DeMille films, including, "Why Change your Wife?" which featured Gloria Swanson and Thomas Meighan, before her signing with Nazimova. Metro feared censors reactions, and thus shelved the "Aphrodite" idea. Her first film for Nazimova was "Billions" in 1920. She met Rudolph Valentino, her future husband, on the set of "Uncharted Seas" in 1921. [18] They began working together on "Camille" soon after. From the start she used Valentino as her canvas, insisting the greased back hair look would not do for a character new to the city as his Armand was.

Her work on Camille is generally cited as some her best, stealing the picture. [19] Rambova used symbolism (Marguerite's dress is draped in Camellias) and many of the sets are based on German Expressionism which had not quite reached the US yet. Hans Poelzig and Emil-Jaques Ruhlmann were her inspiration for various sets on the film. Rambova was determined to bring the art deco look to America, as it was transforming filmmaking in Europe. Though

The infamous Faun Photo

Rambova receives praise today, the film flopped, with many contemporary critics finding it too odd. The failure of "Camille" eventually forced Metro to terminate their contract with Nazimova.

In addition to her design work, Rambova took on teaching design and selling some of her jewels to help make ends meet. She earned more than Valentino, who had notoriously bad contract deals. [20] Her next film with Nazimova was, "A Doll's House".

By 1922 Rambova had left Metro to join Nazimova on her independent artistic productions. By this point Valentino had negotiated a slightly better contract and was now earning more than Rambova. Rambova's designs for "Salome" were seen as extremely daring and risqué. [21] She based them off drawings by Aubrey Beardsley for Oscar Wilde's version. In addition to costume design Rambova contributed to the film's scenario under the alias "Peter M. Winters". [22] The film cost $350,000 to make and flopped at the box office. It was one of Nazimova's last releases. [23] It was also the last film Nazimova and Rambova would work on together.

Valentino signed with Famous Players-Lasky in 1921, a move Rambova was shocked and horrified to learn of (Valentino only informed her after the fact). [24] Rambova felt that the contract was for possibly thousands less than Valentino was worth, and that it would hamper his ability to make artistic films. Before their marriage, a public controversy erupted over pictures Rambova had taken of Valentino (wearing only black paint and a small piece of cloth) as a Faun or Pan like God. They claimed the pictures had been taken by Rambova as part of a series of faun pictures for a magazine called 'Shadowland' that featured art and dancer photos. Paul Ivano recalled the photos had been taken more as a loving gesture on a trip in San Francisco, however Rambova could not keep them to herself and they eventually found their way to the press. [25] The pictures were damaging to Valentino's image, and were also seen as evidence that he was carrying on with Rambova during his divorce from Acker (which indeed he was). He and Acker had separated long before he met Natacha but a divorce had not been sought until that point. With Valentino now a star making good money, Acker seemed more insistent about their relationship. [26]

Soon after the faun controversy, Valentino began work on "Blood and Sand". Rambova had begun to exert small amounts of control during the filming by mediating disputes between Valentino and the director, as well as encouraging Valentino to request filming on location in Spain. [27] That request was denied, with a promise to shoot Valentino's next Spanish themed movie, "The Spanish Cavalier" in Spain.

The pair had moved in together less than a year after meeting, but had to separate (or at least pretended to) as the divorce proceedings began. The divorce was final shortly after the filming of Blood and Sand had wrapped. The pair married soon after on May 13th, 1922 in Mexicali, Mexico. [28] However the law at the time required a year to pass before remarriage and Valentino was jailed as a bigamist. [29] Valentino's studio refused to post bail, possibly trying to teach him a lesson. June Mathis, George Melford, and Thomas Meighan eventually were able to raise enough money to post bail.[30] Rambova had been sent to New York by the studio before Valentino's jailing, and was informed at a stop in Chicago. She reportedly broke down in tears. Throughout the bigamy scandal she refused to speak to the press. [31] The pair had to wait a year to remarry (less risking Valentino being jailed again), and were forced to live in separate apartments with roommates. They legally remarried during a stop on the Minervala tour in Indiana on March 14th, 1923. [32]

As the bigamy scandal raged on, Rambova began work on costumes for Valentino's next picture, "The Young Rajah". The film contained Indian themes and Rambova's costumes were glittery and elaborate representations of such. They were based off Leon Bakst's designs of Nijinsky's role as a Golden Slave in Scheherazade. [33] Rambova likely made the sketches before she was forced to leave California and separate from Valentino. Valentino complained his separation from her distracted his acting, causing a subpar performance. He also complained to Rambova that everything from the sets to the cast was cheap. The film flopped and was one of the first major flops of Valentino's leading man career. [34]

Outraged over the bigamy trial and the way his wife had been treated (at least in his eyes), Valentino declared a one man strike against his studio with Rambova's support. [35] Valentino claimed in addition to those complaints that he wasn't making what he was worth, and that artistic control over his films lay at the heart of the matter. [36] Famous Players sued and won an injunction barring Valentino from seeking any form of employment. This was later reduced to employment in pictures. [37] Rambova stated she was not worried, and could keep them afloat with her designs. She also mentioned offers of being an actress herself, though she had yet to appear as anything more than an extra in film. [38]

Eventually Valentino hired a new manager, George Ullman. At first Rambova worked well with him, but the two eventually clashed in a battle for superiority. [39] Ullman presented the idea of having Valentino promote Mineralava Beauty Products. He then suggested Valentino and Rambova partake in a dance tour to help the promotion and keep Valentino's name in the spotlight. The pair agreed and the tour was a major success. Rambova was credited under her legal name 'Winifred Hudnut'.

Once the tour wrapped the pair were legally remarried and the press praised Rambova for her "business sense", the very thing not a year later she'd be criticized for. [40] By 1924 Rambova had negotiated a contract with J.D. Williams for Valentino to sign with Ritz Carlton Pictures. [41] The deal would require two films to fulfill his obligations to Famous Players, and then four films that he and Rambova could make as they pleased at Ritz Carlton. Rambova would be seen as his artistic collaborator for the first time. [42] By the time "Monsieur Beaucaire" was released the press began to blame Rambova for all his missteps, claiming she was controlling him and power hungry. [43] Rambova was blamed for his strike, for his choice in pictures, and for his artistic goals. Whether those claims were fair or not, Rambova had become Valentino's prime business advisor, mainly because she took charge, he trusted her, and he felt with her English she could understand legal terms better than he could. [44]

Valentino's comeback film "Monsieur Beaucaire" was a comedy about a 17th century Duke. Rambova was the costume designer and art director for the film. Famous Players was sure the film would be a hit, being Valentino's first screen appearance in two years. They were given a huge budget, with Rambova spending $215,000 on costumes alone. [45]

Rambova's troubles began during filming with many finding her cold and snooty. [46] Valentino asked the crew to call him "Rudy" while she asked to be called "Madame". Actress Lois Wilson would be the only one to defend her saying she was talented. [47] However actress Jetta Goudal dropped out of the production, after clashing with Rambova one too many times. She claimed Rambova was a 'know it all'. [48] Rambova also managed to upset an unnamed journalist and publicist Harry Reichenbach. When the journalist came to interview Valentino, he was told he could speak with "Mrs. Valentino" instead. Angered, he left without taking an interview, canceling his article. Reichenbach was furious and publicly aired his grievances. [49]

Rambova claimed that Famous Players made them choose the film, when in reality the Valentinos were offered a choice between "Monsieur Beaucaire" or a sea adventure. When "Monsieur Beaucaire" flopped, most of the blame went to Rambova. Jesse Lasky held her personally responsible saying, "*...she insisted on Valentino doing perfumed parts like Monsieur Beaucaire in powdered wigs and silk stockings. We had to take him on her terms to have him at all.*" [50]

With the public watching them, the Valentinos began work on their next picture, "A Sainted Devil" (sometimes called "The Sainted Devil") which would follow in Valentino's early Latin Lover styled roles. Rambova took control of the production, especially the costumes and the casting. Though Joseph Henabery was the official director, Rambova took over this role with his blessing. [51] The costumes were again lavish and Rambova brought on two designers who would go on to successful careers: Norman Norell, and Adrian (who would design for The Wizard of Oz). [52]

There were again issues with Rambova behind the scenes. Jetta Goudal was brought on once again, only to leave after clashing with Rambova over her character and costumes. [53] "A Sainted Devil" flopped, this time damaging Valentino's career to the point where reviewers declared he had lost his great lover title to John Gilbert. [54] Rambova blamed the story, which she claimed had a war element when they originally agreed to make the picture; with the studio removed it fearing it would offend European audiences. Rambova said of the film, "...*lost sight of that if beauty is only used as shallow satisfaction for the eye and not combined with food for the soul as well...it is but an empty gilded shell.*" The film is now lost. [55]

The Valentinos began work on what they now seen as their chance at a real picture, "The Hooded Falcon". Rambova wrote the initial scenario and it was again to be her production. Valentino visited his friend June Mathis, asking her to write the full script, which she agreed to. However the project would be plagued with problems from the start. [56] Much to the couple's horror, they learned their Ritz Carlton pictures would be distributed via Famous Players-Lasky. [57] Ritz Carlton also did not have much financing, crushing their dreams of filming on location in Spain. To work around this they traveled first to France, then Spain, in search of costumes and scene ideas. [58] They had a $40,000 budget for costumes and props, yet spent $100,000. [59] The picture had a total budget of $500,000, half of which would be used before the film was finally shelved all together. [60]

During production for "The Hooded Falcon" Rambova clashed frequently with Valentino's friends and co-workers. [61] Rambova and George Ullman were once again in a battle for control of Valentino's career. Ullman seen Rambova as a dominating woman who used her charms to get her way. [62]

Rambova, alongside Valentino and Henabery, decided Mathis' script for "The Hooded Falcon" would not do and a script doctor should be used. When Ullman informed Mathis of the decision Mathis promptly quit speaking to both Rambova and Valentino ending her long friendship with both of them (see page

300 for more details). Rambova felt she was unfairly singled out, and with Mathis' departure the press slammed her more claiming she now had full control over Valentino. [63] Valentino and Rambova tried to fight back, by granting interviews claiming that '*Valentino is not a Henpecked Husband*. [64]

With "The Hooded Falcon" on hold, Williams insisted Valentino began work on "Cobra" which took place in a modern setting. Most of the crew from "The Hooded Falcon" worked on "Cobra" as well. Rambova only took part in two scenes before leaving the film claiming modern stories bored her. In the short time she worked on the film she managed to clash with Mario Carillo and other actors as well. [65] "Cobra" flopped and both Valentino's popularity and career were in serious jeopardy. The Valentinos had been keeping to themselves, but as Rambova took more blame in the press they began to try and make more appearances at parties and events, hoping to soften Rambova's image. However, after a final fight between Williams and Valentino over Rambova, Williams announced to the press that "The Hooded Falcon" would be postponed indefinitely, and Valentino's contract terminated. Rambova again took the blame in the press. [66]

With the knowledge United Artists would likely be signing Valentino; Rambova went to speak with Ullman about the contract terms. [67] Valentino was finally offered a decent contract, but one of the stipulations was that Rambova would not be allowed on set or have any part in his films. [68] Knowing he did not have a choice (as he was severely in debt and his career was in serious jeopardy), Valentino took the offer. Rambova was furious, and the move eventually cost them their marriage. [69]

Though they shared similar passions, Valentino and Rambova held very different views when it came to home and personal life. Valentino cherished old world ideals of a woman being a housewife and mother, while Rambova was a feminist who wanted to continue to work and had no plans of being a housewife. [70]

In fact Valentino was known as an excellent cook, while Patsy Ruth Miller suspected Rambova didn't know 'how to make burnt fudge'.[71] Valentino deeply wanted children, Rambova did not. Nita Naldi, a close friend to the pair, claimed Rambova had three abortions. [72] Though this is impossible to prove, Rambova said herself she would see to it she never had children. Ironically the only person to defend Rambova on this matter was Ullman, who noted in his book Rambova also wanted children, but the couple had agreed to wait until their careers were over.

Rambova also did not get along with Valentino's friends and family. Rambova complained during their trip to Italy, and she never

The Rudolph Valentino Medal Ceremony

got along very well with either of his siblings. [73] She eventually sparred with Douglas Gerrad, June Mathis, and George Ullman. The marriage began to strain as the press scrutinized Rambova and blamed her for Valentino's failures. [74]

After Valentino had signed his contract with United Artists, Ullman offered Rambova $30,000 out of his own pocket to create a film of her own choosing. Rambova began work on "What Price Beauty?" which she wrote, produced, and appeared in. Nita Naldi starred, and a small part was given to Myrna Loy in her first screen appearance. [75] Loy would defend Rambova later on, saying she was unfairly judged for Valentino's choices. The film ran over budget, costing $100,000. It received a limited and delayed release. It is now lost. [76]

Rambova turned completely cold to Valentino, forgetting his 30th birthday, mocking him for staying home all day while she went to work (he was waiting for his contract to finalize), sparring with him in public, embarrassing him in front of Hollywood elite on the night of his 'Rudolph Valentino Medal' ceremony, and eventually cheating on him with her cameraman on "What Price Beauty?" [77]

Teresa, and a friend of Valentino's both tried to mediate, but the marriage was broken beyond repair. Rambova left four weeks after Valentino began shooting "The Eagle". Soon after she announced their separation to the press, catching Valentino off guard. [78] The pair took to sparring back and forth in the press. Valentino hoped for reconciliation, but Rambova announced she would be heading to Paris to seek a divorce. Valentino became suicidal soon after. [79]

After divorce proceedings from Valentino began, Rambova produced and starred in another picture originally titled, "Do Clothes Make the Woman?" [80] She had brought 40 trunks back from Europe for the picture and would act opposite Clive Brook. Eventually it was retitled to "When Love Grows Cold" much to Rambova's horror. [81] In addition the distributor promoted the film with her name as "Mrs. Rudolph Valentino". [82] Rambova was so horrified she never acted or worked in film again. [83] Most of the film is lost except small fragments from a promotional trailer.

When Valentino suddenly took ill in August 1926, Rambova was in Europe. At Valentino's request, Ullman sent a telegram to Rambova. [84] Rambova and Ullman both believed a reconciliation had taken place and the two sent telegrams right until the final moments of Valentino's life. [85] When Valentino died, Rambova locked herself in her room for 3 days, not speaking or eating. [86] She did not attend the funeral, though she did send a request to Ullman that Valentino be buried in her family crypt (Ullman decided against this, still waiting on Valentino's siblings decision). [87]

During his illness she had conducted séances. After he died she wrote a book about their life together (likely to counter Ullman's own book) as well as her conversations with him from beyond the grave. The book was released in 1926 and 1927.

After Valentino's death, Rambova appeared on stage via vaudeville and Broadway. She wrote a play titled "All that Glitters" which supposedly detailed her time with Valentino though by the end of the play the couple happily reconcile unlike in real life. [88]

Rambova opened an elite couture shop on Fifth Avenue in 1927. She urged women to express themselves through fashion. She would later close the shop after meeting her second husband. Rambova met Alvaro de Urzaiz on a trip to Europe in 1934. Urzaiz was a British educated, Spanish aristocrat who physically resembled Valentino. [89] After closing her shop, Rambova moved with her husband to the island of Mallorca. They began a business of buying up old villas and modernizing them for tourists; a venture she financed with her inheritance from Hudnut who died in 1928. Some of these villas still stand.

When the Spanish Civil War erupted, Urzaiz was on the pro-fascists nationalist side, becoming a naval commander. Rambova initially shared his views, but changed after she witnessed a pro Franco bishop who wouldn't provide sanctuary to a woman when leftists were rounding up people and shooting. [90] Rambova took pictures of the destruction she witnessed during this time. She then fled to Nice, where she suffered a heart attack at the age of 40. Soon after, she and Urzaiz divorced ending another childless marriage. Rambova would never marry again. [91]

After divorcing her second husband, Rambova remained in France where she began to relax her style and allow herself to be photographed not all done up. She remained in France until the Nazis invaded, at which point she returned to New York. [92] Through the 1940s Rambova's interest in the metaphysical grew, with her supporting the Bollingen Foundation, which she believed helped her see a past life in Egypt. [93] Both Rambova and Valentino were Spiritualists. Rambova had been interested in ancient religions since her teen years. She believed in reincarnation and psychic powers. She attempted to write a book on spirituality before Valentino's death, though it was never published. [94]

Rambova became an Egyptologist[95], and a follower of Madame Blavatsky and George Gurdjieff. She published various articles on healing and astrology during this time. Eventually she helped decipher ancient scarabs and tomb inscriptions which led her

to edit a series of publications titled, "Egyptian Texts and Religious Representations". She conducted classes in her apartment about myths, symbolism, and comparative religion.[96]

She did not speak of Valentino publicly, turning away reporters on the 25th anniversary of his death and threatening to sue if an upcoming picture about him had a caricature of her in it.[97] In the mid 1960s she was struck with scleroderma, and became malnourished and delusional as a result.[98] A cousin brought her to Pasadena, where she died of a heart attack on June 5th, 1966. She was 69.[99] Her collection of Egyptian antiquities were donated to the Utah Museum of Fine Arts. She willed a huge collection of Nepali and Lamaistic art to the Philadelphia Museum of Art.[100] Ironically her death certificate described her as a 'housewife'. Rambova's ashes were scattered in Arizona.[101]

Her papers are held at the Library of Congress. Part of her collection and Egyptology research was donated to Yale University in 2009.

BIBLIOGRAPHY
"Rudy: An Intimate Portrait of Rudolph Valentino" in 1926, (also released as "Rudolph Valentino Recollections by Natacha Rambova" in 1927, and as this text "Rudolph Valentino: A Wife's Memories of an Icon by Natacha Rambova in 2009)
"Volumes 1-4, Egyptian Religious Texts and Representations Bollingen Series XL (1954-1964)"

FILMOGRAPHY

The Woman God Forgot (1917, Costume Designer)
Why Change Your Wife? (1920, Costume Designer)
Something to Think About (1920, Costume Designer)
Billions (1920, Artistic Director, Costume Designer; **Lost**)
Forbidden Fruit (1921, Costume Designer)
Aphrodite (1921, *Never Made*)
Beyond the Rocks (1922, Valentino's Costumes only)
The Young Rajah (1923, Costume Designer, **Lost**)
A Doll's House (1923, Artistic Director, Costume Designer, **Lost**)
Salome (1923, Artist Director, Costume Designer, Writer)
Monsieur Beaucaire (1924, Artistic Director, Costume Designer)
A Sainted Devil (1924, Artistic Director, Costume Designer, Director, **Lost**)
The Hooded Falcon (1924, Writer, Artistic Director, Costume Designer, *Never Made*)

What Price Beauty? (1925, Director, Artistic director, Costume
Designer, Writer, Producer, **Lost**)
When Love Grows Cold (1925, Actress, Artistic Director, Costume
Designer, **Lost**)

Surprisingly Natacha has a pretty high survival rate though
she worked on very few (and very powerful) films. She also worked
on the never realized **Aphrodite** and **Hooded Falcon**. Why Change
Your Wife?, Camille, Beyond the Rocks, Salome, and Monsieur
Beaucaire have been released on DVD. Fragments of The Young
Rajah and When Love Grows Cold have both been released on The
Valentino Collection DVD set.

Rudolph Valentino at a radio appearance, circa 1923

RUDOLPH VALENTINO
BIOGRAPHY AND FILMOGRAPHY

For more in Rudolph Valentino
please see rudolphvalentino.org/rudy.html

Though silent movies have long been forgotten, the name 'Rudolph Valentino' has not. His short career earned him great popularity with roles such as 'The Sheik' and the 'Latin Lover'. His untimely death at age 31 prompted a type of mass hysteria that had never been seen before, making him an eternal icon setting the trend for other celebrities such as Marilyn Monroe, James Dean, Elvis, and Michael Jackson.[1] Yet in his icon immortality, pop culture has forgotten just what they had exactly lost with the early death of Valentino. Nothing like his Sheik image, Valentino was a quiet, sweet, giving man who took great pride in his work and hoped to be remembered for his talent, not his undeniable sex appeal.

The man to be known as Valentino was born Rodolfo Alfonzo Raffaelo Pierre Filibert Guglielmi di Valentina d'Antonguolla (in his early days he was usually known as Rodolfo Guglielmi) in Castellaneta, Italy on May 6th, 1895.[2] One of three surviving children, Valentino's Italian born father was strict with him, while his French born mother favored and spoiled him. Able to get away with anything, Valentino did poorly in school (for instance failing French despite that being the language he spoke with his French born mother at home[3]) and was constantly getting into trouble. Through his mother's prompting, he earned a degree in agriculture, though he did not wish to pursue it as a career.[4]

After finishing school Valentino left for Paris, where he reportedly learned to tango and had his heart broken by a French chorus girl.[5] He wasted and gambled away his money, forcing him to return to Italy in 1912.[6] His mother and uncles decided to send him to America where they figured he would either sink or swim. They provided him with a hefty amount of money which he promptly wasted by living the good life when he arrived in New York City.[7] Unable to disappoint his mother again, he wrote all was well and spent time living on the streets and taking odd jobs.[8]

During this time, a dancing craze was sweeping America; particularly the tango. Dancing cafes (or taxi dance halls) sprung up all over New York City. The dance halls employed male dancers (referred to as taxi dancers or gigolos, though no sexual favors were implied or exchanged) who were paid a dime to dance a single song with a female patron.[9] Valentino was naturally talented at dancing, something he perfected in Paris, and found taxi dancing preferable to his other mundane and poor paying jobs. He eventually rose up the ranks and was quite well known in New York society, dancing with a number of well known partners including friend for life Mae Murray.[10]

During this time, Valentino fell madly in love with a married society woman named Blanca de Saulles. de Saulles had been unhappily married long before she had met Valentino, eventually divorcing her husband John. Perhaps trying to win de Saulles over (she reportedly had never returned his affections, though others dispute this) Valentino testified at the trial. John de Saulles was extremely powerful, and as payback, had Valentino arrested on trumped up vice charges (the exact nature is unknown as the records have been wiped clean). [11] The arrest was highly publicized. Further compounding matters, Blanca shot and killed her husband over a custody dispute soon after the divorce. [12] Valentino had already been unable to find work because of the first scandal, and decided to avoid the second. He left New York with a traveling musical (that included Al Jolson) and changed his name from Guglielmi, to the now known Valentino (and a few variations of it). [13]

It is interesting, for all that is known about Valentino, that his entry into acting is still a bit of a mystery. It is extremely unlikely he ever seen a film in Italy, and just as unlikely in Paris. By the time he arrived in New York the popular flickers were starting to turn into features. How and when he seen his first film is unknown. To make matters even more complicated, many of his early films are lost, so the number is in dispute (in these films he likely worked as nothing more than an extra, the earliest known example being "Patria" in 1916.[14])

The film industry was still based in New York in the late teens, though by the 20s it had mostly gone to California. Extras usually made around $5 a day and finding it was quick and easy work. It is possible during his odd jobs in New York Valentino took such a part, but if so the films or his scenes do not survive.

When Valentino made his way to California, he landed in San Francisco and again began taking odd jobs. A friend named Norman Kerry convinced him to go into silent pictures. [15] Valentino joined Kerry in Los Angeles where he began taking extra and bit work. To make ends meet Valentino kept dancing, but he was growing tired of it. On one studio application a question asked why he wanted to enter pictures. He wrote, 'tired of dancing'. [16]

With his finances a bit more secure, Valentino found a room of his own and began taking bigger parts. He was usually cast as a 'heavy' or villain due to his dark and foreign looks. Film was extremely cut and dry at the time. Handsome Irish or English 'White' men were the romantic types (Jack Pickford, Douglas Fairbanks, Thomas Meighan) while anyone deemed not white (a group that included Italians and Latinos), was unable to obtain such roles.[17] Foreign looking actors usually were given nothing but evil villain roles (Sessue Hayakawa, and Anna May Wong are two tragic examples) [18] Valentino would eventually be the first to change this (with the help of June Mathis). Despite playing heavies, Valentino's early roles show his natural acting talent. At a time when some stars still overacted (remnants of early 1900 stage acting), Valentino portrayed his characters in a natural way. He also showcased his skill for comedy during these years in films like "All Night" in 1918.

Valentino grew sick of playing stereotyped roles, and briefly considered moving back to New York. [19] His personal life hadn't been going well either. His beloved mother died shortly after his arrival in Los Angeles, something that devastated him deeply. [20] He fell into a heavy depression and those who seen him at the time said he looked the part. Shortly after his mother's death, he rushed into a marriage with fellow b film star Jean Acker. Acker was a lesbian, who was caught in a love triangle with another b film actress, Grace Darmond...and the very powerful film star Alla Nazimova. [21] She saw marrying Valentino as a way out of the conundrum, saving her career. [22] The impulsive marriage was never consummated and Valentino was devastated at her rejection. [23] He had not been told of her sexuality and thought he had done something wrong; sending her love notes and gifts for months afterwards. [24] Eventually it must have been explained to him, as he moved on and towards the end of his life, befriended Acker again.

After this hectic marriage, Valentino was sent to Florida to film another b movie titled, "Stolen Moments". While there he read the popular anti war novel, "The Four Horsemen of the Apocalypse". When he found out Metro Pictures had the film rights, he decided to approach them for a small role. [25] By chance, Metro Executive and screenwriter June Mathis had seen Valentino in a small role in "The Eyes of Youth" and had her heart set on casting him as one of the leads, "Julio" (it is possible she might have seen him in a 1918 production "The Isle of Love" which starred her friend Julian Eltinge. However Mathis always stuck to the Eyes of Youth story.) [26] Mathis had been a prominent screenwriter and quickly became the

243

first female film executive in history when she joined up with Metro (this title does not include women who had acted in front of the camera). [27] Mathis had a knack for writing preachy spiritual films that dabbled in karma and the occult (in step with her spiritualist beliefs). She and Valentino remained friends till the end and he considered her his mentor. [28]

Despite protests from her higher ups, Mathis got her way. "The Four Horsemen of the Apocalypse" was released in 1921 and became a smash hit. The film was the first to make a million dollars the box office, was the top grossing film of 1921[29], and the 6th best selling silent film ever. [30] The film made Valentino a star and he became known as "The Latin Lover" due to the role. [31]

However Metro did not think so, continuing to pay Valentino his small salary of $350 a week (when most stars made several thousand a week). [32] Valentino was never wise with business dealings and suffered from similar contract and money issues his entire career. [33] When he died his estate was heavily in debt, something not expected of a star of his stature. [34] To add to his troubles, Metro threw him into a b picture, "Uncharted Seas" (now lost), which would foreshadow his artistic and power struggles with studios and movie moguls his entire career.

However some good came of it. It was on this film set that Valentino met his future wife Natacha Rambova. Rambova had grown up in a wealthy family where she rebelled and took joy in dancing, mythology, and art. She eventually began an affair with the well known married 32 year old dancer Theodore Kosloff (she was just 17). Kosloff kept her as part of his 'arty harem' abusing and controlling her. When Kosloff entered films with Cecil B DeMille he ordered Rambova to design costumes for which he took credit (her work can be seen in such films as "Why Change Your Wife?" and "The Woman God Forgot"). When eccentric actress Nazimova hired Kosloff to design costumes for a film of hers, she discovered Rambova was the designer and hired her as an artistic director on the spot.

Valentino would soon get more time to know her as work began on his next picture, Nazimova's "Camille", for which Rambova designed the sets and costumes. The film was a flop as audiences found it 'too arty', though Valentino enjoyed making it. [35] Many critics praised his natural performance (an excellent example would be the scene where Armand finds Camille's note to him) and apparently some of his scenes were cut as Nazimova feared being upstaged. [36] Rambova and Nazimova were of

Gloria Swanson and Rudolph Valentino in Beyond the Rocks, 1922

The wedding couple

the artistic mind frame and wanted to make films into high art, whether it would be commercially successful or not (ironically 'Camille' was basically the death knell in Nazimova's career). Valentino and Rambova soon grew close over their shared interests, and while he trusted his scripts and business moves to Mathis, he trusted Rambova with her artistic and creative advice.

Despite wanting better and more creative films, Valentino was still desperately in need of money. He signed with Famous Players Lasky, where he would make $500 a week (still much less than other stars). [37] However, Famous Players was much more commercially focused, and Valentino had made the move without consulting anyone, including his friends and Rambova. [38] Though she believed this would hinder their artistic vision and that he was making much less than he deserved, she soon joined him as did Mathis. [39]

Valentino's first film for Famous Players was, "The Sheik", also released in 1921. The film is the one appearance where Valentino abandons his naturalistic style (as portrayed in all his early films and Four Horsemen) for a more exaggerated one, sadly leading some to believe all his film portrayals were as such. It seems this misstep was at the suggestion of the director, George Melford. [40] Despite this, Valentino got along well with the crew and cast and the film was a major success. [41] The term "Sheik" entered popular vocabulary and the fashion and styles from the film became major fads. Valentino became a certified star, with this role usually overshadowing his Latin Lover one in modern times.

Valentino was given some less stereotypical roles with his follow up vehicles, such as "Moran of the Lady Letty" (where he played a white man) and co-starring with Gloria Swanson in "Beyond the Rocks". However these films weren't as successful as his previous ones, and Valentino was once again given 'exotic styled' roles. [42] With Mathis writing his screenplays once more, the films relied less on stereotypes and more on story. [43]

Work began on "Blood and Sand" which was released in 1922. Valentino and Rambova were told they could shoot on location in Spain, but were upset when the film took place on a Hollywood back lot. [44] He was also upset that he was forbidden to do his own bull fighting stunts, feeling the final look was silly and cheap. [45] Despite the couples artistic complaints, the film did extremely well and kept up the demand for more Valentino films. Critics hailed it as something on par with D.W. Griffith's "Broken Blossoms". [46] It was the 4th top grossing movie of the year. [47] Valentino would later consider it one his best films. [48] "Blood and Sand" was also the first film Valentino acted alongside vamp Nita

Naldi, who would be a close friend and his most frequent co-star. [49] Naldi was one of the few friends of his who also liked Natacha, even starring in her one production "What Price Beauty?" (now lost).

After filming wrapped, Valentino and Rambova married in Mexicali, Mexico on May 13th, 1922. [50] However his divorce to Acker had taken place less than a year before and an overzealous district attorney charged Valentino with bigamy (at the time it was illegal to remarry in California if one's divorce had not been finalized in under a years time). [51] Valentino was arrested and put in jail on a Friday, making it so he could not be bailed out until Monday. His studio refused to bail him out (fearing negative press and scandal) and it took the combined efforts of his friends including June Mathis and actor Thomas Meighan before he was freed. [52]

The couple was forced to separate until the heat died down, with Rambova going to New York. Valentino was devastated by the separation and extremely bitter at those he perceived as forcing it. [53] Despite being separated, the pair began work on his next film, the Mathis penned, "The Young Rajah" (now all but a few seconds lost). Valentino complained the entire time and felt the production was again cheap.[54] He also felt his performance was affected by his personal troubles. The film was his first flop since his stardom and Valentino was extremely unhappy about it.[55] Despite the studios claims that he was beginning work on "The Spanish Cavalier", Valentino consulted with Rambova and his lawyers about how to leave his studio. He was already bitter over the handling of the bigamy charges, the reneged promise of filming "Blood and Sand" in Spain, "The Young Rajah" handling, and now once again he was told he would not be able to film in Spain despite the studios earlier promises. [56]

Probably eschewing their advice, Valentino began a self proclaimed 'One Man Strike' against Famous Players. [57] He began refusing his paychecks (despite owing them for paying off Jean Acker) and swore he would not make any more pictures for them until they paid him enough (he was still earning only $1,250), and gave him creative and artistic control. [58] He wasn't kidding about the artistic part: when the studio offered him $7,000 a week to behave, he threw it back in their faces. [59] He then wrote a letter to Photoplay, pleading his case for artistic control. Many fans saw it as a ploy for more money, which Famous Players played up in a publicity war.[60] Famous Players sued him and got a ruling barring him from any work of any kind.[61] Rambova refused to take money from her wealthy parents, and Valentino soon found himself $80,000 in debt. [62] He eventually had the ruling reduced to barring him from acting work only. [63] The effects of this probably will never be fully known. Other studios, including Goldwyn, had wanted to hire him. Joseph Schenck was interested in playing him opposite the extremely popular Norma Talmadge. But barred from acting Valentino was unable to legally accept any of these offers.[64]

Valentino soon met a man named George Ullman, who would become his manager.[65] Ullman secured him a deal promoting Mineralava Beauty Clay, which led to a dancing tour. The Mineralava Dance Tour took place during most of 1923 and involved Valentino and Rambova touring several cities in the US and Canada. They would dance, a beauty contest was held, and Valentino usually got in a rant about the movie industry and how they wouldn't let him be artistic.[66] He also made radio appearances about this time (during one such interview he got so upset they had to cut him off before his words got too fiery).[67] At the end of the tour, a final beauty contest was held at Madison Square Gardens. A short film titled, "Rudolph Valentino and his 88 American Beauties" was later sold newsreel style of the events. During the tour the Valentinos were able to at least pay off some of their debts, and were finally able to legally remarry, which they did on a stop in Indiana on March 14th, 1923.[68]

After a trip to Europe where he finally got to visit his family for the first time in a decade, Valentino returned to the States and signed what looked like a great deal. Ritz Carlton Pictures offered him $7,500 a week, full creative control, and permission to film in New York.[69] Rambova negotiated the deal, though the pair later found it was not as it seemed.[70] The films would be distributed through their old enemy, Famous Players, to whom they still owed two pictures, and eventually they found their budget and location restraints too constricting.[71]

Valentino's comeback picture was, "Monsieur Beaucaire", which was released in 1924. The pair were given full artistic control, with Natacha designing the costumes and sets.[72] However it was a poor story choice for bringing back the virile, popular, Latin Lover and many small town viewers found it 'too artsy and effeminate'.[73] The film is usually blamed as Natacha's misstep, though Natacha claimed they were given the choice between only two stories and this was the better of the two.[74] The film flopped, and whether fairly or not, the blame was given fully to Natacha.[75] Despite this, "Monsieur Beaucaire" holds up better over time, being one of the rare films Valentino was allowed to do comedy.

Their next film, "A Sainted Devil" (now lost), was again blamed as a Natacha misstep.[76] The film went for a stylized, Latin Lover story, but again did poorly at the box office. Glad to be done with Famous Players the pair set about their pet project, "The Hooded Falcon".

Vilma Banky and Rudolph Valentino in The Eagle, 1925

"The Hooded Falcon" was a disaster at every turn. Rambova started on a script but felt her writing ability wasn't strong enough.[77] Valentino asked Mathis to work on it, but Rambova rejected Mathis' work. Thus ended the friendship, as June refused to speak to either of them until the divorce (for more on this see page 300).[78] Several other writers were brought in, but a suitable script seemed out of reach. Rambova spent too much on costumes, blowing twice the original budget before the film had been shot.[79] Ullman feared the film would flop anyways; it was the story of a Moorish Prince in which Valentino would wear a beard. He indeed grew the beard, which was the subject of much debate in the press. [80] Before "The Hooded Falcon" fully imploded, Ritz Carlton convinced Valentino and Naldi to work on a quick film, "Cobra". "Cobra" used most the same cast and crew as Hooded Falcon, but was much less artistic. The film once again flopped thus meaning Valentino had not had a box office success since 1922's "Blood and Sand". [81]

Ritz Carlton had enough and terminated the contract.[82] United Artists approached Valentino and offered $10,000 a week, a percent of profits, and again creative control.[83] However a stipulation was Rambova would be barred from his sets. [84] Desperate to keep his career going (and pay off his massive debt), Valentino took the deal.[85]

Rambova was given a peace offering of $30,000 to finance her own film, with which she made, "What Price Beauty?" (now lost). [86] While she made this film, Valentino was waiting for his contract to finalize and unable to work. During this time their marriage fell apart.[87] Natacha was deeply hurt by his acceptance of the contact and felt her help with his career was not fully appreciated (indeed she had handled the business side better than he ever had).[88] She began an affair with her cameraman to get back at him. [89] There had been deeper troubles before this. Valentino had wanted a housewife and mother, not an independent career woman (which indeed Rambova was). Rambova hated children and according to Naldi had no less than three abortions during the marriage (of course this is impossible to prove).[90] Ironically, one of the few people to state Natacha wanted children was George Ullman, who did no get along with her.[91] Meanwhile, Valentino had desperately wanted children. As Rambova left for New York for what was to be a quiet separation, she announced it to the press unbeknownst to Valentino.[91] He was deeply hurt and divorce proceedings soon began. The divorce took place before the end of 1925.[92]

Valentino set to work on "The Eagle", which was the first of his pairings with Vilma Banky. Likely they were just friends, as Valentino embarked on an affair with Pola Negri soon after.[93] Negri threw a grand performance during his funeral, which damaged her public reputation. She claimed they were to be married but those who knew the pair said they were just having fun and no engagement took place.[94]

"The Eagle" was released in 1925 and did moderate box office. [95] Compared to his last few films it was a smash hit. To this day it is one of his best performances, mixing comedy and action. As one reviewer noted it was like an early James Bond film.

Valentino then began work on "Son of the Sheik". He had hated the Sheik image his entire career, yet knew the money would be too good to pass up. [96] This time around, the film had a solid writer (Frances Marion), solid co-stars (Vilma and the incredibly funny Karl Dane), and authentic costumes he had bought during his travels. [97] The film uses less stereotypes and his acting is superb. In full irony it is one of his best films, and it makes one wonder what he could have done had he lived.

"Son of the Sheik" opened in 1926, right before his death. The film had great fanfare and box office, which went into overdrive when Valentino died on August 23rd, 1926.[98] He had been ill for sometime, complaining of stomach pain. [99] Several friends, including June Mathis, tried to persuade him to see a doctor, but he refused. [100]

On August 15th he collapsed at the Ambassador Hotel and underwent surgery for a perforated ulcer.[101] The surgery went well, but infection set in, which is what caused his death. He had been wiring Natacha during his illness (she was in Europe), and both Ullman (who was with Valentino during his final days), and Natacha, believed a reconciliation had taken place.[102] She was devastated to learn he died.[103] Valentino himself seemed optimistic, telling his doctor he would take him on a fishing trip for being so good to him. Ullman said during one of his last days he asked for a mirror, 'so he could see what he looked like when he was sick, so he can act it right in film'.[104]

Valentino's death caused a mass hysteria the likes of which had never been seen before.[105] A few stars had died before him during the height of their own careers: John Bunny (the first fat comedian), Olive Thomas (the first flapper), Wallace Reid (matinee idol), and William Desmond Taylor (director). Yet none of their deaths sparked the reaction his did. A 100,000 people lined the streets to see his body, and his funerals were marked with publicity stunts.[106] His estate had been in debt at the time of his death, leaving no money to bury him. June Mathis offered to loan her crypt at Hollywood Forever Cemetery.[107]

The arrangement was supposed to be temporary, as Pola claimed she would build a large monument, and a committee of

Italian Americans were formed to create a proper memorial. [108] Led by June Mathis, and her Italian husband Silvano Balboni, the idea was to create an Italian park in Hollywood, with statues of Valentino in various film roles. [109] However, June herself died unexpectedly in 1927 of a heart attack, and plans soon fell through. [110] Valentino was moved to her husbands crypt, where he is still interred. [111]

With the onset of the depression, most memorial plans fell through. In the early 30s a statue was dedicated in De Longpre Park in Hollywood. Sadly it's now a ghetto area, with the statue being the only attraction. [112] For the longest time, even Hollywood Forever Cemetery was in disrepair, though thankfully it has been lovingly restored in recent years. [113]

Valentino's legacy has been a mixed one. Immediately after his death, Natacha announced he was speaking to her from the grave and wrote a book supposedly about it. Valentino had been a spiritualist in life and did believe in the occult. [114] This led to his legacy almost solely being overshadowed by The Sheik and the afterlife. The Valentino Memorial Guild, created after his death to be a charity for children, eventually became a charity run but self proclaimed mediums, who really did nothing charitable. [115] The guild ended in the early 1990s with the death of its eccentric president. Perhaps the only good thing they did was save the snippets we now have of The Young Rajah.

A Lady in Black has visited his grave every year since his death and been the subject of much speculation and press. Likely it was originally created as a publicity stunt since his films were re-released well into the late 30s. [116]

Every year since 1928, a Valentino Memorial Service has been held on the date of his death, at supposedly the time of his death (they fail to account for the time change between New York where he died, and California where he is buried). [117] At first it was a Valentino family sponsored event, but became circus like in the following years. [118] As of late, it has tried to become more solemn, but still is full of Ladies in Black (and other costumes), people promoting their Valentino death books, and other unsavory self promoting people.

During the passing years when silent film wasn't easy to view, a few movies and specials were made about Valentino. However they are extremely inaccurate and in some karmic justice didn't do too well at the box office. Natacha threatened to sue the 1951 version and Valentino's brother did indeed sue the 1977 version (Natacha had passed away by that time).

Though his death now overshadows his life, we are lucky to be able to still view most of Valentino's work. While something akin to 70%-90% of all silent films are currently lost; over 60% of Valentino's survive. [119] He was a method actor before the term was used (Natacha recalled he stayed in his Blood and Sand character the entire time they filmed...even when not on set) and had an extreme knack for it. Much like Marilyn Monroe, his image and good looks overshadow his talent and ambitions, but it is not justified. Valentino was nothing like the Sheik, and those who knew him said he was an extremely generous, polite, sensitive, and sweet man. Hopefully someday these qualities, alongside his acting, will overshadow his death legacy.

BIBLIOGRAPHY

"Day Dreams" (1923)
"How You Can Keep Fit" (1923)
"My Private Diary" (1929)

FILMOGRAPHY

The Battle of the Sexes (1914, **Lost**)
My Official Wife (1914, **Lost**)
The Quest of Life (1916, **Lost**)
Seventeen (1916, **Lost**)
The Foolish Virgin (1916, **Lost**)
Patria (1917)
Alimony (1917, **Lost**)
A Society Sensation (1918, **partially lost**)
All Night (1918)
A Married Virgin/Frivolous Wives (1918)
Delicious Little Devil (1919)
Virtuous Sinners (1919)
The Big Little Person (1919, **Lost**)
A Rogue's Romance (1919, **Lost**)
The Homebreaker (1919, **Lost**)
Out of Luck/Nobody Home (1919, **Lost**)
The Eyes of Youth (1919)
An Adventuress/Isle of Love (1919, **Partially Lost**)
Passion's Playground (1919, **Lost**)
The Cheater (1919, **Lost**)
Once to Every Woman (1919, **Lost**)
The Wonderful Chance (1919)
Stolen Moments (1919, **Partially Lost**)
The Four Horsemen of the Apocalypse (1921)

Uncharted Seas (1921, **Lost**)
Camille (1921)
The Conquering Power (1921)
The Sheik (1921)
Moran of Lady Letty (1922)
Beyond the Rocks (1922)
Blood and Sand (1922)
The Young Rajah (1923, **Lost**)
Rudolph Valentino and his 88 American Beauties (1923)
Monsieur Beaucaire (1924)
A Sainted Devil (1924, **Lost**)
The Hooded Falcon (1924, **Never Made**)
Cobra (1925)
The Eagle (1925)
Son of the Sheik (1926)

Many of Valentino's films still exist. A Married Virgin, All Night, A Delicious Little Devil, The Eyes of Youth, The Four Horsemen of the Apocalypse, Camille, The Sheik, Moran of Lady Letty, Beyond the Rocks, Blood and Sand, Rudolph Valentino and his 88 Beauties, Monsieur Beaucaire, Cobra, The Eagle, and Son of the Sheik all fully exist and have been released on DVD.

Fragments of A Society Sensation, Stolen Moments, The Young Rajah, have also been released on DVD.

Virtuous Sinners, The Isle of Love, The Wonderful Chance, The Conquering Power, all fully exist in archives but have not been released on DVD. Fragments of Patria exist in an archive as well.

Nita Naldi, circa 1922

NITA NALDI

BIOGRAPHY AND FILMOGRAPHY

For more on Nita please see rudolphvalentino.org/ nita.html

By 1930, newspaper articles made note of how 'the younger generation' wouldn't know the name Nita Naldi.[1] By the time she passed in 1961, this was once again reiterated. One obituary written by an acquaintance, compared her fame to that of Elizabeth Taylor or Marilyn Monroe.[2] All vamps must fade, but Nita was arguably one of the greatest. Though many of her films are lost, we are lucky to have her vamping Rudolph Valentino in "Blood and Sand" and "Cobra".

Deemed by more than one person as a 'salty broad', Nita was known for speaking her mind, telling the most inappropriate stories in the fanciest of settings, using language that would put Mabel Normand or Olive Thomas to shame. One reporter, when interviewing her on the set of "Blood and Sand", noted a first impression of Nita. Worrying over her dress Nita declared, "I hope I don't lose the god damned thing before I get back to my dressing room, because I haven't a fucking thing under it!"[3] Despite her naughty mouth, Naldi was known for her intelligence and wit, often making self deprecating comments about herself and her work.[4]

Nita was born Nonna Dooley in March 1895.[5] She was named for her great aunt Mary Nonna Dunphy, who founded The Academy of Holy Angels in Ft. Lee, New Jersey. Not much is known about her parents. Her father Patrick Dooley was born in December 1864, and immigrated from Ireland in 1886. In 1892 he married Julia Cronin, who was born in New York to Irish immigrants.[6]

257

Naldi was the oldest child, with her brother Daniel Francis (Frank) being born in April 1898, and her sister Mary being born later. Julia is enumerated as having 5 kids, with only 2 living in 1900. There is a bit of a mystery surrounding who Mary Naldi might have been.*

Much like the first vamp Theda Bara, who fed the press stories of an Egyptian childhood, Naldi had her own mythology. As her star rose, the press was told of her Italian childhood, her father supposedly an Italian diplomat.[7] It is unlikely she had any Italian blood in her, though even obituaries made note of it. Naldi was actually said to be a 'proud Irish'. As a child, she could be found passionately arguing over Irish issues with friends and hanging St. Patrick's Day cards over her bed (threatening anyone who would dare to take them down with a punch).

Naldi's childhood must have been rough to some extent, with problems caused by her father. In 1900 the family was living with her maternal Grandparents. By 1910, her maternal Grandfather had passed away, and her father had left the family.[8] Naldi always claimed he had 'died'; a common explanation amongst silent film stars with absentee fathers. Patrick appears to still have been alive in 1910, being enumerated in a boarding house not far from where his family lived.[9] Of the boarders there were two German widowers, and a 28 year old Irish immigrant named Martha who was also said to be widowed. She had immigrated in 1906, leaving the possibility that Naldi's parents had ended their marriage due to some sort of affair.[10]

To make matters worse, Naldi's mother soon took ill. Julia spent some of 1910 with her mother and children, but eventually was enumerated in the St Lawrence Hospital that year.[11] Possibly because of this, Naldi would attend her Great Aunt's Catholic school at some point during the year.[12] There, she was said to be a prank maker, putting Epsom salts in the nun's drinking water. She claimed to have been almost expelled over her frequent use of the blasphemous phrase, "Oh my God!", something she gleefully taught her fellow students. Naldi claimed it was there she first seen films being made.[13] Indeed many of the early films were shot in Ft. Lee, NJ until about 1910.

---

*Whether there is actually a blood sister named 'Mary Dunphy' or 'Mary Naldi' is, as of this publication, hard to confirm. Nita made several references to her 'sister' in interviews during the 1920s. When caught running around with the married Barclay, Nita claimed again to be living with her sister named Mary. A Mary Dunphy is indeed buried in the family plot. When Naldi died some reports made mention of a 'sister in Spain'. However no mention is made of her in census records at all. Whoever she was, she was important to Nita. Whether she was a blood relative is still hard to determine. No such name appears on the 1910 Convent School records either; making it all the more confusing.

Even then there were several holdouts, including Theda Bara who entered film in 1914.

Naldi's mother was a 'cloak model' during this time, a job Naldi herself would soon have. Her mother died in November 1915, presumably of an ongoing illness. [14] The whereabouts of her father and Grandmother are unknown, but by all accounts Naldi was left to care for her teenaged siblings alone. The rift with her father was so great that only her mother would be buried under the name 'Dooley', everyone else was buried under 'Dunphy'; likely an influence from Mary Nonna, or the fact that this was their Grandmother's maiden name. [15]

In addition to cloak modeling, Naldi took other various odd jobs and eventually entered vaudeville. She and her brother Frank created a song and dance act. Frank would revive the act with a new partner in 1928 at the New Castle Theater. [16]

Naldi debuted on Broadway in 1918 at the Winter Garden in "The Passing Show of 1918". [17] By 1919 she was a Ziegfeld Follies Girl, but for what years or roles is currently unknown. She played her first vamp role that year in "Aphrodite". Her performance in "The Bonehead" was well received. After this show, noted producer William A. Brady, engaged her for his Broadway play "Opportunity" in 1920. [20]

Naldi had been approached to enter film, a now established, albeit new, art form. She agreed to appear in a picture with Scottish comedian Johnny Dooley (no relation). The film was titled "Hearts and Arts" with Nita playing a Spanish girl. She agreed to work for free as she admired the performer, however once she found he was friendly with Gertrude Vanderbilt she quit in a huff with the picture apparently being shelved.

It seems by the time she entered the Follies, Naldi had taken on the stage name 'Nita Naldi'. This has led to the belief her birth name was Anita, though where she came up with Nita is currently unknown. One obituary claimed the name came from a fellow chorus girl who she was friends with.[18] She chose Naldi as a shortened form of 'Rinaldi', the last name of her best friend from school, Frances Rinaldi.

Despite the belief that John Barrymore snatched her away from the Follies, Naldi claimed her first picture was "A Divorce of Convenience" with Owen Moore. Her second film appears to have been "Experience" which may have been produced around the same time. [19] Either way, Naldi had entered film long before Dr. Jekyll and Mr. Hyde. Despite most reports, Naldi did not sign with Famous Players until "Blood and Sand". [20] Most of her early films were for Selznick Picture Corporation. She also had a part in "Life" in 1921, a

William A Brady production, and an independent Owen Moore production in 1922.

No matter how many films she made, Dr. Jekyll and Mr. Hyde was the one that brought her attention from the film world. Though never romantic, Naldi claimed she and John Barrymore had a great friendship. He teasingly nicknamed her the 'Dumb Duse'. In the late 20s Naldi would say he and Valentino were the most handsome men on earth.

Naldi's breakout role came when she was personally chosen by author Vicente Blasco Ibáñez to play Dona Sol in "Blood and Sand". Naldi recounted the meeting in one of her oral history sessions later in life. She claimed Ibáñez declared she was a wicked woman, that she was his Dona Sol, and he would mark her with that image for life. Indeed Naldi would become best known for her vamping roles. [21]

The vamp craze started in 1897 when a poem titled "A Fool There Was" accompanied a painting of a woman vamping. The poem was turned into a play, and the play became a film in 1915 which gave then almost 30 year old actress Theda Bara her big break. Overnight Bara became a sensation, and though the word 'vamp' does not appear in the film or poem, it soon came in use to describe such a woman, shortened for vampire. Vamps were said to be heartless, soulless, demon women who sucked the essence, money and acclaim out of their victims without even thinking twice. They were also notorious for luring men away from their good Edwardian homes, with Theda Bara's version of the vamp taking great joy in such a horrifying act for the time.

Though Theda had her imitators, none had outshone her, and by 1918 Bara had all but retired (she would make one more little known feature in 1926). Though the flapper craze began in 1920 with Olive Thomas, vamping was still in demand. Naldi's depiction of Donna Sol would give her fame, with many considering her Bara's successor. [22]

Naldi reluctantly relocated to California for filming, though she considered it temporary as she didn't think Hollywood was 'wild' enough. In one of her first interviews she noted how she missed her sister and that she wished she had brought her to Hollywood. [23]

Naldi got along well with her co-star Lila Lee, who she was still friends with later in life. She also got along well with the film's

Still from Blood and Sand, 1922.

star Rudolph Valentino; who had recently become a superstar for his role in "The Sheik".

Valentino had begun his love affair with Natacha Rambova, who would become his second wife after filming wrapped. Most of Valentino's friends did not get along with Rambova, finding her cold and off putting. Naldi and Rambova became friends, with the press speculating Naldi was the only woman Rambova trusted to act with her husband.[24] Indeed Naldi would become Valentino's most frequent co-star, appearing with him in "Blood and Sand", "The Hooded Falcon" (never made), "A Sainted Devil" and "Cobra". In fact she appeared in all but two films made during Valentino and Rambova's relationship.

Of Valentino, Naldi noted she did not find him attractive citing her fake Italian heritage, "Fall for Valentino I shall say not! Why Should I fall for him? Down in Little Italy where I was a kid I knew a hundred boys better looking than Rudy is!"[25] However, Naldi found him a dear friend, "He is most generous. No matter what his income he would spend it on others. He is very grateful aiding in a great degree people who were friendly with him in his less prosperous days."[26]

Naldi also found him a good actor, "Valentino is the most sincere actor I know. He lives the part even in the love scenes. Niblo (Blood and Sand director) would call 'That's enough Rudy...don't get too rough!'"[27]

It is perhaps interesting to note, that in her roles with Valentino, Naldi was the one seducing. Valentino, known for being the Great Lover, would usually play a man taken under her wicked spell. Naldi's characterizations were the opposite of most of his leading ladies, particularly his Sheik films.

After "Blood and Sand", Valentino was brought up on bigamy charges, stemming from his quick marriage to Rambova. The studio ordered him to begin work on "The Young Rajah", which he had little say in. After "The Young Rajah", Valentino was set to make another June Mathis penned film, "The Spanish Cavalier". Naldi was to co-star. However Valentino refused to make the film and went on a 'One Man Strike' that would keep him off the screen for two years. Naldi would not work with him again until he had made his final picture for Famous Players in 1924.

Naldi also had her own relationship troubles at this time. She had met millionaire sportsman J. Searle Barclay in 1919, when she was still performing on Broadway and with the Follies.[28] She claimed later in life fellow Ziegfeld Girl, Lilyan Tashman, introduced them.[29] Barclay, born in 1869 (he sometimes claimed a birth year of 1872), had been married to Isabelle (Isabella) Hunnerwell Harrington for 16 years. [30] Barclay and Naldi had lived together in an upscale apartment in New York City since 1920. Mary Naldi was officially said to be living with her sister at the apartment, with Barclay living in the same building.[31] On several occasions, reporters had interviewed Naldi with Barclay present, with her claiming him to not be Barclay, but her lawyer. [32]

When Naldi relocated to Hollywood for "Blood and Sand", Barclay joined her. It was at this time Isabelle filed for divorce, and named Naldi in the suit, though she was ordered to keep quiet to the press. Asked if she was indeed in a relationship with Barclay, Naldi denied it saying she had already married her lawyer, but would not give any details. When the reporter kept asking, Naldi stated, "You can say I am happy. When I get ready to reveal my husband's name I will do it...and not a day before!" [33]

Naldi would marry Barclay sometime in 1928 in France. With all subtlety, she noted in an interview around the time of the divorce suit, "I love tall men, especially men over 40. A man has no sense until he's reached that age" [34]. Naldi was 28 at the time.

Perhaps her father's abandonment influenced her decisions toward men. Later in life she said of her dating days, "In my day, if men found you could converse, they wouldn't take you out again. So I'd just sit there with my head in my soup plate." [35] When asked what type of beaus she had she replied, "Married men, of course. They're the only ones who had the do-re-mi. I got fed up with the Racquel club." [36]

Naldi would never have children, and after Barclay she would not remarry. When asked in interviews during the 1920s if she would like children or marriage, Naldi would give a neutral reply, stating both would be fine but she was 'meant for more'. By the 1920s she was already being labeled a 'man hater' for some of her comments, a claim that would increase with time.[37] In one interview she noted, "The girl pays and pays...but if she's a smart little girl she gets away with an awful lot of change!"

The divorce suit didn't seem to damage Naldi; perhaps because of the vamp image she had been given. In 1924 she said to a friend, "My stars, boy, how women loathe me!"[38] Fan letters to movie magazines back up this claim, with one stating how she hated Naldi for stealing Valentino's character away from the sweet Lila Lee.

Naldi said of this time in her career, "After Blood and Sand Valentino was given trashy stories to do, and he was the first screen star to go on strike. While this was going on I was featured in a series of shockingly bad pictures in which I always did the same thing - the vamp - which I loathe." [39] Indeed Naldi's vamping career continued unabated with, "Lawful Larceny" (in which she opened the film portraying Cleopatra), "The Glimpses of the Moon" with Bebe Daniels, and "You Can't Fool Your Wife". Naldi was given the role of Sally Lung in Cecil B DeMille's epic "The 10 Commandments". Her work must have impressed the DeMille brothers as her follow up film was "Don't Call it Love" directed by William DeMille. Naldi, however, was unimpressed, saying of 10 Commandments, "I hit a new low in movie characterizations, for in this opus I was not only a moral leper but a physical one as well." [40]

Valentino had finished his one man strike soon after this string of vamp films. In 1924 he owed two pictures to Famous Players-Lasky before he could begin his contract with Ritz Carlton Pictures. He made "Monsieur Beaucaire" which was not well received. His final film for Famous Players, "A Sainted Devil" reverted to his Latin lover image. Naldi was given the leading lady role of Carlotta. Unfortunately this picture is one of Valentino's few lost films.

Before "A Sainted Devil" was released, Naldi received criticism for appearing 'plump' in her last few films. [41] She insisted it was just a bad fitting dress, and that she was as slim as ever. Naldi, who consistently claimed a height of 5ft 8in during her lifetime, had always been full figured as most vamps were. The press claimed she had weighed upwards of 150-160lbs, which for her height would not be too scandalous. [42]

The claims intensified, adding gossip that Naldi had dyed her skin yellow and bobbed her hair. Naldi denied both claims. [43] As for her weight, she originated the 'pork chops and pineapple' diet, one Vilma Banky would be put on soon after. The press speculated that Naldi had been sick for months over the diet, comparing her to Barbara LaMarr who had also had similar weight issues. LaMarr had a drug problem, something Naldi herself would be accused of, especially in her final years (particularly an unflattering shot in Hollywood Babylon 2). Whether Naldi actually used drugs is unknown, though it is possible the weight criticisms could have prompted her to try such things.

However she did it, Naldi claimed to have lost 25lbs for her role of Carlotta. She claimed she now weighed 123lbs. [44] The press speculated her contract required her not to weigh more than 130lbs. By the time Valentino died just a few years later the press claimed she was once again too heavy.

Eager to start their contract with Ritz Carlton, the Valentinos immediately started work on their pet project "The Hooded Falcon". Set in Spain, Valentino and Naldi were to play Moorish royalty. Newspapers noted it would be one of Naldi's first non-vamp roles, playing a sympathetic character who helps Valentino's in the story.

Ritz Carlton refused to let the Valentinos shoot in Europe, so with Naldi they left for France to 'research'. Naldi was fitted for costumes. While in France, Naldi's brother (possibly encouraged by a press agent) declared she had eloped with D. Gircimel Sanges, supposedly a great dueling man. Naldi returned with the Valentinos and her dog, denying such claims. [45]

After returning from France, Valentino approached old friend June Mathis, to write the script for the film. Mathis had penned "Blood and Sand" and said of Naldi, "She's the most interesting personality I've seen in some time. I'd love to write for her." Naldi remembered Mathis fondly telling of the friendship between Mathis and Valentino. [46]

Unfortunately, Mathis never had the chance to write for Naldi after "Blood and Sand". Mathis wrote a script for The Hooded Falcon, which the Valentinos felt was not up to par. Valentino's manager, George Ullman, delivered the news. Mathis promptly stopped speaking to the Valentinos and would not reconcile with Rudy until months before his death.

With Mathis off the project, several more things fell through, making The Hooded Falcon a costly quagmire. To try and salvage some of the funds, Ritz Carlton ordered Valentino to begin a modern film, a quickie titled, "Cobra". Naldi played Elise Van Zile the 'cobra' of the story. It is, perhaps, the most definitive film of her acting opposite Valentino. Sadly it would be their last film together.

Naldi's weight was again under scrutiny, the press would become even more vicious once they thought she had retired from film. By 1925 Naldi was no longer the reigning vamp. Foreign Pola Negri was said to have usurped the vamp throne. Other actresses vied for the title, but soon the vamp would be out of style. It would morph into the femme fatal with Louise Brooks and Greta Garbo. [47]

As with Valentino's last three pictures, Cobra did only middling box office. With $150,000 already spent on the still unfilmed Hooded Falcon, Ritz Carlton cut the cord and ended their association with Valentino.

Valentino and Rambova's marriage began to fall apart in 1925. When Valentino signed with United Artists it was stipulated Rambova (who had been blamed for his failures) would not be allowed on set. As a consolation prize Ullman offered Rambova $30,000 to make her own film. Rambova wrote, produced, and designed the film titled, "What Price Beauty?" Naldi starred as the subtly named Rita Rinaldi. The film is notable for using the fashions

265

of Adrian Greenburg, as well as giving Myrna Loy her first film role. Unfortunately it is now lost.

"What Price Beauty?" had distribution problems, playing from 1926 to 1928 in various cities. It was not a success. It appears Naldi ended her friendship with Rambova during this time, though the reasons are unknown. Rambova admitted to having an affair with her cameraman during filming, and perhaps this was a factor in Naldi's change of heart. Later in life she would claim she accompanied Rambova to three abortions, though this is obviously impossible to verify.[48]

Valentino only made two more films before his sudden death in August 1926. If Naldi saw him around this time, it is unknown. She would speak fondly of him later in life saying, "He was a sweet darling...kind, sweet, and generous". Rambova's biographer asserts the theory that Naldi did have a sexual relationship with Valentino after his divorce, but before he began his relationship with Pola Negri.[49] While possible, Naldi had been involved with Barclay for several years and would marry him by 1928. Only two people (Valentino's make up artist/yacht captain and his brother) claimed to have witnessed her affair with Valentino, and like other such things, it is hard to verify. Asked for a statement when he died Naldi said, "He was a fine actor and a cultured and educated man."[50]

After "Cobra", Naldi performed in a handful of films, all for independent production companies. It was said she had signed a five year contract in 1922 with Paramount. It appears she broke this contract to work on Valentino's independent productions, as most of her films during this time appear to be as an independent contractor (unless she was loaned out by Paramount, another possibility). With "Cobra" it could be said Naldi reached the peak of her career, something she would abruptly end when she left for Europe not a year later.

Perhaps the most interesting of these high profile films is the lost, "The Miracle of Life", which dealt with birth control. After filming "Do Clothes Make the Pirate" a comedy with Dorothy Gish, Naldi was said to have left abruptly for France in October 1925. It would be the last film she would make in the US. The press claimed it was a publicity stunt for her new picture, "The Desert Healer" (using a story from E.M. Hull, author of "The Sheik"). Naldi was supposed to return in a few weeks to begin filming.[51] One reason she may have left was to film "Queen Calalia" (another Ibanez story), with Jack Meador in Spain.[52] The film was never made.

Rumors spread that she had sailed to wed, but why so spontaneously is hard to discern.[53] Ship records for this travel have, as of this writing, not been found. Nita was said to be filming in the UK in 1926, and judging by release dates this could indeed be accurate.

There is no record of her traveling till November 15th, 1927, at which point she sailed for France.[54] Barclay himself arrived at the same time. It is unclear when he and Isabella actually divorced, though one wonders if it had not been finished until this point. Both Barclay and Isabella traveled quite often, before and after Nita. But Isabella traveled to France no less than 6 times between October 1926 and September 1929. In addition she and Barclay both traveled to Glasgow and the UK, but never together. Whether this had something to do with Naldi's filming of "The Mountain Eagle" is unknown, but possible.

France was the place to go for an easy divorce. No actual marriage certificate for Naldi and Barclay has yet been found, however if they did marry it would have likely been in 1928 or 1929. Given how long they had been together, and under what circumstances, it's possible they never even bothered with the legal route.

Naldi claimed to the press the trip was meant to be only a few months long but she would come to stay '13 years'.[55] However she would only spend about six years in Europe before returning to New York City, without her husband. If indeed she really married Barclay, the marriage was short.

By 1927, the US press announced that she had retired, despite the fact Naldi had never made such an announcement. At the time, most believed she had retired because of her marriage, ill health from weight loss, or from being too heavy to play in films. None of which appear to be true as she worked through 1926 on "The Mountain Eagle".

Many modern fans and reporters believe she retired due to talkies. However The Jazz Singer premiered after she left for France. Somehow in the time that has passed a 'bronx honk' has been attributed to Naldi. This type of 'talkie myth' usually stems from the popular film "Singin' in the Rain", which contains a character named Lina Lamont who suffers from an atrocious Bronx accent. In real life, no silent film star suffered from such a fate (not Clara Bow, not Marie Prevost, and definitely not Nita).

Like other silent stars, Naldi's voice was fine, though it took on a British accent in her later years.[56] She had been on stage before entering film and she would be on stage long after she retired from the screen. Naldi would never make a talkie, despite being active until the 1950s. Perhaps the most believable reason came from Naldi herself during an interview in the 1950s. As she lamented her 'silly' vamp roles, the reporter noted that she had 'grown tired of such roles' and as a way out, married Barclay. [57] With most of her 1926 films lost and her European films hard to access, it's hard to judge whether this is true or not.

Instead of retiring, Naldi actually went the opposite route, starring in a handful of films before she left the screen for good. She starred as Beatrice in Alfred Hitchcock's "The Mountain Eagle", which was filmed in the UK. In the summer of 1926 it was reported she was ill (supposedly from either diet or drugs), though this seems unlikely as she was probably filming with Hitchcock at the time. The film would be released in the US in 1927.

Naldi was then asked to make a film for Paramount France, which would be released in the US as "The Lady from Montmartre" in 1928. Known by the French title "La Femme Nue" it was one of the few films Naldi spoke of in the 30s, and appears to still exist in the French archives. [58]

Naldi then made "Pratermizzi" in Austria. This film had color sequences and still exists in fragmented form. [59] Her final film was the Italian production, "La Maschera d'Oro" (The Golden Mask). The current status of this film is unknown.

Few of these films were released in the US (and with very limited runs at that); with most of her home audience assuming Naldi had long retired.

It's not clear when Naldi's relationship with Barclay began to crumble, or why. The pair had been together at least eleven years when they separated. It is also unclear when Barclay lost his fortune. He was referred to as a 'millionaire' during the 20s, but it is possible he lost his wealth in the stock market crash. When he died in 1945 he was said to be penniless. [60]

Naldi returned to New York, without her husband, in late 1931 under the name Nita Naldi Barclay.[61] In December 1932 she filed for bankruptcy claiming to only have the clothes on her back and the jewelry she returned with.[62] By the time the proceedings started, Naldi claimed she had pawned her last jewel.

In need of money, Naldi returned to the stage in 1932 with "The Firebird" and "Queer People" in New York.[63] The papers were abuzz about her weight once again.[64] One newspaper review of "Queer People" cruelly noted, "Remember Nita Naldi, the bold, bad vamp of silent picture days? Well, during the first act of 'Queer People,' what seemed to us like four hips, eight bosoms, and three faces, walked across the stage. It was Nita Naldi.". [65] Naldi sued in 1934 for $500,000. The suit was dismissed in 1938. [66]

Naldi kept on working, performing in a troubled production of "Black Crook" in 1934.[67] She was spotted at the Algonquin looking 'vacant'. She met with old friends including Lila Lee, Lilyan Tashman, Mae Murray and oddly Gypsy Rose Lee.[68] Naldi told the press she enjoyed reading, especially thrillers. She was said to enjoy horseback riding, croquet, and ping pong as well.[69]

The press once again might have been insinuating a problem with Naldi's health. She was noted as saying in 1932, "I don't drink! Two drinks and I act crazy so I don't drink!" Naldi would have a problem with alcohol in the coming decades.[70]

It seemed the only people who remembered her were her colleagues. During an interview around this time, director Rex Ingram cited Naldi, his wife Alice Terry, and Gloria Swanson as the best silent actresses.[71]

By 1936 Naldi's stage career had stalled. Many reports thought she had just returned from Paris, when in actuality she had been back for a few years. She met with the Ziegfeld Girls Club that same year, claiming she was the oldest one there. By this time the press began to speculate on the separation between Naldi and Barclay. However articles from the late 40s (after his death) state her as still married.[72]

In 1940 Naldi came to Boston with the play "Worth a Million". An article from that time claimed Naldi weighed 250lbs.[73] However this seems exaggerated. She must have put on some weight as other magazines claimed a similar story; but this number would be quite exuberant. The '250lbs' figure would go on to haunt her, carrying on years after her death. Pictures of Naldi from the 1950s show her not much heavier than she had been in the 20s, meaning this spike in weight was probably temporary.

Within the year "Blood and Sand" was slated for a remake. Hedy LaMarr was set to take Naldi's Donna Sol role, though it eventually went to Rita Hayworth.

In 1941 Louella Parsons announced in her column that Naldi would be making her first talkie starring in "For Whom the Bell Tolls".[74] The film would eventually be made in 1943 with Ingrid Bergman and Gary Cooper. Naldi was said to have made a screen test, but she seemed to have no further film offers. The fact she was considered for a new high profile film probably indicates, once again, that she was not as heavy as the gossip hounds claimed.

Along with Mae Murray, Naldi took part in "The Silent Screen" at Bill Rose's Diamond Horseshoe Club in New York.[75] Naldi recited the poem "A Fool There Was" for full kitsch effect. She made twice weekly appearances and was said to be the only vamp not in retirement. Whether Naldi and Murray got along is up for debate. One report had it they insisted on separate dressing rooms. [82] However Naldi mentioned Murray fondly in interviews saying when asked to say how old she was, Murray told her to always say '29'. [76] Indeed the feud may have been a publicity stunt, Murray and Naldi were constantly seen around New York together in the 1930s.

One headline at the time summed up how Naldi was thought of, "Buxom Vamp who made Grandpa Shiver now only gets a laugh!" Of course the same article also believed the Italian press release story. [77]

With the new press attention, Naldi claimed she had left Spain because of the Civil War (the very thing that forced Natacha Rambova out of the country); despite the fact she had been living in Paris. [78] In 1949 an article announced Naldi and Pola Negri were both working on their memoirs. [79] Unfortunately only Negri's would be published. If Naldi did write her memoirs, there whereabouts are currently unknown.

In 1952 Naldi returned to Broadway in "In Any Other Language" with Uta Hagen. [80] Naldi received good reviews for her role. When interviewed with Gloria Marlowe, Naldi was asked how it felt to be on Broadway once more. Naldi replied, "I feel like an antique because most of the people I started out with are dead!" [81]

During the same interview, Naldi was asked about her husband, who was now deceased, "My husband could have covered me with square cut diamonds, of course the money made him... well...more interesting!" Sadly, Naldi was noted during the 50s to still be dieting, 'to maintain' she claimed. [82]

Naldi kept up appearances, keeping active well into 1956. Publicity photos capture her at many silent film events. In 1956 she coached Carol Channing on vamping for a new show of hers titled "Vamp!" [83] Channing would be nominated for Best Actress in a Musical for that role. Asked what she thought of vamps now, Naldi noted she thought the censorship would be too limiting, but that she did indeed think vamping was making a comeback. [84] Actress Nita Talbot was named for her. [85] Reporters compared actresses Greer Garson, Jaynes Mansfield, and Bridget Bardot to Naldi in temperament.

1956 also brought the rumor that Naldi was to wed a Park Avenue man named Larry Hall. The union never took place. [86] During this time, Naldi was said to be doing television work. Two known appearances were the show Home in 1956 and the Tonight Show in 1958. In 1959 Naldi was interviewed by Joan and Robert Franklin for Columbia University's Oral History Research Office. These recordings are still held at Columbia, with excerpts released on a CD collection.

271

Naldi had lived in the Hotel Wentworth in room 522 from 1945 until her death. During her final years she had financial assistance from The Actor's Fund. [87] When friend Diana Barrymore died, she left Naldi $5,000 in her will (however the estate was not settled by the time Naldi passed, so she never was able to claim it.[88])

Friends report she turned them away at the very end of her life (she had been active well into the late 1950s), embarrassed by her health and circumstances. [89] Naldi's eyesight had been failing and she had some heart trouble during the final year of her life. [90] Naldi died on February 17th, 1961 aged 65. She had been dead for two days when she was found by a hotel maid. [91] The cause of death was reported to be a heart attack. Her brother Frank paid for the funeral expenses (which the Actor's Fund had intended to cover). [92] Naldi was buried at the Calvary Cemetery in New York, Section 1W, Range AA, Plot 13/14, Grave 5. She is buried with her mother, sister, and brother. [93]

When Naldi died, most of her obituaries got several things wrong, from birth name to age to place. Worst yet, in the coming decade, everyone from Buster Keaton to silent film buffs remembered her as a 'big' girl...many citing the '250lbs' figure (though that would obviously be absurd during her starring years).

Naldi died in the decade when silent film was beginning to be rediscovered, when society woke up and realized these stars would not be around forever. Unfortunately she did not live to see the many retrospectives of her work that would take place just a few years later. Looking at her work today, it is a shame she has not been remembered as well as other silent stars.

FILMOGRAPHY

Divorce of Convenience (1920, **Lost**)

Experience (1920, **Lost**)

Life (1920, **Lost**)

Common Sin (1920, **Lost**)

Last Door (1920, **Lost**)

The Devil's Daughter (1920, **Lost**)

Snitching Hour (1920, **Lost**)

Dr. Jekyll and Mr. Hyde (1920)

Reported Missing (1922, **Partially Lost**)

The Man From Beyond (1922)

For your Daughter's Sake/Common Sin/Warren's Daughter (1922, **Lost**)

Channing of the Northwest (1922, **Lost**)

Anna Ascends (1922, **Partially Lost**)

Blood and Sand (1922)
You Can't Fool Your Wife (1923, **Lost**)
The Ten Commandments (1923)
Lawful Larceny (1923, **Partially Lost**)
Hollywood (1923)
The Glimpses of the Moon (1923, **Lost**)
A Sainted Devil (1924, **Lost**)
Don't Call it Love (1924, **Lost**)
The Breaking Point (1924, **Lost**)
Marriage Whirl (1925, **Lost**)
Lady Who Lied (1925, **Lost**)
The Hooded Falcon (1924, **Never Made**)
Cobra (1925)
What Price Beauty (1925, **Lost**)
The Unfair Sex (1926, **Lost**)
The Miracle of Life (1926, **Lost**)
Clothes Make the Pirate (1926, **Lost**)
The Mountain Eagle/Fear O' God (1926, **Lost**)
La Femme Nue/The Model from Montemarte (1928,
Partially Lost)
Die Pratermizzi (1928, **Partially Lost**)
La Maschera d'Oro/The Golden Mask (1929, **Lost**)

Sadly, Many of Naldi's films are thought lost. Dr. Jekyll and Mr. Hyde, Blood and Sand, The Man From Beyond, The Ten Commandments, Cobra all fully exist and have been released on DVD.

Fragments of Die Pratermizzi exist and have been released on a DVD in Germany and Austria. La Femme Nue appears to exist in the French archives, though to what extent is currently unknown. Fragments of Reported Missing, Anna Ascends, Lawful Larceny all exist in various archives but have not been released.

June Mathis

JUNE MATHIS BIOGRAPHY

For more on June please see rudolphvalentino.org/junemathis.html

When June Mathis died unexpectedly in 1927 at the age of 40, Jesse Lasky said of her, "When the history of motion pictures is finally written June Mathis's (sic) name will be recorded as one of the most brilliant craftsmen ever associated with the screen." [1] Sam Goldwyn and others echoed his remarks.[2] June Mathis had brought art to film, and pioneered a woman's place in the industry. However history would not be so kind.

Today Mathis is solely remembered for having discovered Rudolph Valentino. If it weren't for June Mathis, there would be no Rudolph Valentino as we know him. Adela St. Roger's said of June and Rudy, "Without June Mathis there would be no Valentino. Only two women were ever important to Rudy. Natacha was one. June Mathis was the other." [3]

Like many other people in Valentino's life, June Mathis has been reduced to some stereotypical frumpy mother figure suited for a bad play (and in fact many films on his life have done her a great injustice). While he may have been one of her greatest achievements, he was certainly not her only one. Mathis was the first female executive and producer. She was voted the 3rd most important woman in the film industry by WAMPAS in 1926 and was part of the forming Academy when she died (she, however, was not a founding member as she passed too soon). [4]

Originally a stage actress of some renown, she left the stage to pursue a writing career while film was still young. Though she had no previous training, Mathis quickly rose through the ranks becoming the first female executive in filmdom with Metro Pictures. There she took full control of her own project, "The Four Horsemen of the Apocalypse"; made Valentino a superstar, and worked on many Alla Nazimova films.

After a string of successes with Valentino, Mathis continued her executive career, becoming more renowned and well paid then the year before. Not only was she not an old frumpy woman, but she was a bit of a man eater, dating many of her protégés. At a time when so few women had power, Mathis ruled the film world despite being completely behind the scenes.

June Mathis was born June Beulah Hughes in January 1887 in Leadville, Colorado to Virginia 'Jenny' Hughes. [5] Virginia claimed a birth year of 1860; while June's maternal Grandmother Emily Hawkes claimed a birth year of 1852 (obviously one or the other was not telling the truth; Emily was probably born in 1842 as she claimed to marry in 1869). The family came from Illinois. Her father is harder to verify. Mathis claimed in articles he was Dr. Philip Hughes from Wales, and that his family in the UK was quite illustrious. She also claimed he died when she was a baby, forcing her mother to move to Salt Lake City and herself to enter vaudeville to help earn her keep.

The real situation is harder to discern. Jenny was said to have married 'fellow widower' William D. Mathis in 1887, when June was either a newborn or a toddler. W.D. had three children from his first marriage (Laura, George, and Samuel), all of whom were older than June. [6] The youngest child, Samuel, was born in 1882, and was thus only a few years older than June. Mathis adored W.D. calling him her father and taking his name during her childhood.

Philip doesn't appear anywhere. June's Salt Lake Obituary (where many who knew her still lived) mentioned her as coming from a 'theatrical' family. This could explain why her mother and maternal Grandparents were so willing to travel around the vaudeville circuit with her, leaving her stepfather and stepsiblings in Utah.

Mathis always cited her birth father as dead, well into the 1920s. It is extremely unlikely he was so illustrious, or even a doctor. Silent film stars would usually cite an absentee parent as dead to save embarrassment.

No Philip Hughes appears in the census (and if indeed a man by that name was a vaudeville performer he could be hidden in some obscure corner of the US during the census). However, a John T. Hughes appears in the 1900 census, having been born in 1854 and immigrated from Wales in 1876. He married a Margaret A. Hughes in 1897. The couple lived in Pennsylvania at the time. June first appears in the Utah papers that very year, which might give some very strong evidence that this indeed was her father. Indeed John could have left the family sometime in the 1890s, whether for another woman or just to leave. Either way, June would always refer to him as 'dead', even on her passport applications.

However they came about, the new family had settled in Salt Lake City, Utah, where William ran 'Mathis Drug Store' at 330 South Main Street. He was quite popular with the locals who called him 'Pop'. William was so proud of Mathis he plastered clippings of her achievements all over his drug store walls. [7] Mathis would mention missing him on a trip to Utah after his passing. [8]

Mathis was said many times to have entered vaudeville to help support her mother, but with such a small time period between marriages this is probably unlikely. From descriptions, Mathis was an endearing child who loved attention, growing to quite a bit of renowned in her adopted home town. There she was known as the 'Cleverest Child Elocutionist in this part of the country'.

It seems she took to entertaining at a young age, with many public performances occurring in 1898, when she was likely 11. The first such performance came reciting at the Ladies Auxiliary of the Democratic County Committee in October 1898 (despite the name, it was a gathering of Republican women). [9] A few weeks later she held another such performance with the paper remarking, "Little June Mathis recited in her usual charming style." [10] Mathis' performances became a stable of these meetings well into 1899. [11]

Mathis continued performing, this time at the Utah Camp No. 338 at K. of P. Castle in February 1899. The paper singled out her performance remarking, "This little lady shows a remarkable presence of mind and memory, accompanied by a graceful carriage and splendid elocution. She recited "Tit for Tat" in true Irish brogue, and for an encore "Hol' Dem Philippines" in the Negro dialect. Both were well rendered and vigorously applauded." In addition she also sung a song. [12] In March 1899 she gave another recitation, this time at the Blue Night at the YMCA parlors membership drive.

As a child Mathis had attended Whittier School. As a teen she attended Salt Lake High, though it is very likely her education was interrupted during her many travels. [13] It appears she dropped out of school by the time she moved to San Francisco.

Mathis moved to San Francisco at the age of 13 in 1900. Her mother, Grandmother, and Grandfather traveled with her. Her stepfather remained in Salt Lake where he proudly informed everyone of her accomplishments. There she was engaged to appear in a vaudeville act at Fishers. Mathis was eventually allowed to put together her own act of imitations and dances. [14] After Fishers, she was hired by The Archie Levy Amusement Association who said of her act, "The Archie Levy Amusement association takes great pleasure in announcing the appearance of the very clever and capable little child artist, June Mathis, appearing in a choice selection of her own bright ideas. This capable and clever little genius is, beyond a question of doubt, the greatest in her respective line." [15]

In 1901, Mathis was engaged to play the Orpheum in San Francisco, which was the highest one could go in San Francisco at the time. [16] Her stepfather was so excited he shared the telegram with the local newspaper. [17]

Mathis did well with vaudeville, signing with the Keith Circuit in Chicago. [18] There she played the Haymarket, Olympic, and Grand Theatres. [19] While in Chicago, Mathis received a telegram asking her to appear in a May Vokes play.[20] Mathis made her professional stage debut in 1903, with Vokes in "Where are You?". [21] Though she was 16 years old (and likely already shaving years off of her age), Mathis was still billed as a 'baby' which was the common practice for teenagers at the time.

Mathis was a success as 'Baby' and toured "Where are You?" well into 1904, eventually performing back in Salt Lake to wild acclaim. [22] After this she was offered the role of Janey in Ezra Kendall's "The Vinegar Buyer", again to much acclaim. [23] Mathis was put under contract for this play and her salary was said to have rose substantially.

Mathis was then signed with Burrows and Lancaster where she played the larger cities in a variety of plays including "When Georgina was 18", and "Jolly Jolliers". [24] After this she was engaged to play with Will T. Hodge in "Eighteen Miles from Home". [25] In only four years, Mathis' star had risen from a nobody to a featured and well reviewed player.

In 1907 she was given her first star billing in, "The Girl Patsy", which was written by Jane Mauldin Feigl. [26] At the age of 20, Mathis was said to be one of the youngest leading ladies in the profession. [27] The role gave Mathis so much acclaim that she was eventually selected by Julian Eltinge in 1908, for a major role in his play, "Brewster's Millions".[28] Eltinge, a wildly popular drag performer, would become a close friend of Mathis', the two working together for many years. [29] It is quite possible that Mathis first spotted her own protégée Rudolph Valentino in one of Eltinge's films in 1918.

Mathis made her way to New York City in 1910 where she lived with her Grandparents, mother, and some boarders. [30] Again William was in Salt Lake. It was said in 1910 she did a play called, "Going Some" which may have brought her out to the East Coast. It must not have gone well for very long, as Mathis mentioned in an interview towards the end of her life, "Years ago I tried to be an actress on the speaking stage. I wasn't much a success. Yet no matter how discouraged I felt, how weary I became doing the rounds of the manager's offices, I always had one place of comfort. The office of Mrs. DeMille, who was a casting agent. She was the mother of Cecil and William De Mille.

She worked very hard and I certainly meant nothing in her life. But no matter how...I went there. She always spared time to see me and send me out again with fresh courage.

When Cecil was beginning to win his first great success I met the brothers out there. William didn't remember me, but Cecil did. 'Mother would love to see you again' he said and sent me to call on her. There she was as great as ever ready to help me. I can't forget that kindness and the only way I can repay it is by trying to extend it to others." [31]

Making the rounds in New York could be quite dreadful and heartbreaking, as many silent film stars described. Likely in need of some income; Mathis described her first foray into film during the 'off season' (Summertime).[32] Mathis had decided to pursue 'flickers' which were considered 'vulgar' at the time. Only an actor or actress down on their luck would dare pursue them.

Not wanting to soil her reputation, Mathis performed under a fake name in a comedy shot in New England during this time. [33] Mathis confided in another interview it had been a part of a 'Zulu' woman in a slapstick comedy (thus likely being a short in blackface). [34] Unimpressed with acting, Mathis decided to go behind the camera. She hung around sets learning about directing, filming, lighting and writing techniques. [35] Judging by her description, her foray into film must have occurred around 1910 though it could have occurred as late as 1912.

Despite her many goals and aspirations, Mathis had been a very sickly child from a young age. Her heart troubles began as a child and had never quite gone away (eventually it would cause her death).[36] After ending her time with Brewster's, Mathis had to take rest as she had become severely ill (from what, is not mentioned). Mathis grew better and claimed she had healed herself with the power of positive thinking. [37] An insistent Spiritualist, Mathis' beliefs would become more powerful and profound through the years.

With her health intact, Mathis was signed to play once again with Eltinge in 1912 with, "The Fascinating Widow" a play that would give them both great acclaim. She toured with the production, which would go on to sell out 20 weeks in Chicago.

Mathis noted that while touring Widow, a local newspaper had asked her to write an article for them. After she had done so, the editor commented that she was a good writer; why not try that for a profession? Mathis was flattered but still unsure about leaving the stage. [38]

She possibly returned to Salt Lake for a brief visit, but soon left for San Francisco. While there she took up several 'dreadful' musical comedies and small roles (Mathis was said to be a soubrette).

[39] Though Mathis enjoyed comedy, she hated performing in musical comedies. [40] The company traveled to Los Angeles where a friend in film noticed her sketches (she was said to have a gifted artistic bent from a young age) and suggested she enter film. Again Mathis was unsure.

However, after another performance of the dreadful comedy, Mathis packed her trunks and decided she was done with the stage for good. Mathis was convinced she could be a wonderful scenario writer (screenwriter). In her opinion film adaptations of literature always fell short of a climax, something she felt she could do better. [41] Having saved enough money, Mathis took her mother and moved to New York, where she studied under an editor friend for two years. [42] Mathis said of the time that she studied during the day and attended the movies at night. [43] Oddly, she also seemed to make one last foray into stage, with the one off Broadway performance of the unfortunately titled, "Granny Maumee" in April 1914. [44]

Mathis was adamant for the rest of her life that most screenwriters never took the time to study, and that's why many of them failed. [45] She hated 'half baked' attempts and would say so in many interviews. In addition to her studies, Mathis read every piece of literature she could find, insistent on studying the greats. [46]

Mathis' writing style would be quite consistent over the years. If it was drama it would contain comedic elements, and if it was a comedy it would usually stay light-hearted. Most of her films were somewhere between the two genres, using drama and humor, with a heavy dose of spiritualist themes about redemption and the power of belief. Mathis' masterpieces seem to be quite long, considering they stay consistently entertaining speaks well of her skill.

Many have said that Mathis was a firm believer in the Bible and book of Revelations in particular (thus a draw to "Four Horsemen"). In 1926 she said, "All our moral pictures have shown the effect of the Bible. Every time a writer writes a subtitle pointing out the paths of good and evil he draws his similes from the pages of the Bible. There are no pictures which do not show at some point of contact with The Holy Book". [47]

However for an adaptation of Sir Gilbert Parker's "Right of Way", Mathis eliminated the religious propaganda and chose to treat religion as a great, universal thought of God instead of a sect idea. [48] More often than not Mathis' films seemed to contain vague spiritualist and occult ideas, rather than strictly Christian ones.

When speaking of Christianity and film, Mathis would usually proclaim that she believed in clean comedy, finding European films 'vulgar'.[49] This was a common thing to do during the 20s, while trying to keep a step ahead of vicious moral codes. It seems in private Mathis felt differently, as she inserted several clever and scandalous comedic bits into many of her films (such as the children picking up a discarded cigarette in the background of "Turn to the Right"). In Four Horsemen, she deliberately inserted a small bit of German soldiers cross-dressing, admitting in the press she had done it for those who knew to what she was alluding.[50]

It seems likely her time on the road, particularly with Eltinge, had given her some liberal beliefs that would not please the women's church clubs of the time. In an interview she declared, "You can't portray life and obey the censor!"[51]

George Henderson remembered Mathis' skill dealing with censors noting, "After Miss June Mathis, one of the most noted screen writers, had completed her version of Four Horsemen, 137 cuts in the film were made by the censors in Pennsylvania.

Yet Miss Mathis has had years of experience in evading or complying with censorship rules and the whole expert force of Metro Studios was working with her. While I was talking with Miss Mathis a director appeared at her door and asked, "What kind of wine glasses will we use in that trading post scene?"

"Champagne glasses," answered the writer. "Use a white wine so we can claim it is white cider they are drinking when the censors object.""[52]

Likely in early 1915, she entered a film story writing contest. Though Mathis did not win, she received many offers from film studios who liked her writing style. Finally, the notable Edwin Carewe was able to convince her to join Metro Pictures. Mathis' first film was "The House of Tears".[53]

Many of Mathis' films, particularly before she was an executive, were directed by Carewe. One wonders if there was a romantic relationship there, though such things are hard to prove. Mathis seemed to have a habit of partnering or later on mentoring creative men who she would share relationships with, and leaving them creatively once the relationship had ended.

As a writer for Metro, Mathis quickly rose through the ranks working with Carewe. By 1917 she had moved to head of the Scenario department, making her the first female film executive in history.[54] While Mathis was constantly lauded as the top female in the film industry during her career, some clarification is needed. Mathis likely tied America's Sweetheart, Mary Pickford, for the title.

Pickford was an extremely astute and powerful businesswoman; however this knowledge was kept quiet from the public to preserve her image of innocence at a time when females in positions of power were not encouraged. [55]

Other than acting, Pickford had her own production company (run by her mother, the equally brilliant Charlotte Pickford Smith), approved everything from scripts to costumes to casting, and eventually was 1 of the 4 founders of United Artists. Pickford gained almost full control of her films in 1915 and 1916, meaning she would be the first female producer just a year before Mathis. However this does not account for Helen Gardner, (the first vamp type) who had her own production company in 1912. However, Mathis would become an executive before Pickford, and Gardner, again just by a few years. [56]

Unlike the other women, Mathis was strictly behind the scenes, and no such expectations were made of her to preserve some sort of image. Though Mathis never achieved the independence and wealth that Pickford did (ironically in the last year of her life, Mathis was rumored to be signing with UA) she was likely the highest achieving, ranking, and paid female in the industry who did not appear on camera.

Unlike Pickford, Mathis was hands on in directing, crew selection, production, casting, editing, writing, and scouting. No other writer (including Anita Loos or Frances Marion, though Marion possibly earned more as the exclusive Pickford scenarist) or even acting female would out rank her in such power. Mathis is constantly overlooked as a female pioneer in this regard (as is Pickford as well).[57]

Through 1917 Mathis made several important films including "The Millionaire's Double" (Lionel Barrymore), "The Call of her people" (Ethel Barrymore), "Somewhere in America" (Mary Miles Minter), "The Jury of Fate" (Tod Browning), "The Legion of Death" (Tod Browning), and "Aladdin's Other Lamp" (Viola Dana). In fact Viola Dana would credit Mathis for 'discovering' her, though she had been in film since 1914.

In 1918 Mathis began another important year. She wrote "Red, White, and Blue Blood", which ironically was directed by Charles Brabin (who would cause her much grief several years later during Ben-Hur). With War in the air, Mathis wrote several propaganda films including "To Hell with the Kaiser" (which gave Karl Dane a key role) and "Why Germans Must Pay!" What Mathis really thought of the Great War is anyone's guess; however her epic blockbuster, "The Four Horsemen of the Apocalypse" was notable as one of the first anti war films. Much of Hollywood was pressured into making propaganda films, something many filmmakers openly regretted (including D.W. Griffith and Raoul Walsh). [58]

In 1918 Julian Eltinge began work on his own war film, "Over the Rhine". However the film took too long to shoot, with the war over by the time it was to be released. With war films now out of style, Eltinge shelved the picture. The film would be recut and released in 1920 as "An Adventuress". The final cut in 1921, "The Isle of Love" is the only one that survives today. [59] In the film were two nobodies in small roles: Virginia Rappe (soon to be the cause of the Fatty Arbuckle lynching) and Rudolph Valentino. Mathis claimed she first seen Valentino in Clara Kimball Young's picture, "The Eyes of Youth" (a film that would definitely speak to her Spiritualist beliefs). [60] However one must wonder if she had seen him in a cut of Eltinge's film, or even met him during the production. Mathis had a long association with Eltinge, she would even write a skit for his 'Revue of Nineteen Nineteen'.

However he was found, Valentino would always speak fondly of Mathis saying, "For seven long years, working hard, playing small parts in sometime atrocious pictures I labored to be 'found'. But it was June Mathis who opened the door of opportunity for me. It was she who saw me for the part in the Four Horsemen." [61] For another interview he said, "She discovered me, anything I have accomplished I owe to her, to her judgment, to her advice and to her unfailing patience and confidence in me."

In addition to being trusted with Frances X. Bushman, Viola Dana, and Mae Murray; Mathis was given control over eccentric Russian actress Alla Nazimova. Mathis had penned "Toys of Fate" which became Nazimova's breakthrough film; launching her into film superstardom. Now a guaranteed star, Nazimova demanded to move to Los Angeles and that Mathis pen her future films as well. In October 1918, Mathis left New York to work on "A Red Lantern" for Nazimova. Of note, "A Red Lantern" was Anna May Wong's first film role (lost in a crowd of extras). [62]

Mathis was able to cut down on her output during 1919, something she had hoped to do for quality control. By 1920 her output stayed study. One interesting film from that year is "The Saphead" which would be Buster Keaton's first feature film. During these years, Mathis would be noted as a dramatic writer who added a heavy dose of spiritualism into her films. However Mathis had a knack with comedy, even inserting it when writing a dramatic film.

June and Valentino on set of "Blood and Sand" 1921

This would become more noticeable especially during 1922 with such films as "Turn to the Right" which features her heavy dose of spiritualism and believe to achieve attitude, many dramatics, but also many funny bits inserted usually between the dramatic scenes. With a lesser hand this could be tiresome, but with Mathis it was brilliant.

Mathis had begun work on adapting Vincent Blanco Ibanez's "The Four Horsemen of the Apocalypse" which she intended to make fit her lofty vision. Mathis was certain one needed to be 'far sighted' to see the big picture. She had been certain from a young age she could make a spectacle bigger and better than anything before it.

Mathis would succeed, launching both Rex Ingram and Valentino into stardom.[63] Four Horsemen would be the highest grossing film of 1921 beating out Charlie Chaplin's "The Kid". It would gross $9 million (in 1933 dollars) and be the 6th best selling silent film ever.[64] It would be remade in 1962 as a talkie.

In 1920, Mathis 'discovered' Rex Ingram. Ingram had been directing b pictures since 1914. He and Mathis worked together on his first film for Metro, "Hearts are Trumps" which was possibly made while Four Horsemen was in the works. The duo were said to be inseparable, spending extremely long days at the studio working on her masterpiece.

Mathis was never one to be shy with the opposite sex. She enjoyed telling the story of a drunken leading man who tried to rape her in her dressing room. Mathis bit him on his shoulder and 'held on like a little bulldog' until he let her go. Ironically they had to go out and play a love scene soon after, with Mathis proudly playing the sweet ingénue in love once again.[65]

As much as the accusations of 'frumpy' and 'motherly' have been lobbed at her, it seems Mathis had just as many relationships as anyone else, though such things are so terribly hard to verify 90 years later. Most sources use a terrible photo of Mathis with frizzy hair and bad lighting, furthering the impression of her being a frumpy, ugly, old woman. However other photos prove that though she was no Ziegfeld girl, Mathis wasn't as dull and haggard as she is usually made out to be. In her teens, her looks and fashions were highly praised by the press and critics.[66] As an executive she would buy the finest clothes from Paris, which shows in photos.[67]

Another claim often lobbed at her is 'overweight'.[68] Mathis had been ill as a child and was still suffering from a heart condition during her film years. She would jokingly note in interviews she had a little fat for 'health'.[69] Though not as stylish or slim as Anita Loos or Frances Marion, Mathis made up for her looks with a wit and a

June Mathis, Rudolph Valentino, and Rex Ingram during filming of
The Four Horsemen of the Apocalypse, 1921

noted bubbly personality. One interviewer said of her, "She has wide cheeks, full grey eyes and what she frankly calls 'fat, to nourish the nerves.' Her poise is perfect. She gives the impression of tremendous reserves of energy...Miss Mathis is thoroughly feminine, even concealing her age, which I guess in the late 30's." (she was 36 at the time). [70]

Relationships with both Ingram and Valentino have been written off as 'inaccurate', though no one has ever cited why. It appears much of this came from a Nazimova biography, as there were many rumors swirling around during the 1920s about her romances.

In fact, the story of probable affairs with either Ingram or Valentino are tangled together, all seeming to cumulate in 1921. Mathis thought fondly of both men, and believed she had lived lifetimes with both before (Mathis was a big fan of reincarnation). [71] She felt a motherly type tendency towards both, believing she had been a mother to both men in a previous lifetime, particularly Valentino (in somewhere like Egypt she noted). [72]

There seems to be some solid evidence that she did indeed have an affair with Ingram. She took and mentored him, giving him a major film to show off his talents. Before Valentino was chosen for the role of Julio (something Mathis seemed to have intended all along), it seems the relationship was bordering on serious. [73]

Was there a relationship with Valentino? It doesn't seem as impossible as most assume. Mathis adored him as a friend, with others noting they seen each other once a day for the first several months after they had met. [74] Mathis' friendship with Valentino seemed to overshadow whatever relationship she indeed had with Ingram. Ingram did not like Valentino, in fact to such a point it might be evidence that he and Mathis were romantically involved.

Four Horsemen was Mathis' film through and through. She wrote the story, had a hand in crew and casting, and worked right alongside Ingram during filming. Mathis mentored Valentino during filming, something he mentioned as being extremely thankful for. [75] However it might have been more than just mentoring, as Ingram refused to direct Valentino and barely spoke to him, making such extra help necessary.

By the time Four Horsemen was released, the bad blood boiled further. Ingram had thought this film would be his breakthrough, but instead it became Valentino's. [76] Ingram never had another major success and all but retired by 1924. Valentino, however, would go on to fame and critical acclaim until his death.

Ingram became almost obsessive with his mission to prove he was better than Valentino. In a 1921 interview touting his new

June and her beloved parakeet

find 'Ramon Samaniegos' (aka Ramon Novarro), Ingram insisted it was the director who made such stars and that Valentino was nothing, he would prove it with this new Latin Lover (even going as far to make a film titled "The Arab" ripping off the The Sheik). [77]

Apparently the bad blood never went away, as Alice Terry would tell film historian Anthony Slide how certain she was both Pola Negri and Rudolph Valentino were gay (though both had well noted relationships with each other and other member of the opposite sex). [78]

Though Adela St. Johns is known for making colorful versions of events, she quite possibly revealed the truth in the 1950s, "In the first months of their friendship, June and Rudy saw each other every day, every night. It is ridiculous to dismiss her merely as the woman who discovered Valentino, for she molded his thought, taste, work and soul.

FIRST woman executive in the industry, June didn't fall in love with him. She had already given her heart; as well as her brains to Rex Ingram. But she did see Rudy as Julio and insisted that he play the part: For Valentino to build Rex Ingram's "Four Horsemen" at the box office might have been O.K. But audiences didn't even see the beauty of Ingram's sets, nor the skill he'd used with lighting. They were watching Valentino dance. Forever after "the Four Horsemen" was to be known as the picture that made Valentino.

Oh, it was a famous victory for June, the triumph of Valentino. But soon, finding beautiful Alice Terry, an extra girl he'd promoted to dance with Valentino asleep on the set, Rex Ingram woke up, took her to dinner, and married her.

The marriage rocked Hollywood. What would June do? In public June showed the magnificent condescension of a duchess. If her heart broke in private, nobody except her friend Rudy knew it. Nothing could shake the friendship between June and Rudy, but Ingram did break up what might have been the greatest three-way combination in all picture history." [79]

Perhaps most telling is Ingram had divorced his wife Doris Pawn in 1920; before he likely met Terry, but about the time he would have been with Mathis. [80] Mathis, Valentino, Ingram, and Terry would all go on to work on, "The Conquering Power". It would seem that whatever business was between Mathis and Ingram, it did not come to a head until that time, as the now trio (sans Valentino) worked on one final film, "Turn to the Right", which was released in 1922 (however production had begun in 1920). Before being spotted by Ingram, Terry had indeed been nothing more than an extra girl.

Ingram and Terry secretly eloped in November 1921 while working on their first non Mathis film, "The Prisoner of Zenda". [81] It would be during this time that Ingram grew vocal in his hatred for Valentino, and began to push Novarro as a new star. It doesn't seem he, nor Mathis, had much to say about each other after the marriage. Though both he and Terry would have plenty of mean things to say about Valentino.

Ironically, somehow with the silence, Mathis was written out of her creative partnership with Ingram. During the 20s it was believed she had a hand in discovering Ramon Novarro as well, and that she deserved more credit for collaborating with Ingram than she got. [82] Most Ingram fans to this day refer to his movies as 'Ingram/Terry pairings' when in reality his major films were 'Mathis/Ingram' pairings.

As for Valentino, Mathis' friendship with him grew stronger. Before "Turn to the Right", Mathis began work with both Nazimova and Valentino on "Camille". Some have suggested Mathis did not write this film, though they have given no reason why.

Nazimova seemed to hold a high opinion of Mathis and its likely she sought her out. Mathis introduced Nazimova to Valentino, who in turn introduced Valentino to her art director, Natacha Rambova.

When Mathis had previously worked with Nazimova, Rambova was not yet in the picture. [83] It seems by most accounts that Rambova and Mathis got along during these early years. Mathis, her mother Virginia, Rambova, and Valentino would constantly dine together. Mathis' mother died in January 1922 [84] (her stepfather would die a little over a year later on September 14th, 1923). All three were deeply affected by her death, as both Valentino and Rambova had admired her greatly. According to Rambova, it was at this time Mathis and a friend of Mathis introduced her and Valentino to spiritualism and automatic writing.

This is quite an explosive, yet obvious, claim as all Valentino and Rambova biographers have seemed to overlook it. Mathis was a proud Spiritualist, believing in the occult, the power of thinking, automatic writing, reincarnation, and séances. [85] Of reincarnation Mathis said, "If you are vibrating on the right plane, you will inevitably come in contact with the others who can help you. It's like tuning in on your radio. If you get the right wave-length, you have your station." [86] Never shy of her beliefs, it was said she chose George Walsh for the lead in Ben-Hur because of his 'orangish-yellow aura'.

She incorporated her beliefs into her films from the very start, and never made shy of her beliefs to the press. A press release for "Why Women Love" describes Mathis writing method, which sounds very similar to the description the 'soul of Rudy' gives in Rambova's book.[87] Rambova is usually cited as introducing and encouraging Valentino towards Spiritualism, but it does not seem unlikely that his 'little mother' would not have had some influence on him.

Rambova mentioned how Valentino wrote Day Dreams with a belief that certain spirits of deceased writers were the ones responsible for the poems and credited their initials in his book. Mathis held a similar belief, believing that General Lew Wallace had aided her to adapt "Ben-Hur"; that she had received psychic inspiration from F. Marion Crawford in transposing "The Palace of the King"; and that Frank Norris had communicated with her regarding "Greed".[88]

After completing three pictures for Alice Lake, Mathis joined Valentino by moving to Famous Players-Lasky. [89] Valentino wanted her to write "The Sheik", but the script had already been written. [90] After putting Valentino in two quickie pictures, Famous-Players finally utilized her in writing what would be one of his greatest films commercially and critically, "Blood and Sand".

Following in the Latin Lover vein, the film furthered Valentino's superstar status. It was also the first of his many pairings with Nita Naldi. Mathis adored Naldi and said of her "She's the most interesting personality I've seen in some time. I'd love to write for her." Sadly, Mathis would never get to write for Naldi again. Blood and Sand would be one of the top four grossing films of 1922 (making two years in a row the duo had been on the list), and only one of two Valentino/Mathis films to be remade as a talkie. On his death bed Valentino cited it as his greatest performance. [91]

Mathis wrote two follow up films, "The Young Rajah" and "The Spanish Cavalier" both of which were to be released in 1922 and 1923. Once filming on Blood and Sand had wrapped, Valentino and Rambova eloped in Mexico, violating the bigamy laws of the time (Valentino's divorce to Jean Acker had not been finalized for one year). Valentino was arrested and very upset with his treatment by Famous Players. Against his will he made "The Young Rajah" which would be his last Mathis penned film.

"The Young Rajah" is all but lost today (surviving in just a few seconds worth of film) but it is a quintessential Mathis film. Extremely heavy on spiritualism and her religious beliefs, the film did poorly. It was the first major flop for both Mathis and Valentino in a long time. Valentino, angered by his treatment at the studio, began on a one man strike that would bar him from any form of employment (later downgraded to just film employment). Some wish

June Mathis and Charles Brabin

to blame Mathis for the failure, though it is hard to really judge without having the film to view. For her part Mathis felt it was a failure herself saying, "The film was terrible. Valentino kept displaying that wonderful profile to the camera, but the part didn't need it. He looked lost - and it showed." [92]

"The Spanish Cavalier" was turned into "The Spanish Dancer" and given to Pola Negri. Realizing there wouldn't be much for her to do without Valentino, Mathis signed with Goldwyn on November 21st, 1922 (about the time Young Rajah was released) as an editorial director. [93] It was the highest office she had ever held and her pay was said to be extraordinary, somewhere around $750 to $1500 a week. [94] Samuel Goldwyn would later try to take a lot of credit for Mathis, saying he had signed her at Metro (though he was probably ousted out by the time she was signed), that he had insured her life for $1 million (this happened either at Goldwyn or First National), and that he had thought highly of her despite the disasters to come.

As Valentino began to fight his battles with the court and film industry, Mathis began preparations for a new major super production, "Ben-Hur". She wished to have Valentino play Ben-Hur (a role that would eventually go to Ramon Novarro in the end) but his injunction made that impossible. [95] Mathis began picking her cast and crew including director Charles Brabin, who she had worked with once before. She mentioned admiring his few films with Theda Bara, who was, by this point, his wife. Mathis chose Kathleen Key to play Tizrah (a role she would keep), Frances X. Bushman as Messala (a role he too would keep) and George Walsh to play Ben-Hur. The cast and crew left for Italy in March 1924 to shoot on location, something costly and expensive. The production was expected to cost $3 million, with $1 million being for the rights alone. [96]

When Mathis would return in the fall of 1924, rumors swirled she was engaged to Walsh. [97] Whether Mathis' relationship with Balboni started in Italy or upon her return to the US is hard to discern. It's possible she could have had a relationship with George Walsh, but there isn't very solid evidence for it. Miriam Cooper (Walsh's sister in law), makes no mention of Mathis in her autobiography. [98]

Other than supposedly meeting her future husband, the trip and production would prove a massive disaster for Mathis, Brabin, and Goldwyn. Any and everything that could go wrong did. There were translation problems, costly equipment problems, and finally creative problems. Brabin did not get along with Mathis, feeling it was his picture instead of hers (despite the fact she was his boss and in charge of the film). It reached the point that Brabin would not

Eric von Stroheim posing with Mathis, 1923.

even speak with her, or pretend to listen and then do his way anyways.

By June 1924, newspapers were abuzz that resignations were imminent. By July the original crew was off the picture with production and a mostly new cast moved to Hollywood for reshoots (ironically Ingram would claim to help direct the new film). [99] Mathis would make subtle digs at Brabin in the press, and would almost ironically and boldly give a speech at the "Optimists Club" just a few months later titled, "Filming Ben-Hur under difficulties". [100]

While at Goldwyn, Mathis was pegged for another major fiasco: editing Erich von Stroheim's ten hour epic masterpiece, "Greed", down to a more manageable size. [101] Mathis and von Stroheim were friends and respected each others work. In fact, they were brought to Goldwyn at the same time, with von Stroheim rumored to direct "Ben-Hur". [102] Stroheim himself reluctantly knew the film had to be edited and asked Rex Ingram to do so. This took the film down to a length of about two hours. Mathis herself never edited it, being preoccupied with Ben-Hur (production on Greed started in 1923, and Mathis would be gone during most of the fiasco), but left a note to a staff editor to do so. [103] Mathis has been unfairly blamed for the editing over the years. Her name was likely associated with the film due to her position (Editorial Director) and her prestige. The press never seemed to have a bad word to say about Mathis, every film was her latest 'masterpiece'. Promoting "Greed" as such would surely bring in people who may not have attended else wise. Though she received a contractual credit; Mathis never touched the film.

Mathis returned to the US in July 1924 from France alone. [104] On August 2nd, 1924 Mathis signed with First National Pictures. She was again an executive, signed by Richard A. Rowland who had given her one of her first promotions at Metro many years before. Mathis was said to be making $50,000 a year or $1,000 a week. [105]

On Rowland's advice, Mathis was set to write and edit films for Colleen Moore and Corinne Griffith. Many people have retroactively decided this was a downgrade, despite the fact she was still an executive and still making a high salary (quite likely one of the highest she ever earned). Mathis had enjoyed writing comedy her entire career, and judging by her time at First National it suited her.

Mathis' first project for Moore was said to be "Bobbed Hair". However Moore had to finish filming "So Big" (ironically directed by Brabin) before she could begin work on Mathis' film. "Bobbed Hair" would eventually be made by Marie Prevost. Meanwhile Mathis began work on "Sally".

Valentino had, by this time, ended his strike and returned to the screen finishing his obligations to Famous-Players. He was set to make his own film, "The Hooded Falcon", which was to be Natacha and his masterpiece. Mathis was rumored as a writer for the project, and was officially attached by the end of August 1924. [106] Fearing she would be too busy trying to make good with Colleen Moore's deadline, she presented a preliminary script to Valentino, Rambova, and the director.

Mathis and Valentino had not seen much of each other since his first marriage to Rambova in 1922, as Mathis had left to work on Ben-Hur and Valentino had left on a national dance tour with Rambova. Adela St. Johns suspected this was the moment their relationship became strained. [107] Until the marriage, Mathis had been friendly with Rambova. When Valentino was arrested, Mathis along with Thomas Meighan and George Melford fronted the bail money for his release. [108] Perhaps the incidents that followed lowered Mathis' opinion of Rambova. Rambova, for her part, felt the world had unfairly turned against her in the past two years. She was seen as controlling and manipulating her husband into a whiny artistic bore. [109] How much is her fault is still debatable, though at the very least it can be said she never forced Valentino to do anything.

In an ironic twist, many contemporaries saw Mathis as being not only the Spiritualist influence on Valentino, but the artistic one as well. He met Mathis before he met Rambova, and surely Mathis' direction and advice on Four Horsemen and The Conquering Power meant something to him. It almost appears that with "Monsieur Beaucaire", Rambova was trying to be like Nazimova, while Valentino was trying to be like Mathis in their artistic goals. Or perhaps even more so "The Hooded Falcon" was such a mission. Either way, both films were a disaster.

Valentino, Rambova, and the director agreed that Mathis' script would not do. George Ullman, Valentino's manager, delivered the news to Mathis. Mathis, who was known for her temper and strong will (ironically she always claimed to fight fair and never lose her cool), promptly refused to speak to either Rambova or Valentino ever again. [110]

Mathis' strong will was legendary in its own sort of way. Mathis did not deny it, only claiming that she fought 'fairly' and only for things she was certain should be left in her films. Even her husband would not be immune from such debates. One article noted Mathis was said to be 'indignant' when George Walsh was fired from Ben-Hur, despite her denial of their relationship. Judging by her actions, Mathis did not take perceived wrongs lightly. However, when it came to those nearest to her, she never said a word to the press. She never remarked on her break up with Ingram (personally or professionally), and she never remarked about this spat with Valentino.

According to all those around the duo, Mathis and Valentino thought very highly of each other personally and professionally. Mathis had written "The Spanish Cavalier" for him, and according to Natacha, Mathis had also written a Cellini project for him (she said this was before the strike, but it sounds like something that occurred perhaps shortly after; based on various reports). It would be quite odd for Mathis to just simply walk away from such a relationship. Surely something else had led up to such a drastic decision.

Unfortunately, both Ullman and Rambova wrote just the basics of the situation in their respective books (Ullman rewrote his memoirs shortly before his death; sadly he didn't include any further details on this situation). Rambova felt she had been unfairly blamed once again, which would indicate Mathis had cited Rambova as the source of her frustration. Press reports from the time note that, "All of Hollywood" was waiting to see which woman would win the battle for superiority, which by December the press had decided Rambova was (in their portrayal, unfairly,) the winner. Rambova had taken the heat for Valentino's last two failures, but it seems the spat with Mathis was the climax of the presses hatred of her.

Rambova had written the original outline and once again tried to doctor the script. Perhaps, Mathis felt she had no right to criticize her work, being an amateur in the screenwriting field. Still something more seems to lie underneath the situation. Sadly what it is seems impossible to find in a way satisfactory of historical research, as of this writing.

Valentino gave an interview shortly after the incident stating how he still cared for and respected Mathis, and hoped things would be resolved soon, "I cannot tell you how sorry I was not to be able to accept her script. But it just would not do, and we were wasting so much money so we just had to postpone that production. I shall make this modern picture 'Cobra' while the script is being rewritten."[111]

He also almost cryptically added after being asked what kind of boy he was, "A very troublesome little boy, who occasioned his mother much sorrow," [112] perhaps a reference to his and Mathis' belief they had been mother and son in a past life. The article goes on to mention that he smiled and as the reporter explained, "You would never, never, guess what kind of sorrow. His besetting sin, if you please, was falling in love with grown up ladies as old as his own

298

mamma!" [113] (the only two possible women to match that description were Blanca de Saulles and Mathis).

One further event occurred to make the situation even more cryptic. Mathis married Silvano Balboni soon after declaring to never speak to the Valentinos again, in early December 1924.[114] Silvano Balboni (just as often spelled Sylvano, on official documents he used Silvano), was an Italian cameraman from Genoa. He was born in 1894, though later he would claim 1904 for awhile (June's age fibbing must have rubbed off on him).[115] When he married June the press was told he was an 'Italian nobleman' who worked as a director for 15 years in Italy. That is unlikely, though he may have had a family of some prestige as his brother was a doctor. Not much else is known of him before or after his time with June. There were definitely two sides to him, and it seems the relationship had more aspects to it then most realize.

The couple were said to have met while on production for Ben-Hur.[116] This is the most accepted story, but there is a kink in it. Balboni traveled to the US in September 1922, two months before Mathis was hired at Goldwyn.[117] One reporter, who claimed to be friends with the couple, noted Balboni mentioning how when he was a poor cameraman and didn't know who June was, he'd 'steal flowers from her garden because they were so pretty'.[118] Odd enough in and of itself, the story also seems to verify that he had spent some time struggling in California before Ben-Hur. One newspaper report notes he was brought in for Ben-Hur, possibly meaning he and Mathis met before the production traveled to Italy. How much involvement Balboni had is really hard to discern, though his language skills were probably extremely valuable. Mathis said she wasn't very impressed with him at first. Of the moment she fell in love with him she explained, "It was one day when I had got some sand in my eye, and he took it out so tenderly that when I was able to see again the first thing I saw was my Sheik!"[119]

Mathis soon insisted him into all of her work, as a cameraman and as a director. How happy the relationship was is disputable. Indeed they did one joint press interview, and attended many Hollywood parties and events, but a private understanding is lacking here. No one seems to have thought it important to record for posterity. While they put on a happy show, Balboni's actions after her death might hint at something deeper, though again the conclusions are hard to draw.

Mathis apparently made the decision to marry on the spur of the moment (some reports called it a 'secret' wedding), insisting she wanted orchids and all the trimmings. But by the time arrangements had been made everything near Los Angeles was

299

June and Silvano at their home

closed. Balboni suggested marrying in Santa Ana, CA where they could still marry without delay. Mathis had a fit insisting nothing good came of quickie Santa Ana marriages, but apparently she was eventually convinced to try Riverside instead, as they married at the Mission Inn in Riverside, CA. [120]

So why did Mathis stop speaking with Valentino over the rejection of one script? What did she hold against Natacha that caused Natacha to feel she was unfairly blamed? Why did she rush a script for someone so dear to her in the first place, considering the fact that if it did well it surely would have redeemed them both in the film world? And why did she marry Balboni so suddenly (practically eloping) after the spat?

Many films have unfairly portrayed Mathis as a frumpy woman with an unrequited love for her protégé (not that anything in those films is accurate to begin with). Many women who knew Valentino remembered him more for his cooking than his smoldering sexuality, claiming whatever it was on the screen they did not see in real life. [121] Mathis and Valentino had been extremely close in an almost daily friendship that lasted three years. Mathis obviously saw great potential in him as an actor, who also happened to possess unnaturally good looks. But what her private opinions were remains unknown.

One could look at her actions as unrequited love. Perhaps feeling she had lost her chance when Rambova came along. However that does not account for her and Rambova's cordial friendship during the time Rambova and Valentino were dating/living together. However the rush marriage to Balboni seems to point to something of this nature.

Contrary to reports, Mathis did not 'bring Balboni back with her'. She signed her contract with First National on August 2nd, 1924. Balboni didn't return from Naples until September 1st, 1924 (add to that June had returned from France, not Italy, as Balboni did). [122] He signed a 'declaration of intention' (the first step to citizenship, it would be valid for up to seven years from that date) on September 16th. [123] Mathis was attached to The Hooded Falcon right before Balboni returned. The fight likely occurred sometime in November, with news of it breaking in early December.

It would seem Mathis must have had some sort of relationship with Balboni before November...but when did it start? The couple could have known each other as early as 1922, or could have started dating as late as September 1924. Given the whispers about her relationship with George Walsh, it probably indicates Mathis and Balboni were not a couple until their return, as the Walsh rumors usually accompanied news of her departure from Ben-Hur.

Reports of Mathis' marriage broke December 15th, 1924; the same time the spat reports were also breaking. This seems extremely telling, why such a rush to marry Balboni so near a personal rough patch?

Given this evidence, there might be a strong indication that Mathis and Balboni had barely been together romantically, when her spat with the Valentinos occurred. Such a quick marriage to an Italian, who reminded her of a 'Sheik', while Valentino himself referenced older women giving him love trouble, might be some solid evidence that either Mathis did, at some point, have a romantic relationship with Valentino; or at the very least, had unresolved romantic feelings for him.

In addition, Mathis and Valentino ended their creative partnership soon after his marriage to Rambova. There was no reason Mathis had to do this. Valentino was a bankable star, and though "Young Rajah" failed, it was obvious neither thought there was a reason to end the partnership (given the future films ready to produce). Once the strike began, Mathis left for Goldwyn, where she wanted Valentino for the role of Ben-Hur, but was unable, legally, to get him. Whatever had been boiling between that time and the end of her stint on Ben-Hur obviously came to a head over The Hooded Falcon.

And indeed, Rambova had been around most of that time. Before the marriage, maybe Mathis did not feel threaten. And after, there was obviously tension (both reasonable and unreasonable). It is my opinion based on all this, that Mathis at least had some sort of romantic feelings for Valentino; and there might be a strong indication of an actual romantic relationship of some sort, particularly given what had happened with Ingram before Natacha was in the picture. I doubt the full story will ever be uncovered, but maybe someday, some more information will be found to shed more light on the matter whatever it may be.

Onto a less controversial theory, perhaps with no romantic intentions what so ever, Mathis felt Rambova was (or had become) vindictive and controlling, as other people with Valentino had begun to feel. Natacha seems to hint at this in her book, saying those around Valentino had begun to tell him how harmful she was. Whether she specifically meant Mathis or not is unknown.

Both Rambova and Mathis had, at one point, been in control of Valentino's career direction, maybe Mathis felt shut out. Both Rambova and Mathis were strong, power hungry women with major artistic skills including drawing, direction, production, and casting. However Mathis excelled at writing and never did much with costuming (on occasion she designed a few costumes); while

302

Rambova did the opposite. While Mathis succeeded for being a strong woman involved in every aspect of production, Rambova did not. And though much of her work is lost, it does indeed seem Rambova's work was unfairly misjudged in her own time. Films such as Monsieur Beaucaire prove she indeed possessed some skill and insight.

One almost wonders if Rambova aspired to become just as powerful as Mathis. Not only did she begin to assert herself behind the scenes more in 1924, but the film proceeding "The Hooded Falcon" had been "A Sainted Devil". It was Valentino's one and only Latin Lover film without June, and stills alone reveal the film to resemble Rambova's take on Mathis' previous Latin films. Almost a more stylized version of The Four Horsemen of the Apocalypse. It was also based on a Rex Beach story, an author Mathis had mentioned admiring greatly since the start of her career. The film was the second flop for the Rambova/Valentino film pairing (in fact, Valentino would not have another success until The Eagle). Did this, perhaps, set off some spark between the two women?

Whatever bad blood there was, it seemed fresh to Rambova. In 1926 when she wrote her memoirs (a year before Mathis died) she constantly referred to June by her full name, would barely mention her to begin with, leaving her out in obvious spots (such as speaking about her mother Virginia), and explicitly leaving her out of 'Rudy's' soul's messages. In several places, Natacha (or 'Rudy's Soul') goes into great detail about theories Mathis had discussed with the press years before, almost word for word. Yet even though Natacha has Rudy's 'soul' devote a whole chapter to the magic of writers, Mathis isn't even mentioned once in that section.

After marrying Balboni, Mathis began production on "Sally". Once again it was almost entirely her production, from script to editing to crew. "Sally" was a major hit and Mathis was quickly put to work on "Irene" and "Classified". Some of her final films were noted vehicles for Anna Q. Nilsson, Blanche Sweet, and Barbara LaMarr.

Mathis' films did so well she was said to be unable to take a honeymoon until a year after the wedding (at which point she, or the press, would claim she had just married, in December 1925…a year after the fact). When she returned, she began putting Balboni to work, their first pairing was "The Far Cry". Soon after, Mathis took trips to her hometown as well as New York City.

By early 1926, Mathis negotiated to do four films a year with Balboni, which were to be "June Mathis Productions". [124] She only completed "The Masked Woman" and "The Greater Glory" before leaving to freelance.

On October 31st, 1926 she left First National over production disputes. She began freelancing as a scenario writer for most of 1927.[126] Mathis was rumored to be signed with both MGM and UA months before her death.[125] Mathis' final films would be "An Affair of the Follies" and "The Magic Flame" (with Vilma Banky). One final film, "Reno" would be made as a talkie in 1930.

Despite her vow never to speak to Valentino again, Mathis luckily changed her mind. After returning to Los Angeles she attended a preview screening of "Son of the Sheik" in Santa Monica, CA in May 1926 with some friends.[127] Valentino spotted the group and went over to say hello. All of the ladies were touched and many tears were said to have been shed.[128] Mathis and Valentino became instant friends again, spending time together and advising each other on various troubles. Mathis was one of the friends who insisted he should see a doctor for the pain he was having, but Valentino did not listen.[129] Mathis attended the premiere of "Son of the Sheik" at the Million Dollar Theatre in Los Angeles, CA. It was probably the last time she saw him alive.

Valentino died unexpectedly while in New York in August 1926. Mathis was deeply affected, swearing she had seen his apparition in her living room at the very moment he passed (eerily similar to a scene in Four Horsemen). To the press, she gave a touching statement saying, "My long association with Rudolph Valentino endeared him to me, as he has become endeared to everyone who knew him, my heart is too full of sorrow at this moment to enable me to speak coherently. I only know that his passing has left a void that nothing can ever fill in that the loss to our industry is too great to estimate at this time."[130]

She and Balboni attended both the NY and CA funerals. Valentino died $150,000 in debt with no money available for his burial expenses. Mathis owned a block of crypts in a mausoleum at Hollywood Forever Cemetery. Her mother and father were buried there, and spaces awaited her, Balboni, and her Grandmother, Emily Hawkes.

Rambova offered to bury Valentino in her family crypt in New York, but Ullman (who was in charge of his estate) declined. Mathis offered her crypt, saying he could stay until she needed it herself. Sadly that would only be a year later, almost to the day.

Balboni and Mathis sat on a committee of Italian Americans who were attempting to give Valentino a more proper resting place. The original idea was an Italian Garden in the heart of Hollywood, featuring statues of him in various costumes, as well as a movie theatre. Sadly all such plans would fall through when Mathis died.[131]

Mathis began work on her own films once again. In October 1926, WAMPAS named her the third most influential and important woman in the film industry (ranking just behind Mary Pickford and Norma Talmadge). [132] Mathis beat out the other three major female writers including Anita Loos, Frances Marion, and Jeanie Macpherson. It was her 10th year as a writer. When she died, AMPAS passed a resolution of mourning, noting she was one of the founders of the Academy (though according to the Academy she is not on the founding list, probably meaning she passed too soon to take any part its formation). [133] Mathis was constantly cited as the highest paid and most talented screenwriter during this time.

She made a trip to New York City without Balboni in May 1927. With her Grandmother Emily Hawkes (occasionally spelled Hawks or referred to as 'Millie') on July 27th, she watched "The Squall" in a Broadway Theater. Her last words were reportedly, "Oh Mother I'm dying!" which has led to confusion over who she was with at the time of her death. However her mother had passed a few years prior in 1922. Mathis was 40.

Two doctors and two nurses were in the audience and tried to assist her, but she had already passed. [134] Until the coroner could arrive, Mathis' body had to lay in an alley surrounded by a crowd. [135] Her 85 year old grandmother was in shock, stroking her hand and insisting if she could take her granddaughter home, everything would be okay. She reportedly kept saying, "June! June! Speak to me!" [136] The official cause of her death was a heart attack, likely brought on by her life long suffering from valvular heart disease, which she had been born with. Such disease is fatal when not treated with some kind of surgery, something impossible in 1927. [137]

Balboni wasn't alerted until the next night, at which point he left for New York. One report said he was so distraught he needed medical assistance. Mathis' funeral was held at the same church as Valentino's in New York. A reporter noted that the craziness of Valentino's funeral was absent, though the church was filled with sincerely grieving mourners. Mathis' body was sent back to California for burial. [138]

There her body laid in state at the funeral chapel of W.P. Strother on Hollywood Blvd for two hours on August 5th, 1927. Hundreds of cinema and literary elite were said to have paid their respects. A service was held at the Hollywood Forever Cemetery,

Silvano and June dressed for a costume party

with flower tributes sent from George Ullman, Charlie Chaplin, Tom Moore, Colleen Moore, and Alberto Valentino. [139] Mathis had offered to write a screenplay for Alberto if he ever entered film as he had intended, shortly after Valentino's death. [140] Mathis' grandmother was said to be so upset she had to be carried out of the mausoleum.

Valentino's body was moved into her husband's future crypt, while Mathis took place in her own crypt. George Ullman was said to be handling the funeral arrangements and the rest of the decisions appear to have been made by her stepsister Laura. Balboni isn't mentioned anywhere. In the 1930s Balboni sold the crypt to the Valentino family, making it Valentino's official final resting place. Mathis said of the borrowed crypt, "He is my guest in my future home and I don't intend to ask him to leave." [141] They remain side by side to this day.

Mathis' estate became a mess, bringing out an ugly side of Balboni. In September 1927 his brother Dr. Tulio Balboni was appointed the administrator of Mathis' estate by Silvano's lawyers. [142] Mathis' had written a will before a surgery shortly before her death, but had failed to properly date it. [143] She had specified a life long stipend for her Grandmother (who was 85 years old) and her estate was originally estimated to be worth $200,000. She also asked that her step-sister be provided for. When her Grandmother passed, Mathis had willed the rest to Balboni (including $12,300 in securities and $10,000 in property). [144] Without the proper date, the will could be broken by inheritance laws; leaving everything to Balboni.

Days later, Mathis' will was ruled ineligible for probate, due to the missing date, which was believed to be March 1927. [145] A legal battle broke out over the trust for her Grandmother, and the remaining half of her property. Balboni's lawyers tried to have Hawkes barred from protesting, insisting Balboni would 'provide for her'. Nothing was mentioned of her sister. [146]

In March 1928, Balboni got his way and won the battle, receiving all rights to Mathis' estate and disinheriting her now nearly 85 year old Grandmother and step-sister. [147] Her estate was worth $100,000 total when he won it. He also took low blows at Hawkes in court saying with her bobbed hair and 'short skirts' she, "was equipped with a wardrobe that would be the envy of any flapper." [148] He even went as far as to insinuate that Hawkes wanted her inheritance for an extravagant wardrobe. Hawkes appealed, but it appears nothing came of it. Emily Hawkes died in 1933 at the age of 90 or 91. [149]

Balboni seems to be a man with two faces. One reporter noted on New Years Eve 1928 he attended a Hollywood ball, but

307

mostly sat silent.[150] He directed a few films that year, none of particular note. Balboni left for Italy in 1930. While back in Italy, Silvano married De Gasperis Louise (also called Luisa) on October 29th, 1930 near Rome. [151] She was eight years younger than June had been. The couple had a son on June 29th, 1931.[152] Silvano named him Paolo Antonio (also called Paul Anthony). At some point, Balboni traveled to Bremen before returning to America in January 1933. [153] In September he left back to Genoa.

In February 1934 Balboni returned to California, this time with his family. In 1924, shortly before her married June, he had signed a 'Declaration of Intent' (the first of a two step system to becoming a US citizen). Upon returning in 1934, Balboni again signed a declaration (each declaration was only valid for 7 years). [154] Quite crassly, Silvano sought press, hoping to get some work as a cameraman (he also failed to mention his new family). [155] It seems he was not successful, as it appears he was making movies in Italy in the 1950s. When he returned to Italy is not known, though it could have been at some point in the 1930s.

Mathis' death sent shock waves across the industry. Many saw her as a sincerely powerful and pioneering force in film, and they were certain her name would live on for such works. Sam Goldwyn said of her death, "The untimely death of June Mathis is (sic) come as a blow to us. A truly brilliant scenarist, Miss Mathis was, a tremendous personal factor in the successful growth of the art of picture making. The vast continuity done by her was for my productions the magic flame, which makes her loss all the more poignant to me personally." [156]

Jesse Lasky said of her death, "The motion picture industry has lost its wisest counselors. The death of June Mathis comes as an overwhelming shock to all of us. She pioneered women's place in the new world of entertainment. When the history of motion pictures is finally written June Mathis' name will be recorded as one of the most brilliant craftsmen ever associated with the screen." [157]

Unfortunately none of that came to pass. Unlike her contemporaries, Mathis barely lived to see talkies exist, let alone succeed in them. Today, no-one realizes her films are her own, or that her films are the only Valentino films that were remade as talkies. No one remembers the work she did, or why she did it. Her memory is regulated to a footnote as the frizzy, frumpy, fat woman who discovered Valentino, despite the fact that she did so much more than that.

Unlike Frances Marion or Anita Loos, there hasn't been one single biography written about her. Not only did Loos and Marion live long enough to write their own accounts (to much acclaim at that), but both women had had numerous biographies and studies written about them. Mathis has nothing. Reportedly, a biography is in the works, but if anything will ever come of it no one knows. Poor Mathis will probably end up on a McFarland rack, overpriced and under promoted. A recent Frances Marion author gave a lecture which included numerous references to Anita Loos and Mary Pickford, but not one of Mathis.

Perhaps one of the greatest things to mourn about her early death is the fact Mathis was unable to record her own thoughts for posterity, as both George Ullman and Natacha Rambova did the year she died. Mathis' insight would have been invaluable to understanding the life and career of Rudolph Valentino, let alone her own works. Unfortunately so much of this story is lost to history. Considering Mathis' influence and work with Valentino alone she deserves better. But alone, on her own merit as a female film executive she deserves better.

FURTHER READING

RUDOLPH VALENTINO

"Dark Lover: The Life and Death of Rudolph Valentino" by Emily Worth Leider

"The Valentino Mystique" by Allan Ellenberger

rudolphvalentino.org

affairsvalentino.com

"Affairs Valentino" by George Ullman and Evelyn Zumaya

"Conversations with Rodolfo: A Novel" by Hala Pickford

NATACHA RAMBOVA
"Madam Valentino: The Many Lives of Natacha Rambova" by Michael Morris

rudolphvalentino.org/natacha.html

NITA NALDI
rudolphvalentino.org/nita.html

JUNE MATHIS
rudolphvalentino.org/junemathis.html

SILENT FILM (REVELATIONS SECTION)
"Wallace Reid: The Life And Death of a Hollywood Idol by E. J. Fleming

"Alma Rubens: Silent Snowbird" by Alma Rubens

"Enrico Caruso: His Life and Death" by Dorothy Caruso

"Enrico Caruso: My Father and My Family" by Andrew Farkas and Enrico Caruso Jr.

"The Garden of Invention: Luther Burbank and the Business of Breeding Plants" by Jane S. Smith

forgetthetalkes.com

polanegri.com

SILENT FILM (GENERAL)

"Dark Lady of the Silents" by Miriam Cooper

"Karl Dane: A Biograph and Filmography" by Laura Petersen Balogh

"Pickford: The Woman Who Made Hollywood" by Eileen Whitfield

"Lulu in Hollywood" by Louise Brooks

"Douglas Fairbanks" by Jeffrey Vance and Tony Maietta

forgetthetalkies.com

thesilentmovieblog.wordpress.com

silentsandtalkies.blogspot.com

claroscureaux.blogspot.com

silentcomedians.com

silentstanzas.blogspot.com

aandfproductions.com

johnbunny.com

pandorasbox.com

marypickford.com

karl-dane.com

CONTRIBUTORS

Forgetthetalkies.com

Halapickford.com

1921PVG.com

Rudolphvalentino.org

Claroscureaux.blogspot.com

SPIRITUALISM (GENERAL AND HISTORY)

"Talking to the Other Side: A History of Modern Spiritualism and Mediumship: A Study of the Religion, Science, Philosophy and Mediums that Encompass this American-Made Religion" by Todd Jay Leonard

"The Other Side of Salvation: Spiritualism and the Nineteenth-Century Religious Experience" by John B. Buescher

"Talking to the Dead: Kate and Maggie Fox and the Rise of Spiritualism" by Barbara Weisberg

"So you want to be a Medium: A Down to Earth Guide" by Rose Vanden Eynden

"The Secret Doctrine" by H. P. Blavatsky and Michael Gomes

311

SPIRITUAL MATTERS (GENERAL)

"Temples, Tombs, and Hieroglyphs: A Popular History of Ancient Egypt" by Barbara Mertz

"The Astral Plane: Its Scenery, Inhabitants And Phenomena" by C. W. Leadbeater

Mae Murray Motion Picture Magazine Cover

SPECIAL NOTES

As the author of this section, I wanted to add a word about two very special causes near to my heart. In their own way both have a link to Rudy, and both have very deep links to Silent Film.

Saving the Motion Picture Home

In 1918, Mary Pickford along with her soon to be husband Douglas Fairbanks, and Charlie Chaplin, went around the United States raising money for the Great War, now known as World War One. When the war was over, Mary had some money from the bonds she herself had bought, and with this money she decided to make a fund to help out fellow actors. Before film, Mary had been a road trouper through the best and worse of live theatre. By this time she surely realized even her old rivals (such as Florence Lawrence) might not always be as wealthy as they thought they would. Or maybe she was just terribly practical...Mary was smart like that.

So in 1921 Mary, along with her old cohorts and some other fellow actors, incorporated The Motion Picture Fund, which later had the word Television added to it (we shall here on out refer to it as MPTF). In 1932, with the Depression roaring, Mary again came up with a good program...'the payroll deduction program' in which actors would pledge a small percentage of their weekly pay to the fund. In return when they were broke, ill, or in need...they would have help.

Then Fund President Jean Hersholt came up with the idea to create a retirement home and hospital, for stars who no longer had any money or were in dire need of care. Ground was broke in 1942, with the home and hospital opening in 1948.

No matter how big or little the movie person had been (everyone from gofers to leading ladies are accepted), each were given remarkable care and help free of charge. It's the kind of health and elder care that was way ahead of its time, the kind Europeans are now quite blessed with... while we in the United States are not.

Over the years, all sorts of wonderful picture people have lived and died there. Some more modern ones include Yvonne De Carlo (Lily Munster), and Joel McCrea.

As we all sadly know, many silent film stars did not have happy endings. Though Rudy never needed the Motion Picture home, given his spending habits its not unlikely he may have eventually wound up in need of the wonderful place. Karl Dane killed himself once reduced to poverty, and Nita Naldi ended her life much as mentioned in her section of this book...destitute and living on another charity fund, The Actor's Fund, until her death in the 1960s.

MANY MANY silent film stars and related people ended their lives at the Motion Picture Home. Mae Murray, who had a hell of a ride as a falling star, died in the hospital. She was no longer well, but the staff accommodated her and kept her happy. **Clara Kimball Young, Florence Turner, Madam Sul Te Wan, Norma Shearer, Mack Sennett, Dorothy Sebastian, Jobyna Ralston, Betty Blythe, Chester Conklin** are just a few who also lived out their lives in the Home.

Everything was going fine...until January 2009. Jeffrey Katzenberg, the current Chairman, announced the Fund no longer had any money and needed to close the hospital and home. Not only that, but all current residents would have to be moved...people ill, on limited incomes (or no income at all), and upwards of 90 some years old. There were about 100 residents at the time, with an alarming spike in deaths soon after the announcement.

Ready to be angry? Well here's the facts: the Chief Executive receives upwards of $500,000 a year...even getting a raise during this Great Recession of ours. 80% of the patients' costs are covered by Medi-Cal. To add to it, they've wasted millions on consultants, and have used recent celebrity donations for the most useless things (a new pool from Jodie Foster, a Torah from Steven Spielberg...note the Home is not a religious one).

Other than out and out laziness and possible corruptness, a common belief for this sudden need to close is Katzenberg was a victim of the Bernie Madoff Ponzi scheme...and it is believed he may have lost the Fund's money as well in this scheme (though for the record, this is not confirmed as of this writing).

When the Hospital idea was announced, stars from all over Hollywood gathered to put on radio shows and the like to raise money for the Fund. They would donate their entire earnings from these performances to help out their fellow actors. Where is the outrage now? No where.

A grassroots organization, Saving the Lives of Our Own, has been started to try and stop the closure and expose the truth. So far they've managed to delay the closing and they've done some amazing work getting the word out. I am very pleased to share two links below with you. Please visit, and help keep the home open.

Saving the Lives of Our Own:
savingthelivesofourown.org

Petition to keep the home open:
thepetitionsite.com/1/keeptheMPTFhomeopen

Bringing Back Broadway

While I sadly do not yet have a place to direct your attention for film preservation, this cause is important enough for the moment. Between 1900 and 1930 THE place to go in Los Angeles was Downtown.

You must remember that before film folk arrived, Los Angeles was a small city, and Hollywood a rural town. D.W. Griffith brought the first legitimate film company to Hollywood in 1910 for the winter. They stayed at The Alexandria Hotel (5th and Spring, one block off Broadway). This first company included Mary and Jack Pickford as well.

With film slowly trickling to Los Angeles and Hollywood, Downtown sprang up. The first Orpheum opened on Broadway in 1911 (it later became the Palace in 1924), The Globe Theatre (a live vaudeville/play house) opened in 1913, and Sid Grauman opened his first movie house 'The Million Dollar Theatre' in 1918.

Broadway became 'the' place to be, with all the shops, theatres, restaurants, and hotels located nearby. Almost every silent star you can imagine landed there, including Rudy. Rudy first came to Los Angeles and stayed at The Alexandria on Norman Kerry's invite. He then moved to a flop house near 5th and Grand (the Los Angeles Central Library now sits on the site and has since 1927), and many of his films opened at The Rialto (built in 1917, most Metro Pictures opened there), and The Million Dollar (his last 2 films premiered there). In fact the last places Rudy would ever be in Los Angeles were Downtown. He attended the premiere of Son of the Sheik at the Million Dollar, and attended a costume party with Pola Negri at the Biltmore Hotel (near the library; a lot of movie history there).

Frederica Sagor Maas (who is remarkably still alive as of this writing, she is 109) wrote that by the late 1920s most people had moved on to Hollywood, less they had business downtown (humorously she noted the parking was terrible back then...just as it is now). The final gasp of Broadway came in 1928 and 1931. United Artists opened their theatre at 9th and Broadway, and Charlie Chaplin heavily invested in the Los Angeles Theatre in 1931. The Los Angeles Theatre was the final gasp...both silents and the Roaring Twenties were dead. Broadway too was dead.

White flight soon took hold, with the area becoming predominantly Hispanic and African American; while the middle class fled to the newly formed suburbs. In the 1940s the 'world renowned LA rail system' (a name that sounds humorous today given LA's car reputation) was done away with in favor of the highways. Downtown became in short...a ghetto. It wasn't pretty.

Historic theatres and buildings were demolished or gutted. The 'lucky' ones either became flop houses or Spanish language movie theatres (most would close their doors by the 1980s). Junkies and criminals moved in. This kept on well into the early 2000s. To give you an idea of the damage, Clune's Auditorium (where "Birth of a Nation" premiered and Rudy danced as one of his first jobs in LA) was demolished in the 1980s for parking space! Even sadder. The Ambassador Hotel (site of many silent film events and the assassination of Robert Kennedy) was demolished in 2005 to build a crappy underperforming school.

The Los Angeles Conservancy was founded in 1978 to save the Central Library, which greedy developers also wanted to tear down. In 1988 The Los Angeles Historic Theatre Foundation was formed as an off shoot, to help save the theatres.

Currently ground level Broadway is akin to a Little Mexico, filled with cheap shops and merchants shouting at you in Spanish to buy some cheap trinket. But when one looks up, its 1921 again. It has to be one of the few remaining historic 1920s spots on earth. The Million Dollar, Palace, Globe, Tower, Orpheum, and United Artists Theatres all still exist in pretty decent condition. The Cameo, Arcade, and Rialto still exist to a certain extent, but need severe restoration. In fact almost all these theatres need proper restoration...except the Orpheum. Someone bought it in 2003, and after a $3 million restoration it is truly stunning. Most of these theatres show screenings off and on, with film shoots and other events taking up the rest of their schedules.

Theatres aside, many other neat things still stand. Across from the Orpheum, the former Hamburger's Department Store is still intact, complete with the little H's etched on the building. The Alexandria was recently restored as low income apartments. Inside they have placed many silent film star photos and play Jazz music. They recently reopened their bar and also have a live theatre. Their ballroom is also intact.

I want nothing more in this life, than to see Broadway restored. In addition to the other two wonderful organizations mentioned, there is a third specifically made for this purpose: Bringing Back Broadway. They have a 10-20 year plan to revive the area in a style similar to Hollywood Blvd. Their influence can already be seen, and frankly I could not be prouder of them.

It takes a lot of work, time, and money to restore these historic buildings. The people who do this work deserve more thanks than we could ever give them. If you are a lover of silent film you need to do your part...be it in donations, time, or even sending supportive emails when needed. You do not have to be in Los Angeles to give your support, with the internet the whole world can help Bring Back Broadway. And maybe someday...in 2020...you can take a walk to the Rialto and see a new film being played. Please see the links below.

The Los Angeles Conservancy:
http://www.laconservancy.org

The Los Angeles Historic Theatre Foundation:
http://lahtf.org

Bringing Back Broadway:
www.bringingbackbroadway.com

Notes in Rediscovering

Natacha Rambova Biography

1. Leider, Emily. "Dark Lover: The Life and Death of Rudolph Valentino" page 128

2. Leider, Emily. "Dark Lover: The Life and Death of Rudolph Valentino" page 249

3. Leider, Emily. "Dark Lover: The Life and Death of Rudolph Valentino" page 128

4. Leider, Emily. "Dark Lover: The Life and Death of Rudolph Valentino" page 129

5. Leider, Emily. "Dark Lover: The Life and Death of Rudolph Valentino" page 130

6. Leider, Emily. "Dark Lover: The Life and Death of Rudolph Valentino" page 134

7. Leider, Emily. "Dark Lover: The Life and Death of Rudolph Valentino" page 130

8. Leider, Emily. "Dark Lover: The Life and Death of Rudolph Valentino" page 131

9. Leider, Emily. "Dark Lover: The Life and Death of Rudolph Valentino" page 131

10. Leider, Emily. "Dark Lover: The Life and Death of Rudolph Valentino" page 132

11. Leider, Emily. "Dark Lover: The Life and Death of Rudolph Valentino" page 132

12. Leider, Emily. "Dark Lover: The Life and Death of Rudolph Valentino" page 132

13. Leider, Emily. "Dark Lover: The Life and Death of Rudolph Valentino" page 132

14. Leider, Emily. "Dark Lover: The Life and Death of Rudolph Valentino" page 134

15. Leider, Emily. "Dark Lover: The Life and Death of Rudolph Valentino" page 100

16. Morris, Michael. "Madam Valentino: The Many Lives of Natacha Rambova" page 246

17. Leider, Emily. "Dark Lover: The Life and Death of Rudolph Valentino" page 132

18. Leider, Emily. "Dark Lover: The Life and Death of Rudolph Valentino" page 127-128

19. Leider, Emily. "Dark Lover: The Life and Death of Rudolph Valentino" page 135

20. Leider, Emily. "Dark Lover: The Life and Death of Rudolph Valentino" page 140

21. Morris, Michael. "Madam Valentino: The Many Lives of Natacha Rambova" page 89-92

22. Morris, Michael. "Madam Valentino: The Many Lives of Natacha Rambova" page 89

23. Morris, Michael. "Madam Valentino: The Many Lives of Natacha Rambova" page 92

24. Leider, Emily. "Dark Lover: The Life and Death of Rudolph Valentino" page 148

25. Leider, Emily. "Dark Lover: The Life and Death of Rudolph Valentino" page 185

26. Leider, Emily. "Dark Lover: The Life and Death of Rudolph Valentino" page 184

27. Leider, Emily. "Dark Lover: The Life and Death of Rudolph Valentino" page 204

28. Leider, Emily. "Dark Lover: The Life and Death of Rudolph Valentino" page 197

29. Leider, Emily. "Dark Lover: The Life and Death of Rudolph Valentino" page 211

30. Leider, Emily. "Dark Lover: The Life and Death of Rudolph Valentino" page 148

31. Leider, Emily. "Dark Lover: The Life and Death of Rudolph Valentino" page 209

32. Leider, Emily. "Dark Lover: The Life and Death of Rudolph Valentino" page 255

33. Leider, Emily. "Dark Lover: The Life and Death of Rudolph Valentino" page 215

34. Leider, Emily. "Dark Lover: The Life and Death of Rudolph Valentino" page 217

35. Leider, Emily. "Dark Lover: The Life and Death of Rudolph Valentino" page 229

36. Leider, Emily. "Dark Lover: The Life and Death of Rudolph Valentino" page 231

37. Leider, Emily. "Dark Lover: The Life and Death of Rudolph Valentino" page 238

38. Leider, Emily. "Dark Lover: The Life and Death of Rudolph Valentino" page 238

39. Leider, Emily. "Dark Lover: The Life and Death of Rudolph Valentino" page 244

40. Leider, Emily. "Dark Lover: The Life and Death of Rudolph Valentino" page 256

41. Leider, Emily. "Dark Lover: The Life and Death of Rudolph Valentino" page 293-294

42. Leider, Emily. "Dark Lover: The Life and Death of Rudolph Valentino" page 287

43. Leider, Emily. "Dark Lover: The Life and Death of Rudolph Valentino" page 289

44. Leider, Emily. "Dark Lover: The Life and Death of Rudolph Valentino" page 293

45. Leider, Emily. "Dark Lover: The Life and Death of Rudolph Valentino" page 297

46. Leider, Emily. "Dark Lover: The Life and Death of Rudolph Valentino" page 299

47. Leider, Emily. "Dark Lover: The Life and Death of Rudolph Valentino" page 301

48. Leider, Emily. "Dark Lover: The Life and Death of Rudolph Valentino" page 301

49. Leider, Emily. "Dark Lover: The Life and Death of Rudolph Valentino" page 301

50. Leider, Emily. "Dark Lover: The Life and Death of Rudolph Valentino" page 289

51. Leider, Emily. "Dark Lover: The Life and Death of Rudolph Valentino" page 308-309

52. Leider, Emily. "Dark Lover: The Life and Death of Rudolph Valentino" page 311

53. Leider, Emily. "Dark Lover: The Life and Death of Rudolph Valentino" page 311

54. Leider, Emily. "Dark Lover: The Life and Death of Rudolph Valentino" page 312

55. Leider, Emily. "Dark Lover: The Life and Death of Rudolph Valentino" page 311

56. Leider, Emily. "Dark Lover: The Life and Death of Rudolph Valentino" page 148

57. Leider, Emily. "Dark Lover: The Life and Death of Rudolph Valentino" page 314

58. Leider, Emily. "Dark Lover: The Life and Death of Rudolph Valentino" page 314

59. Leider, Emily. "Dark Lover: The Life and Death of Rudolph Valentino" page 317

60. Leider, Emily. "Dark Lover: The Life and Death of Rudolph Valentino" page 333

61. Leider, Emily. "Dark Lover: The Life and Death of Rudolph Valentino" page 322

62. Leider, Emily. "Dark Lover: The Life and Death of Rudolph Valentino" page 322

63. Leider, Emily. "Dark Lover: The Life and Death of Rudolph Valentino" page 324

64. Leider, Emily. "Dark Lover: The Life and Death of Rudolph Valentino" page 324

65. Leider, Emily. "Dark Lover: The Life and Death of Rudolph Valentino" page 326

66. Leider, Emily. "Dark Lover: The Life and Death of Rudolph Valentino" page 331-332

67. Leider, Emily. "Dark Lover: The Life and Death of Rudolph Valentino" page 334-339

68. Leider, Emily. "Dark Lover: The Life and Death of Rudolph Valentino" page 334-339

69. Leider, Emily. "Dark Lover: The Life and Death of Rudolph Valentino" page 334-339

70. Morris, Michael. "Madam Valentino: The Many Lives of Natacha Rambova" page 163

71. Leider, Emily. "Dark Lover: The Life and Death of Rudolph Valentino" page 198

72. Leider, Emily. "Dark Lover: The Life and Death of Rudolph Valentino" page 337

73. Leider, Emily. "Dark Lover: The Life and Death of Rudolph Valentino" page 279

74. Leider, Emily. "Dark Lover: The Life and Death of Rudolph Valentino" page 324

75. Leider, Emily. "Dark Lover: The Life and Death of Rudolph Valentino" page 330-331

76. Leider, Emily. "Dark Lover: The Life and Death of Rudolph Valentino" page 330-331

77. Leider, Emily. "Dark Lover: The Life and Death of Rudolph Valentino" page 336-340

78. Leider, Emily. "Dark Lover: The Life and Death of Rudolph Valentino" page 344

79. Leider, Emily. "Dark Lover: The Life and Death of Rudolph Valentino" page 346-347

80. Leider, Emily. "Dark Lover: The Life and Death of Rudolph Valentino" page 350-351

81. Leider, Emily. "Dark Lover: The Life and Death of Rudolph Valentino" page 350-351

82. Leider, Emily. "Dark Lover: The Life and Death of Rudolph Valentino" page 350-351

83. Leider, Emily. "Dark Lover: The Life and Death of Rudolph Valentino" page 350-351

84. Leider, Emily. "Dark Lover: The Life and Death of Rudolph Valentino" page 381

85. Leider, Emily. "Dark Lover: The Life and Death of Rudolph Valentino" page 381

86. Morris, Michael. "Madam Valentino: The Many Lives of Natacha Rambova" page 186

87. Leider, Emily. "Dark Lover: The Life and Death of Rudolph Valentino" page 396

88. Morris, Michael. "Madam Valentino: The Many Lives of Natacha Rambova" page 193

89. Leider, Emily. "Dark Lover: The Life and Death of Rudolph Valentino" page 411

90. Leider, Emily. "Dark Lover: The Life and Death of Rudolph Valentino" page 411

91. Leider, Emily. "Dark Lover: The Life and Death of Rudolph Valentino" page 411

92. Leider, Emily. "Dark Lover: The Life and Death of Rudolph Valentino" page 411-412

93. Leider, Emily. "Dark Lover: The Life and Death of Rudolph Valentino" page 411-412

94. Leider, Emily. "Dark Lover: The Life and Death of Rudolph Valentino" page 411-412

95. Leider, Emily. "Dark Lover: The Life and Death of Rudolph Valentino" page 411-412

96. Leider, Emily. "Dark Lover: The Life and Death of Rudolph Valentino" page 411-412

97. Leider, Emily. "Dark Lover: The Life and Death of Rudolph Valentino" page 411-412

98. Leider, Emily. "Dark Lover: The Life and Death of Rudolph Valentino" page 411-412

99. Leider, Emily. "Dark Lover: The Life and Death of Rudolph Valentino" page 411-412

100. Leider, Emily. "Dark Lover: The Life and Death of Rudolph Valentino" page 411-412

101. Leider, Emily. "Dark Lover: The Life and Death of Rudolph Valentino" page 411-412

Rudolph Valentino Biography

1. Leider, Emily. "Dark Lover: The Life and Death of Rudolph Valentino" page 8
2. Leider, Emily. "Dark Lover: The Life and Death of Rudolph Valentino" page 9
3. Leider, Emily. "Dark Lover: The Life and Death of Rudolph Valentino" page 23
4. Leider, Emily. "Dark Lover: The Life and Death of Rudolph Valentino" page 35
5. Leider, Emily. "Dark Lover: The Life and Death of Rudolph Valentino" page 40-41
6. Leider, Emily. "Dark Lover: The Life and Death of Rudolph Valentino" page 41
7. Leider, Emily. "Dark Lover: The Life and Death of Rudolph Valentino" page 42
8. Leider, Emily. "Dark Lover: The Life and Death of Rudolph Valentino" page 46-49
9. Leider, Emily. "Dark Lover: The Life and Death of Rudolph Valentino" page 58
10. Leider, Emily. "Dark Lover: The Life and Death of Rudolph Valentino" page 64
11. Leider, Emily. "Dark Lover: The Life and Death of Rudolph Valentino" page 73
12. Leider, Emily. "Dark Lover: The Life and Death of Rudolph Valentino" page 75
13. Leider, Emily. "Dark Lover: The Life and Death of Rudolph Valentino" page 77
14. Leider, Emily. "Dark Lover: The Life and Death of Rudolph Valentino" page 80
15. Leider, Emily. "Dark Lover: The Life and Death of Rudolph Valentino" page 81
16. Leider, Emily. "Dark Lover: The Life and Death of Rudolph Valentino" page 88
17. Leider, Emily. "Dark Lover: The Life and Death of Rudolph Valentino" page 87
18. Leider, Emily. "Dark Lover: The Life and Death of Rudolph Valentino" page 87
19. Leider, Emily. "Dark Lover: The Life and Death of Rudolph Valentino" page 111
20. Leider, Emily. "Dark Lover: The Life and Death of Rudolph Valentino" page 89-90

21. Leider, Emily. "Dark Lover: The Life and Death of Rudolph Valentino" page 100

22. Leider, Emily. "Dark Lover: The Life and Death of Rudolph Valentino" page 100

23. Leider, Emily. "Dark Lover: The Life and Death of Rudolph Valentino" page 102

24. Leider, Emily. "Dark Lover: The Life and Death of Rudolph Valentino" page 103

25. Leider, Emily. "Dark Lover: The Life and Death of Rudolph Valentino" page 112

26. Leider, Emily. "Dark Lover: The Life and Death of Rudolph Valentino" page 113

27. Leider, Emily. "Dark Lover: The Life and Death of Rudolph Valentino" page 115

28. Los Angeles Times (December 21st, 1924). "Secrets of Valentino's Life"

29. Leider, Emily. "Dark Lover: The Life and Death of Rudolph Valentino" page 123

30. Variety (1932-06-21). "Biggest Money Pictures"

31. Leider, Emily. "Dark Lover: The Life and Death of Rudolph Valentino" page 124

32. Leider, Emily. "Dark Lover: The Life and Death of Rudolph Valentino" page 127

33. Leider, Emily. "Dark Lover: The Life and Death of Rudolph Valentino" page 292-293

34. Leider, Emily. "Dark Lover: The Life and Death of Rudolph Valentino" page 402-403

35. Leider, Emily. "Dark Lover: The Life and Death of Rudolph Valentino" page 137

36. Leider, Emily. "Dark Lover: The Life and Death of Rudolph Valentino" page 136

37. Leider, Emily. "Dark Lover: The Life and Death of Rudolph Valentino" page 148

38. Leider, Emily. "Dark Lover: The Life and Death of Rudolph Valentino" page 146

39. Leider, Emily. "Dark Lover: The Life and Death of Rudolph Valentino" page 200

40. Leider, Emily. "Dark Lover: The Life and Death of Rudolph Valentino" page 155

41. Leider, Emily. "Dark Lover: The Life and Death of Rudolph Valentino" page 167

42. Leider, Emily. "Dark Lover: The Life and Death of Rudolph Valentino" page 200

43. Leider, Emily. "Dark Lover: The Life and Death of Rudolph Valentino" page 200

44. Leider, Emily. "Dark Lover: The Life and Death of Rudolph Valentino" page 204-205

45. Leider, Emily. "Dark Lover: The Life and Death of Rudolph Valentino" page 205

46. Leider, Emily. "Dark Lover: The Life and Death of Rudolph Valentino" page 218

47. Leider, Emily. "Dark Lover: The Life and Death of Rudolph Valentino" page 218

48. Leider, Emily. "Dark Lover: The Life and Death of Rudolph Valentino" page 218

49. Leider, Emily. "Dark Lover: The Life and Death of Rudolph Valentino" page 202

50. Leider, Emily. "Dark Lover: The Life and Death of Rudolph Valentino" page 207

51. Leider, Emily. "Dark Lover: The Life and Death of Rudolph Valentino" page 206

52. Leider, Emily. "Dark Lover: The Life and Death of Rudolph Valentino" page 211

53. Leider, Emily. "Dark Lover: The Life and Death of Rudolph Valentino" page 217

54. Leider, Emily. "Dark Lover: The Life and Death of Rudolph Valentino" page 217

55. Leider, Emily. "Dark Lover: The Life and Death of Rudolph Valentino" page 217

56. Leider, Emily. "Dark Lover: The Life and Death of Rudolph Valentino" page 228

57. Leider, Emily. "Dark Lover: The Life and Death of Rudolph Valentino" page 228

58. Leider, Emily. "Dark Lover: The Life and Death of Rudolph Valentino" page 230

59. Leider, Emily. "Dark Lover: The Life and Death of Rudolph Valentino" page 231

60. Leider, Emily. "Dark Lover: The Life and Death of Rudolph Valentino" page 232-234

61. Leider, Emily. "Dark Lover: The Life and Death of Rudolph Valentino" page 238

62. Leider, Emily. "Dark Lover: The Life and Death of Rudolph Valentino" page 238

63. Leider, Emily. "Dark Lover: The Life and Death of Rudolph Valentino" page 240

64. Leider, Emily. "Dark Lover: The Life and Death of Rudolph Valentino" page 236-237

65. Leider, Emily. "Dark Lover: The Life and Death of Rudolph Valentino" page 245

66. Leider, Emily. "Dark Lover: The Life and Death of Rudolph Valentino" page 240

67. Leider, Emily. "Dark Lover: The Life and Death of Rudolph Valentino" page 240

68. Leider, Emily. "Dark Lover: The Life and Death of Rudolph Valentino" page 255

69. Leider, Emily. "Dark Lover: The Life and Death of Rudolph Valentino" page 261

70. Leider, Emily. "Dark Lover: The Life and Death of Rudolph Valentino" page 294

71. Leider, Emily. "Dark Lover: The Life and Death of Rudolph Valentino" page 314

72. Leider, Emily. "Dark Lover: The Life and Death of Rudolph Valentino" page 298

73. Leider, Emily. "Dark Lover: The Life and Death of Rudolph Valentino" page 303

74. Leider, Emily. "Dark Lover: The Life and Death of Rudolph Valentino" page 289

75. Leider, Emily. "Dark Lover: The Life and Death of Rudolph Valentino" page 289

76. Leider, Emily. "Dark Lover: The Life and Death of Rudolph Valentino" page 312

77. Leider, Emily. "Dark Lover: The Life and Death of Rudolph Valentino" page 313

78. Leider, Emily. "Dark Lover: The Life and Death of Rudolph Valentino" page 323

79. Leider, Emily. "Dark Lover: The Life and Death of Rudolph Valentino" page 333

80. Leider, Emily. "Dark Lover: The Life and Death of Rudolph Valentino" page 319

81. Leider, Emily. "Dark Lover: The Life and Death of Rudolph Valentino" page 329

82. Leider, Emily. "Dark Lover: The Life and Death of Rudolph Valentino" page 333

83. Leider, Emily. "Dark Lover: The Life and Death of Rudolph Valentino" page 334

84. Leider, Emily. "Dark Lover: The Life and Death of Rudolph Valentino" page 334

85. Leider, Emily. "Dark Lover: The Life and Death of Rudolph Valentino" page 334-335

86. Leider, Emily. "Dark Lover: The Life and Death of Rudolph Valentino" page 335

87. Leider, Emily. "Dark Lover: The Life and Death of Rudolph Valentino" page 335

88. Leider, Emily. "Dark Lover: The Life and Death of Rudolph Valentino" page 336

89. Leider, Emily. "Dark Lover: The Life and Death of Rudolph Valentino" page 338

90. Leider, Emily. "Dark Lover: The Life and Death of Rudolph Valentino" page 337

91. Leider, Emily. "Dark Lover: The Life and Death of Rudolph Valentino" page 334

92. Leider, Emily. "Dark Lover: The Life and Death of Rudolph Valentino" page 355

93. Leider, Emily. "Dark Lover: The Life and Death of Rudolph Valentino" page 359

94. Leider, Emily. "Dark Lover: The Life and Death of Rudolph Valentino" page 362

95. Leider, Emily. "Dark Lover: The Life and Death of Rudolph Valentino" page 349

96. Leider, Emily. "Dark Lover: The Life and Death of Rudolph Valentino" page 365

97. Leider, Emily. "Dark Lover: The Life and Death of Rudolph Valentino" page 366

98. Leider, Emily. "Dark Lover: The Life and Death of Rudolph Valentino" page

99. Leider, Emily. "Dark Lover: The Life and Death of Rudolph Valentino" page 369

100. Leider, Emily. "Dark Lover: The Life and Death of Rudolph Valentino" page 369-370

101. Leider, Emily. "Dark Lover: The Life and Death of Rudolph Valentino" page 308

102. Leider, Emily. "Dark Lover: The Life and Death of Rudolph Valentino" page 381-382

103. Leider, Emily. "Dark Lover: The Life and Death of Rudolph Valentino" page 396

104. Leider, Emily. "Dark Lover: The Life and Death of Rudolph Valentino" page 383

105. Leider, Emily. "Dark Lover: The Life and Death of Rudolph Valentino" page 387-396

106. Leider, Emily. "Dark Lover: The Life and Death of Rudolph Valentino" page 392

107. Leider, Emily. "Dark Lover: The Life and Death of Rudolph Valentino" page 399

108. Leider, Emily. "Dark Lover: The Life and Death of Rudolph Valentino" page

109. Leider, Emily. "Dark Lover: The Life and Death of Rudolph Valentino" page

110. Leider, Emily. "Dark Lover: The Life and Death of Rudolph Valentino" page

111. Leider, Emily. "Dark Lover: The Life and Death of Rudolph Valentino" page 409

112. Leider, Emily. "Dark Lover: The Life and Death of Rudolph Valentino" page 409

113. Leider, Emily. "Dark Lover: The Life and Death of Rudolph Valentino" page 409

114. Leider, Emily. "Dark Lover: The Life and Death of Rudolph Valentino" page 241

115. Leider, Emily. "Dark Lover: The Life and Death of Rudolph Valentino" page 416

116. Leider, Emily. "Dark Lover: The Life and Death of Rudolph Valentino" page 414

117. Leider, Emily. "Dark Lover: The Life and Death of Rudolph Valentino" page 415

118. Leider, Emily. "Dark Lover: The Life and Death of Rudolph Valentino" page 415

119. Leider, Emily. "Dark Lover: The Life and Death of Rudolph Valentino" page 426-435

NITA NALDI

Nita Naldi Biography
1. Capital Times (January 4th 1930). ""The Spoilers" is being re-made into a talkie"
2. Bluefield Daily Telegraph (February 25th, 1961). "Once she was a star"
3. LA Times (May 14th, 1922). "Actress Tells of the Follies"
4. Bluefield Daily Telegraph (February 25th, 1961). "Once she was a star"
5. Year 1900; Census Place: Manhattan, New York, New York; Roll T623_1123; Page 2A; Enumeration District: 930
6. Year 1900; Census Place: Manhattan, New York, New York; Roll T623_1123; Page 2A; Enumeration District: 930
7. San Antonio Light (May 18, 1941). "Buxom Vamps who made Grandpa shiver now only get a laugh"
8. Year: 1910; Census Place: Manhattan Ward 19, New York, New York; Roll T624_1040; Page 3B; Enumeration District 1043; Image 51.
9. Year: 1910; Census Place: Manhattan Ward 19, New York, New York; Roll T624_1039; Page 17B; Enumeration District 1028; Image 619.
10. Year: 1910; Census Place: Manhattan Ward 19, New York, New York; Roll T624_1039; Page 17B; Enumeration District 1028; Image 619.
11. Year: 1910; Census Place: Ogdensburg Ward 4, St. Lawrence, NY; Roll T624_1075; Page 10A; Enumeration District 160; Image 510
12. Year: 1910; Census Place: Ft. Lee, New Jersey; T624_868; page 28A; Enumeration District 17; Image 527
13. LA Times (May 14th, 1922). "Actress Tells of the Follies"
14. Find A Grave Memorial # 754
15. Find A Grave Memorial # 754
16. New Castle News (October 2nd 1928). "Feature Bill Seen at Capitol"
17. Lowell Sun (October 26th, 1952). "On Broadway with Earl Wilson"
18. Cumberland Evening Times (February 24th, 1961). "Glancing Sideways"
19. Ogden Standard-Examiner (March 13th, 1921). "Filmland Flickers"

20. Oakland Tribune (October 22nd, 1922). "Nita Naldi and Jacqueline Logan Signed by Paramount"

21. San Antonio Light (May 18, 1941). "Buxom Vamps who made Grandpa shiver now only get a laugh"

22. Logansport Pharos-Tribune (October 16th, 1922). "Valentino kissed her, but she didn't fall for him!"

23. LA Times (May 14th, 1922). "Actress Tells of the Follies"

24. Logansport Pharos-Tribune (October 16th, 1922). "Valentino kissed her, but she didn't fall for him!"

25. Logansport Pharos-Tribune (October 16th, 1922). "Valentino kissed her, but she didn't fall for him!"

26. Logansport Pharos-Tribune (October 16th, 1922). "Valentino kissed her, but she didn't fall for him!"

27. Logansport Pharos-Tribune (October 16th, 1922). "Valentino kissed her, but she didn't fall for him!"

28. The Bee (August 28th, 1923). "Screen Vamp is Connected with Domestic Split"

29. Salamanca Republican-Press (June 12, 1941). "Man about Manhattan"

30. The Bee (August 28th, 1923). "Screen Vamp is Connected with Domestic Split"

31. The Bee (August 28th, 1923). "Screen Vamp is Connected with Domestic Split"

32. The Bee (August 28th, 1923). "Screen Vamp is Connected with Domestic Split"

33. The Washington Post (May 6th, 1923). "Big Girl Handicapped in Game of being "His Sweetie," Says Nita"

34. Lowell Sun (October 26th, 1952). "On Broadway with Earl Wilson"

35. The Lincoln Star (February 7th 1926). "All the Theaters This Week"

36. The Lincoln Star (February 7th 1926). "All the Theaters This Week"

37. Lowell Sun (October 26th, 1952). "On Broadway with Earl Wilson"

38. Cumberland Evening Times (February 24th, 1961). "Glancing Sideways"

39. Nevada State Journal (July 27th, 1924). "News Notes from MovieLand"

40. Nevada State Journal (July 27th, 1924). "News Notes from MovieLand"

41. Los Angeles Times (January 31st, 1926). "Nita Naldi thin by dieting and no exercise"

42. Los Angeles Times (January 31st, 1926). "Nita Naldi thin by dieting and no exercise"

43. Nevada State Journal (July 27th, 1924). "News Notes from MovieLand"

44. The Zanesville Signal (December 6th, 1925). "The Love Triangle of Cobra"

45. The Emporia Gazette (September 24th, 1924). "Good Story, But Isn't True"

46. Leider, Emily (2004). Dark Lover: The Life and Death of Rudolph Valentino page 114

47. New Castle News (March 2nd, 1928). "Screen Vamps Grow Slimmer to Suit Public"

48. Morris, Michael. "Madam Valentino: The Many Lives of Natacha Rambova" page 177-178

49. Morris, Michael. "Madam Valentino: The Many Lives of Natacha Rambova" page 177

50. Ellenberger, Allan "The Valentino Mystique: The death and afterlife of the silent film idol" page 167

51. The Syracuse Herald (October 11th, 1925). "Mystery Miss Nita Naldi"

52. The Gleaner (September 8th, 1925). "Facts about people from Screenland"

53. The Lincoln Star (October 25th, 1925). Nita Naldi to Wed?

54. Year 1927; Microfilm Serial T715; Microfilm roll T7154170; Line: 9

55. Oakland Tribune (June 20, 1941). "Nita Naldi on Billy Rose's Payroll; So is Lila Lee; Movie Dames 'Harmless'"

56. rudolphvalentino.org/nita.html

57. Oakland Tribune (June 20, 1941). "Nita Naldi on Billy Rose's Payroll; So is Lila Lee; Movie Dames 'Harmless'"

58. Archives Francaises du Film (1926). "La Femme Nue". How much exists is unknown.

59. Centre national de la cinématographie has a copy labeled 1926. Filmarchiv Austria released clips of the film on a DVD titled "Deutschland auf der Leinwand - Der Prater" in 2005. It was said to have screened in Austria or Germany around the same time, how much exists is unknown.

60. Capital Times (February 18th, 1961). "Nita Naldi Dies; Co-Star in 1920s with Valentino"

61. The Syracuse Herald (January 5th, 1933). "Nita Naldi files bankrupt petition"

62. The Syracuse Herald (January 5th, 1933). "Nita Naldi files bankrupt petition"

63. The Nebraska State Journal (April 24th, 1938). "Theater Topics"

64. Nebraska State Journal (April 24th, 1938). "Theater Topics"

65. The Nebraska State Journal (April 24th, 1938). "Theater Topics"

66. The Salt Lake Tribune (June 3rd, 1934). "Lack of Summer Shows on Broadway Due to Movies"

67. The Salt Lake Tribune (August 24th, 1936). "Highlights of New York as seen by O.O. McIntyre"

68. The Salt Lake Tribune (May 16th, 1936). "Memory Lane"

69. The Salt Lake Tribune (Ma 16th, 1936). "Memory Lane"

70. The Salt Lake Tribune (Ma 16th, 1936). "Memory Lane"

71. The Salt Lake Tribune (October 11th 1939)

72. Lowell Sun (January 24th, 1949) "Louella Parsons"

73. Wisconsin State Journal (June 22nd, 1931). "On Broadway"

74. Waterloo Daily Courier (June 20th, 1941). "Nita Naldi Eyed for Pillar in "For Whom the Bell Tolls""

75. Oakland Tribune (June 20, 1941). "Nita Naldi on Billy Rose's Payroll; So is Lila Lee; Movie Dames 'Harmless"" (many quotes ten commandments blood and sand)

76. Waterloo Daily Courier (June 20th, 1941). "Nita Naldi Eyed for Pillar in "For Whom the Bell Tolls""

77. Lowell Sun (October 26th, 1952). "On Broadway with Earl Wilson"

78. San Antonio Light (May 18, 1941). "Buxom Vamps who made Grandpa shiver now only get a laugh"

79. Winnipeg Free Press (May 10th, 1941). "Former Screen Stars Work in Night Club"

80. Lowell Sun (January 24th, 1949) "Louella Parsons"

81. Lowell Sun (October 26th, 1952). "On Broadway with Earl Wilson"

82. Fitchburg Sentinel (September 27th 1952). "Broadway"

83. The Daily Review (November 16th, 1955). "Age of Vamp is being Reborn"

84. The Daily Review (November 16th, 1955). "Age of Vamp is being Reborn"

85. Salt Lake Tribune (February 4th, 1962). "Gals 'Pursue' 'Cue Ball,' Brad Dexter"

86. The Daily Reporter (January 18th, 1956). "Dorothy Kilgallen's Voice of Broadway"

87. Capital Times (February 18th, 1961). "Nita Naldi Dies; Co-Star in 1920s with Valentino"

88. The Evening Standard (March 1st, 1961). "Miss Naldi in Dream World"

89. The Evening Standard (March 1st, 1961). "Miss Naldi in Dream World"

90. Capital Times (February 18th, 1961). "Nita Naldi Dies; Co-Star in 1920s with Valentino"

91. Capital Times (February 18th, 1961). "Nita Naldi Dies; Co-Star in 1920s with Valentino"

92. The Evening Standard (March 1st, 1961). "Miss Naldi in Dream World"

93. Findagrave.com. #754

JUNE MATHIS

June Mathis Biography

1. Los Angeles Times (July 28th, 1927). "June Mathis to be buried here"

2. Billings Gazette (July 31st, 1927). "Few pause at bier of woman who 'made' Valentino; unlike frenzied mob at Rudy's Rites"

3. San Antonio Light (November 12th 1950). "Laughter and Tears"

4. Los Angeles Times (August 4th, 1927). "Body of Writer Due Tomorrow"

5. Mathis was notoriously quiet about her age. In the 1900 Salt Lake Census she is listed as being born 'January 1887' (cite: Year 1900; Census Place: Salt Lake City, Utah, Ward 2; Roll T623_1684); Page 3B; Enumeration District: 22). However due to performing, she was enumerated again in San Francisco where she claimed a birth year of 1886 (cite: Year 1900; Census Place: San Francisco, CA; Roll T623_105; Page 3B; Enumeration District: 197). When she died a Salt Lake Obituary mentioned her as being '42' giving her a birthdate of 1885 (cite: The Salt Lake Tribune (July 27th, 1927). "Famous Utah Woman Dead"). It must have ran in the family as comparing her mother and Grandmother's census birth years there is only 8 years between them; meaning someone was fudging their age.

6. Year 1900; Census Place: Salt Lake City, Utah, Ward 2; Roll T623_1684); Page 3B; Enumeration District: 22

7. The Salt Lake Tribune (October 10th, 1926). "Career of June Mathis, Former Salt Lake Girl, High Light in Filmdom"; The Salt Lake Tribune (March 5th, 1965). "In the Mail" (address)

8. The Salt Lake Tribune (May 2nd, 1926). "Daughter of Utah's Pride Again Visits Home Town"

9. The Salt Lake Tribune (October 18th, 1898). "First Democratic Tea"

10. The Salt Lake Tribune (November 8th, 1898). "Last of the Democratic Teas"

11. The Salt Lake Tribune (March 12th, 1899). "Democratic Club meetings"

12. Salt Lake Tribune. (February 6th, 1899). "Woodmen of the World"

13. The Salt Lake Tribune (December 8th, 1912). "Zion Girl Leading Lady of Fascinating Widow"

14. The Salt Lake Tribune (December 8th, 1912). "Zion Girl Leading Lady of Fascinating Widow"

15. The Salt Lake Tribune (March 1st, 1908). "With the Theatres"
16. The Salt Lake Tribune (July 14th, 1901). "Clever Salt Lake Child"
17. The Salt Lake Tribune (July 14th, 1901). "Clever Salt Lake Child"
18. The Salt Lake Tribune (March 1st, 1908). "With the Theatres"
19. The Salt Lake Tribune (March 1st, 1908). "With the Theatres"
20. The Salt Lake Tribune (March 1st, 1908). "With the Theatres"
21. The Salt Lake Tribune (March 1st, 1908). "With the Theatres"
22. The Salt Lake Tribune (March 1st, 1908). "With the Theatres"
23. The Salt Lake Tribune (March 1st, 1908). "With the Theatres"
24. The Salt Lake Tribune (March 1st, 1908). "With the Theatres"
25. The Salt Lake Tribune (March 1st, 1908). "With the Theatres"
26. The Salt Lake Tribune (March 1st, 1908). "With the Theatres"
27. The Salt Lake Tribune (March 1st, 1908). "With the Theatres"
28. The Salt Lake Tribune (March 1st, 1908). "With the Theatres"
29. The Salt Lake Tribune (December 8th, 1912). "Zion Girl Leading Lady of Fascinating Widow"
30. Year: 1910; Census Place: Manhattan, Ward 12, New York, New York; Roll T624_1028; page 14B; Enumeration District: 746; Image 570
31. "The Syracuse Herald (February 19th, 1927). "Truth about Breaking into the Movies"
32. The Salt Lake Tribune (October 10th, 1926). "Career of June Mathis, Former Salt Lake Girl, High Light in Filmdom"
33. The Salt Lake Tribune (October 10th, 1926). "Career of June Mathis, Former Salt Lake Girl, High Light in Filmdom"
34. Zulu: Dunkirk Evening Observer (July 24th, 1922). "Persistence, Preparation, Prosperity"
35. The Salt Lake Tribune (October 10th, 1926). "Career of June Mathis, Former Salt Lake Girl, High Light in Filmdom"
36. Ogden Standard-Examiner (July 31st, 1927). "Tributes Paid June Mathis"
37. 74. Leider, Emily. "Dark Lover: The Life and Death of Rudolph Valentino" page 115
38. Dunkirk Evening Observer (July 24th, 1922). "Persistence, Preparation, Prosperity"
39. Sandusky Register (November 15th, 1923). "Miss June Mathis"
40. The Lincoln Star (February 7th 1926). "All the Theaters This Week".
41. Nevada State Journal (July 27th, 1924). "News Notes from MovieLand"
42. Ogden Standard-Examiner (July 31st, 1927). "Tributes Paid June Mathis"
43. Ogden Standard-Examiner (July 31st, 1927). "Tributes Paid June Mathis"

44. The Lincoln Daily Star (April 12th 1924). "Torrence Steps into Limelight"
45. Dunkirk Evening Observer (July 24th, 1922). "Persistence, Preparation, Prosperity"
46. Dunkirk Evening Observer (July 24th, 1922). "Persistence, Preparation, Prosperity"
47. The Lincoln Star (May 9th, 1926). "Motion Pictures Can't Exhaust Bible for Sub-Titles, Stories, June Mathis, Scenarist, Says"
48. Oakland Tribune (December 29th, 1921). "Censor must be pleased or his axe falls hard"
49. Los Angeles Times (November 27th, 1924). "Screen Women appear at club"
50. Slater, Thomas (2007-11-03). "June Mathis: Moving the margins of mainstream". Journal of Humanities.
51. Los Angeles Times (June 3rd, 1923). "Most responsible job ever held by woman"
52. Oakland Tribune (December 29th, 1921). "Censor must be pleased or his axe falls hard"
53. The Salt Lake Tribune (May 2nd, 1926). "Daughter of Utah's Pride Again Visits Home Town"
54. The Gleaner (September 8th, 1925). "Facts about people from Screenland"
55. Whitfield, Eileen (1999). "Pickford: The Woman Who Made Hollywood". Page 145
56. Pickford became a producer in 1916 (depending how one interprets her duties this could have counted as an executive position), while Gardner became a producer in 1912. Mathis would become an executive in 1917, while Mary would not assume that title until she co-founded UA in 1919.
57. Oakland Tribune (February 4th, 1923). "Growing Rich on Dreams"
58. Cooper, Miriam. "Dark Lady of the Silents"
59. A copy survives at the UCLA Film Archive
60. Leider, Emily. "Dark Lover: The Life and Death of Rudolph Valentino" page 113
61. Los Angeles Times (December 21st, 1924). "Secrets of Valentino's Life"
62. Chan, Anthony B. "Perpetually Cool: The Many Lives of Anna May Wong" page 31
63. Leider, Emily. "Dark Lover: The Life and Death of Rudolph Valentino" page 113-116
64. Variety (1932-06-21). "Biggest Money Pictures"
65. Los Angeles Times (June 3rd, 1923). "Most responsible job ever held by a woman"

341

66. The Salt Lake Tribune (March 1st, 1908). "With the Theatres"
67. Leider, Emily. "Dark Lover: The Life and Death of Rudolph Valentino" page 113
68. Leider, Emily. "Dark Lover: The Life and Death of Rudolph Valentino" page 114
69. The Cumberland Evening Times (January 29th, 1923). "Job others scored makes June Mathis good for a million"
70. The Cumberland Evening Times (January 29th, 1923). "Job others scored makes June Mathis good for a million"
71. Los Angeles Times (March 22nd, 1931). "Have you lived on earth before?"
72. Los Angeles Times (March 22nd, 1931). "Have you lived on earth before?"
73. San Antonio Light (November 12th 1950). "Laughter and Tears"
74. San Antonio Light (November 12th 1950). "Laughter and Tears"
75. Leider, Emily. "Dark Lover: The Life and Death of Rudolph Valentino" page 116
76. San Antonio Light (November 12th 1950). "Laughter and Tears"
77. Lowell Sun (January 24th, 1949) "Louella Parsons"
78. Slide, Anthony. "Silent players: a biographical and autobiographical study of 100 silent film actors and actresses"
79. San Antonio Light (November 12th 1950). "Laughter and Tears"
80. Soares, André. Beyond Paradise: The Life of Ramon Novarro.
81. San Antonio Light (November 12th 1950). "Laughter and Tears"
82. Lowell Sun (January 24th, 1949) "Louella Parsons"
83. Rambova began working with Nazimova in 1919. June had already written several films for her by that time.
84. Los Angeles Times (January 26th, 1922). "Dies in New York"
85. Leider, Emily. "Dark Lover: The Life and Death of Rudolph Valentino" page 113
86. Leider, Emily. "Dark Lover: The Life and Death of Rudolph Valentino" page 113
87. Independent (February 20th, 1926). "Why Women Love"
88. Ogden Standard-Examiner (June 17th, 1923). "Spiritual Aid"
89. Leider, Emily. "Dark Lover: The Life and Death of Rudolph Valentino" page 151
90. Leider, Emily. "Dark Lover: The Life and Death of Rudolph Valentino" page 153
91. Leider, Emily. "Dark Lover: The Life and Death of Rudolph Valentino" page 204
92. The Gleaner (November 18th, 1968). "How will today's fans react to the Great Lover's' Charms?"
93. Los Angeles Times (November 21st, 1922). "Miss Mathis gets Plum"

94. Los Angeles Times (June 3rd, 1923). "Most responsible job ever held by woman"

95. Leider, Emily. "Dark Lover: The Life and Death of Rudolph Valentino" page 237

96. Los Angeles Times (June 3rd, 1923). "Most responsible job ever held by woman"

97. Los Angeles Times (August 28th, 1924). "Flashes signs June Mathis"

98. Cooper, Miriam "Dark Lady of the Silents"

99. Soares, André. Beyond Paradise: The Life of Ramon Novarro.

100. Los Angeles Times (October 10th, 1924). "Optimists Club"

101. Slater, Thomas (2007-11-03). "June Mathis: Moving the margins of mainstream"

102. Los Angeles Times (November 21st, 1922). "Miss Mathis gets Plum"

103. Slater, Thomas (2007-11-03). "June Mathis: Moving the margins of mainstream"

104. Year: 1924; Microfilm Serial T175; Microfilm roll T175+3520; Line 12

105. Los Angeles Times (August 28th, 1924). "Flashes signs June Mathis"

106. Los Angeles Times (November 1st, 1924).

107. San Antonio Light (November 12th 1950). "Laughter and Tears"

108. Leider, Emily. "Dark Lover: The Life and Death of Rudolph Valentino" page 211

109. Leider, Emily. "Dark Lover: The Life and Death of Rudolph Valentino" page 289

110. Leider, Emily. "Dark Lover: The Life and Death of Rudolph Valentino" page 323

111. Los Angeles Times (December 21st, 1924). "Secrets of Valentino's Life"

112. Los Angeles Times (December 21st, 1924). "Secrets of Valentino's Life"

113. Los Angeles Times (December 21st, 1924). "Secrets of Valentino's Life"

114. Iowa City Press-Citizen (December 16th, 1924). "Daily Graphic Review of Events"

115. Ancestry.com Selected US Naturalization Records – Original documents – 1790-1974

116. Los Angeles Times (September 26th, 1926). "Disprove Ancient Theory"

117. California Passenger and Crew Lists; 1893-1975; Ancestry.com

118. Port Arthur News (September 7th, 1926). "Film Fax"

119. Los Angeles Times (September 26th, 1926). "Disprove Ancient Theory"
120. Los Angeles Times (September 26th, 1926). "Disprove Ancient Theory"
121. Leider, Emily. "Dark Lover: The Life and Death of Rudolph Valentino" page 241
122. Year: 1924; Microfilm Serial T715, Microfilm Roll T715_3532; Line 10
123. Ancestry.com; Selected US Naturalization Records – Original Documents; 1790-1974
124. Oakland Tribune (January 2nd, 1927). "June Mathis Signed" (MGM) and The Salt Lake Tribune (February 23rd, 1927). "June Mathis Signs Contract" (UA)
125. The Salt Lake Tribune (February 27th, 1927). "Born on High Mountain Top June Mathis has ever lived on the high peak of success"
126. Oakland Tribune (November 14th, 1926). "Movieland"
127. Ellenberger, Allan. "The Valentino Mystique" page 34
128. Ellenberger, Allan. "The Valentino Mystique" page 34
129. Leider, Emily. "Dark Lover: The Life and Death of Rudolph Valentino" page 369
130. Ellenberger, Allan. "The Valentino Mystique" page 62
131. Ellenberger, Allan. "The Valentino Mystique" page 98
132. Independent (October 20th, 1926). "Name 12 for Movie Hall of Fame List"
133. Los Angeles Times (August 4th, 1927). "Body of Writer Due Tomorrow"
134. The Warren Tribune (July 27th, 1927). "Famous Scenario Writer Stricken While at Theatre"
135. The Warren Tribune (July 27th, 1927). "Famous Scenario Writer Stricken While at Theatre"
136. The Warren Tribune (July 27th, 1927). "Famous Scenario Writer Stricken While at Theatre"
137. The Salt Lake Tribune (July 31st, 1927). "June Mathis Carves Niche in Theater of Fame"
138. The Salt Lake Tribune (July 31st, 1927). "June Mathis Carves Niche in Theater of Fame"
139. The Salt Lake Tribune (August 2nd, 1927). "Services Held for June Mathis"
140. Ogden Standard-Examiner (November 30th, 1927). "In Hollywood"
141. Derrick (July 28th, 1927). "Death of June Mathis Saddens Movie Colony"

344

142. Oakland Tribune (August 24th, 1927). "Legal Snarls Seen in Mathis Estate"

143. Oakland Tribune (August 24th, 1927). "Legal Snarls Seen in Mathis Estate"

144. Ogden Standard-Examiner (August 23rd, 1927). "Grandmother Contests Will".

145. Ogden Standard-Examiner (August 23rd, 1927). "Grandmother Contests Will"

146. Los Angeles Times (August 7th, 1927). "Estate of June Mathis Goes to Kin"

147. Ogden Standard-Examiner (February 21st, 1928). "Says Grandma has 5 coats"

148. Daily News (February 22nd, 1928). "Bobbed Grandma Seeks Half of $100,000 Estate"

149. Find a Grave #2060

150. Los Angeles Times (January 22nd, 1928). "And they danced the old year out!"

151. Ancestry.com Selected US Naturalization Records – Original documents; 1790-1974

152. Ancestry.com Selected US Naturalization Records – Original documents; 1790-1974

153. California Passenger and Crew Lists 1893-1957; Ancestry.com

154. Ancestry.com Selected US Naturalization Records – Original documents; 1790-1974

155. "Ogden Standard-Examiner (September 28th, 1934). "Mussolini Loses Man"

156. Billings Gazette (July 31st, 1927). "Few pause at bier of woman who 'made' Valentino; unlike frenzied mob at Rudy's Rites"

157. Los Angeles Times (July 28th, 1927). "June Mathis to be buried here"

CPSIA information can be obtained at www.ICGtesting.com
Printed in the USA
BVOW041342060313

314858BV00002B/252/P